Collected Plays

Volume Three

For several decades, Girish Karnad has been recognized nationally and internationally as one of the pre-eminent playwrights in contemporary India. Born in 1938, he belonged to the generation of writers who came to maturity shortly after Independence and collectively reshaped Indian theatre as a national institution in the later twentieth century. Karnad's *Collected Plays* brings together the playwright's own English versions of all his important plays and makes them available to audiences around the world. Together, these volumes span the varied and celebrated career of Girish Karnad, from his very first play to his later works.

T0364637

Collected Plays

Volume Three

Yayati
Wedding Album
Boiled Beans on Toast

GIRISH KARNAD

With an Introduction by
Aparna Bhargava Dharwadker

OXFORD
UNIVERSITY PRESS

OXFORD
UNIVERSITY PRESS

Oxford University Press is a department of the University of Oxford.
It furthers the University's objective of excellence in research, scholarship,
and education by publishing worldwide. Oxford is a registered trademark of
Oxford University Press in the UK and in certain other countries.

Published in India by
Oxford University Press
22 Workspace, 2nd Floor, 1/22 Asaf Ali Road, New Delhi 110 002, India

Collected Plays, Volume Three © Oxford University Press 2018
Yayati first published by Oxford University Press 2008
Wedding Album first published by Oxford University Press 2009
Boiled Beans on Toast first published by Oxford University Press 2014

The moral rights of the authors have been asserted.

First Edition published in 2018
Oxford India Paperbacks 2020

ISBN-13: 978-0-19-012918-7
ISBN-10: 0-19-012918-2

Typeset in Minion Pro 10.5/14
by The Graphics Solution, New Delhi 110 092
Printed in India by Rakmo Press, New Delhi 110 020

*For Saras,
Radha, and Raghu*

Contents

Introduction

In an interview with me recorded in 1993 and published in 1995, Girish Karnad made the following observation in response to a question about how the lack of serious criticism affects the arts in India.

I must emphasize here that the sudden spurt in serious playwriting in the 1960s was strengthened by the number of committed, intelligent, and active people who came into the amateur or semi-professional theatre scene at that time. Alkazi, Sombhu Mitra, Utpal Dutt, and Habib Tanvir were already there. And suddenly there were Satyadev Dubey, Shyamanand Jalan, Arvind and Sulabha Deshpande, Rajinder Nath, Kavalam Panikkar, G. Sankara Pillai, B.V. Karanth, Om Shivpuri.... We all reacted to each other's work. There was endless discussion.... We playwrights translated each other's work. I miss all that dearly.[1]

What Karnad was evoking implicitly in these comments were the mechanisms and processes by which mainstream urban Indian theatre was formed as a post-Independence field of practice, without the systemic stimulus of a functioning theatrical marketplace. In artistic terms, there were four critical factors that made this unusual performance economy possible—playwrights around the country kept up a steady stream of plays that were notable successes both in print and performance; gifted directors (who also often doubled as playwrights) brought new work quickly onto the stage, in collaboration with their groups of actors, designers, and technicians; a cadre of competent and active translators made new plays, as well as Indian, Western, and world theatre from various other periods, available in multiple languages so that the works could circulate nationally; and a relatively small but loyal body of viewers extended enough support to the entire enterprise to make it viable. In material terms, there was strategic support from national- and state-level public and private institutions, such as the central and regional Sangeet Natak Akademis, the National School of Drama (NSD), the Shri Ram Centre for Art and Culture, and Bharat Bhavan.[2] Through programmes of training, development of repertory companies, grants, fellowships, subsidies, and sponsored events, these organizations offered a range of opportunities that were more or less accessible to individuals and groups, and sustained their work in varying degrees.

Twenty-seven years after Karnad's comments during the interview, the period of creative ferment he recalled with such nostalgia has receded even more irrevocably into the past. There is a widespread sense among all those involved with urban theatre in India that circumstances today are qualitatively different from the formative conditions that had emerged during the 1960s, and were in evidence even until the late 1980s. One explanation for this change is the inevitable generational shift—with the exception of Ebrahim Alkazi and Rajinder Nath (neither of whom has been an active director for some time), the practitioners Karnad mentioned in 1993 are no longer living, and many other iconic careers, including those of Vijay Tendulkar, Badal Sircar, G.P. Deshpande, and K.V. Subbanna, have also come to an end. But there have been substantial artistic, material, sociological, cultural, and political shifts as well to account for the current sense of difference and distance. The majority of new plays now seem to lack the qualities that had transformed a large number of earlier works into 'instant classics', from Sircar's *Ebong Indrajit* (And Indrajit, 1962) and Karnad's *Tughlaq* (1964) to Satish Alekar's *Begum Barve* (1979) and Vijay Tendulkar's *Kanyadaan* (1983). The pressures of a neo-liberal economy and the continuing problem of resources have pushed theatre workers into increased dependence on corporate sponsorship, philanthropy, and institutional patronage.

Hence, annual events such as the NSD's Bharat Rang Mahotsav (India Theatre Festival), the Mahindra Excellence in Theatre Awards endowed by the Mahindra Company, and the calendar of the National Centre for Performing Arts carry disproportionate weight in the process by which good theatre is made available to audiences for a reasonable cost. Other active institutions, such as Prithvi Theatre in Mumbai, the Shri Ram Centre for Art and Culture in Delhi, and Ranga Shankara in Bengaluru have to take on some purely revenue-generating activities so that they can support their own artistic initiatives. The arrival of colour television in India in 1982 dealt theatre a blow from which it has not managed to recover fully, and in many Indian cities, the problems of negotiating traffic keep that television-watching audience at home in the evenings, leading to a significant decline in the audience for theatre. Counterpointing these struggles for survival is the perception that the real momentum in theatre now belongs not to the predominantly male, middle-class, somewhat complacent urban mainstream but to the forms of subversion, resistance, and protest represented by women's theatre, street theatre, Dalit theatre, gay and lesbian theatre, experimental political theatre, and applied theatre of various kinds. With the further weakening of live theatre by the exponential increase in new digital media, and the daily pressures of a polity in crisis, creative energy is said to be seeping out from the metropolitan centre, into oppositional forms at the periphery.

In the early twenty-first century, Girish Karnad is a singularly intriguing figure to place against this narrative of centralization and dispersal because his sixty-year career in the theatre encompasses the post-Independence arc fully, and indeed brings it full circle. There could not be a more remarkable confirmation of this cyclicity than the present volume, which opens with Karnad's very first play, *Yayati* (published in Kannada in 1961), and then moves on to the last two works published in his lifetime, *Wedding Album* (written originally in Kannada as *Maduveya Album*, 2009), and *Boiled Beans on Toast* (written originally in Kannada as *Benda Kaalu on Toast*, 2014; Karnad's final play, *Crossing to Talikota*, was published posthumously in 2019). This unusual conjuncture requires some explanation so that the post-2005 phase of the playwright's career can come more clearly into view. As Karnad noted frequently in print, *Yayati* was written during the period of psychological turmoil in 1960 when his impending departure for Oxford University as a Rhodes scholar created anxiety in his family about his return. At that time, every major feature of the work had taken the twenty-two-year-old author by surprise—that it was a play and not a cluster of angst-ridden poems, that it was written in Kannada instead of English, and that it used an episode from the Mahabharata as its narrative basis instead of creating an Oedipal psychodrama set in the present. 'The myth,' Karnad acknowledges, 'nailed me to my past', and it also initiated a preference for narratives *from* the past which dominated his playwriting for the next four decades. In my Introduction to Volume 1 of his *Collected Plays* (first written in 2005), I mapped this preference as a cycle of myth–history–folklore, which, in different permutations, informed all but one of Karnad's published plays from 1961 to 2005: myth in *Yayati*, *Agni Mattu Malé* (The Fire and the Rain, 1994), and *Bali: The Sacrifice* (2002); history in *Tughlaq* (1964), *Talé-Daṇḍa* (Death by Decapitation, 1990), and *The Dreams of Tipu Sultan* (1997); folklore in *Hayavadana* (Horse-Head, 1971), *Nāga-Mandala* (Play with a Cobra, 1988), and *Flowers: A Monologue* (2004).

The exception was *Broken Images* (2004), the first of Karnad's plays to be set in the urban present, and one that was written and performed almost simultaneously in English and Kannada, but dealt with the specific politics and economics of English as a creative medium in relation to a strong 'regional' language such as Kannada. Manjula Nayak, a self-possessed thirty-something who has been a well-known short-story writer in Kannada suddenly publishes a bestselling novel in English, and becomes a national and international celebrity—'The Literary Phenomenon of the Decade'. Following a live televised address to viewers, a surreal dialogue with her own image on the TV screen in the studio gradually reveals that Manjula has plagiarized the novel from her younger sister, Malini, a lifelong invalid and brilliantly gifted writer in English who had died a few months before the novel appeared. Manjula discovered the novel, signed 'M. Nayak', in her husband Pramod's desk drawer immediately after Malini's death, sent it to a literary agent in England, and decided to seize the opportunity when the agent and the publisher assumed she was the author. The decision has brought her wealth and fame, but ended her marriage to Pramod, who was in love with Malini and knew the truth about the novel. At the end of the short play, Manjula declares that she has morphed into Malini, the dead sister who now clearly controls her body, her mind, and her duplicitous future life.

Placed against this forty-year trajectory, the three plays included in this volume present suggestive patterns of similarity and difference. In one perspective, *Yayati* is a play from 1961, representing myth as primary subject matter, Kannada as the language of original composition, and Karnad's disconnection from the theatre world as the determining condition of its dramaturgical structure. In another perspective, it is a play from 2008 (the year of its publication as an individual work), rewritten in both English and Kannada in light of the insights, suggestions, and critical comments offered by 'professionals who have actually staged it', not to mention the authorial experience Karnad could bring to bear on it after more than four decades of playwriting. The play's exclusion from Volume 1 of the *Collected Plays* in 2005 also reflects Karnad's fastidiousness as an author and translator, which led to his decision not to authorize, especially in the potentially global medium of English, a work with which he 'continued to feel dissatisfied', but which he was eventually persuaded to publish in his own English translation. The unusual textual history of *Yayati* both in Kannada and English, and its anomalously long trek towards publication in English, are reminders of the circuitousness that sometimes interrupts the linear progression of literary and theatrical careers. In contrast, the two other plays, *Wedding Album* and *Boiled Beans on Toast*, are in part continuations of the change in direction signalled by *Broken Images*—although both were written originally in Kannada and then translated by Karnad into English, they are concerned with urban life in the present, and use two Karnataka cities as their setting: Dharwad and Bengaluru in the former, Bengaluru in the latter.

In other important respects, however, all three plays are comparable—each deals in its own particular way with familial conflicts, and each foregrounds the lives of women. These patterns can be outlined in general terms here, and elaborated in the individual discussions that follow. The title character in *Yayati* is a mythic king whose egotism and coarse sensuality would qualify him as an 'anti-hero' in the modernist tradition of Jean Anouilh, and the play follows the counter-Oedipal logic of the traditional Indian family structure, which leads a self-doubting son to surrender to the will of a self-centred father, even though his decision destroys many lives. Much more prominent than the drama of male generational conflict in the play, however, are the volatile relationships between four self-possessed, articulate women—the queen, the mistress, the loyal servant, and the young bride—all of whom, as I noted, 'are subject in varying degrees to the whims of men, but succeed in subverting the male world through an assertion of their own rights and privileges'.[3] In *Wedding Album*, the tensions in the middle-class nuclear family of five run beneath the surface, and the moments of emotional trauma happen mostly offstage. But the patriarch has now shrunk into an inarticulate old man prone to occasional outbursts, and the son has become a facilitator who does not hesitate to use his family members as material for television melodrama, and gives in to a marriage of convenience. Once again, four women claim most of our attention—a somewhat guilt-ridden mother who has done her duty by her husband, but not all her children; a discontented older daughter who is married and lives abroad; a younger daughter who makes a questionable choice of husband in the course of the play; and an old servant whose abandonment of her own daughter forms the understated climax of the action. In *Boiled Beans on Toast*, the 'man of the house' within the main family is a nameless provider who does not appear on stage at all, the teenage son is in the process of finding himself, the life of an ambitious young professional is wrecked with brutal casualness, a vindictive brother forces his sister to break off family ties, and a few other men have walk-on parts (as policemen, autorickshaw drivers, and so on). Much of the focus is on the unusual friendship between two ethically dissimilar women of privilege (a hospice volunteer and an amoral fantasist), and the rivalry between two ethically dissimilar female servants jockeying for position in upper-class homes as they try to survive in the 'monster city' of Bengaluru.

In fact, when the twelve works gathered in all three volumes of Karnad's *Collected Plays* (covering the period 1961–2014) are considered together from the viewpoint of gender, other interesting patterns emerge. The history plays are constrained to a large extent by their historiographic sources, and their focus on a premodern political world that does not allow women much agency. Hence, the Stepmother is the only significant female character in *Tughlaq*, and Karnad's inventive energy goes into creating a range of historical and fictional male alter egos for the title character, especially the master-manipulator Aziz. The same is true of *The Dreams of Tipu Sultan*, in which the queen, Ruqayya Banu, appears with her young sons in only one scene, and dies soon afterwards, unaware that her children are being bartered for the sake of the kingdom. In the crowded historical canvas of *Talé-Daṇḍa*, there are principal male as well as female characters, but the affective emphasis is on the communities of men, women, and children who are destroyed by caste violence when a reformist socio-religious movement becomes a deadly political tool. The plays based on myth and folklore, however, place women at the centre as desirable and desiring subjects, whether we consider the triad of Devayani–Sharmishtha–Chitralekha in *Yayati*, Padmini in *Hayavadana*, Rani in *Nāga-Mandala*, Vishakha and Nittilai in *Agni Mattu Malé*, or the Queen in *Bali*. In a third variation, women in the three 'plays of the present', beginning with Manjula in *Broken Images*, are mundane and in many cases ethically compromised figures, caught up in an urban domestic and social world that lacks charm and charisma. The following discussions reinforce that the value Karnad places on female subjectivity in his fictions of the past (for example, *Yayati*) undergoes an ironic decline in his fictions of the present (*Wedding Album* and *Boiled Beans on Toast*), pointing to a central difference in his imagining of the premodern and modern worlds.

II

Although *Yayati* was not included in Volume 1 of the *Collected Plays*, I had used Priya Adarkar's existing translation to discuss the play near the beginning of my Introduction to that volume because it marked the real and symbolic beginning of Karnad's career as a playwright.[4] The author mentions in his short note to *Yayati* in the present volume that the play went through significant changes in his own translation of 2008, and it seems superfluous now to compare the two versions. The text of the play included here, unchanged since 2008, does not displace my earlier comments based on Adarkar's translation; but it does offer an opportunity to move beyond the critical perspectives of 2005, and focus on aspects of the play that have come more clearly into view now.

The first notable feature of the new version is its structure. Karnad employs the classical/folk convention of the *sutradhar*, but only as a detachable, self-reflexive frame at the beginning and end, leaving the intervening action of the play completely undisturbed by metatheatrical 'intrusions'. In the Prologue, the sutradhar rehearses the conventional claim that he is 'responsible' for the text to be presented as well as its effective performance, but the real purpose of his set piece is to establish the play's modernist credentials. By insisting that 'a play based on myth' is not a 'mythological', he connects *Yayati* to the structures of archetypal human experience ('the fears and desires sleepless within us') rather than to the structures of religious devotion (the desire for 'divine grace' and redemption). The sutradhar also declares that the play contains no gods and deals with death, hence invoking the godless modern universe that was Friedrich Nietzsche's legacy to the existentialist philosophy of Jean-Paul Sartre and Albert Camus, two authors read widely by Karnad's generation of writers and intellectuals in India. The short epilogue at the end of the play is an exercise in pure irony. The sutradhar 'erases' the existentialist despair of Pooru's final cry, 'What does all this mean, O God? What does it mean?' by insisting that the conventions of Sanskrit drama demand a happy ending, and so we must accept the 'authority of the epics that Pooru ruled long and wisely and was hailed as a philosopher king'. Ancient myth yields modernist meaning, but form also subverts content: Karnad continues in *Yayati* the self-undermining use of traditional conventions he had begun in *Hayavadana* and repeated in *Nāga-Mandala*.

Second, what deepens the irony is that the four-act drama sandwiched between the Prologue and Epilogue is a showpiece of

Western-style construction, observing the Aristotelian unities of time, place, and action more scrupulously than any other play by Karnad. The action begins early on the evening of Pooru's return to the capital city with his bride Chitralekha, moves through the quarrel between Devayani and Sharmishtha, Yayati's seduction of Sharmishtha, and Shukracharya's curse against Yayati, and concludes with Chitralekha's suicide that same night, after Pooru's assumption of his father's curse has transformed him into a decrepit old man. The unchanging setting for the entire play is the 'inner chamber' in Yayati's palace which is the royal couple's bedchamber, but also the scene of seduction, Pooru's fond memories of his dead mother, and Chitralekha's final confrontation with Yayati. This continuity in time and space creates an atmosphere of unrelieved crisis, sustained in turn by the perlocutionary thrust of the dialogue. As characters spar with each other and try to 'make things happen' through actions as well as words, details from the past are filled in, and old antagonisms erupt in the present, culminating in the curse pronounced by Shukracharya— the most powerful perlocutionary act of all.

The economy of action is possible, of course, because of substantial deviations from the original story. In the Mahabharata narrative Pooru is Sharmishtha's youngest son with Yayati, indicating that the relationship between the parents is both long-standing and legitimate. In Karnad's play Pooru is the 'half-caste' son of a dead queen who concealed her rakshasa (demonic) identity to marry Yayati as an act of vengeance, and ended her life in bitter vituperation. Only two years have passed since Devayani's marriage to Yayati, and hence Sharmishtha's arrival in the palace as her slave. So Yayati's seduction of Sharmishtha at the end of Act 1 is the first such transgression on his part, prompting Devayani's departure in the middle of Act 2, and the curse soon afterwards. The two remaining acts work out the consequences of the curse on the lives of Pooru, Chitralekha, Yayati, Sharmishtha, and Swarnalata. The relationships are foreshortened to match the accelerated action, making *Yayati* Karnad's most tightly structured play.[5]

The theatrical strengths of the new version have been tested in a number of productions. Arundhati Raja of Bengaluru's Artistes

Repertory Theatre directed the English translation at the Ravindra Kalakshetra in October 2006, and at Ranga Shankara Theatre in February 2007. The Manipuri adaptation of November 2007 by leading playwright-director Ratan Thiyam was described as a 'masterpiece of painting', because of the visual elegance of a large open set with eye-catching wooden surfaces lit with brass lamps. For me the play's dramatic power was confirmed most memorably in a fully costumed and blocked stage reading, co-directed by Joan Brooks and Barbara Clayton, which I had organized as the final event of the 38th Annual Conference on South Asia in Madison, Wisconsin, in October 2009. Enacted by faculty members and graduate students of the Department of Theatre and Drama at the University of Wisconsin, the performance received a standing ovation from the playwright himself, who was a keynote speaker at the conference, and present in the audience!

The third distinctive feature of the revised *Yayati* is antithetical to the first two, because it highlights the invocation of ancient social hierarchies and tribal identities. It is essential to the play's psychosocial codes that Yayati is a Chandravanshi king, Devayani a brahmin queen in a kshatriya palace, Shukracharya a brahmin sage with the power to curse, Sharmishtha an asura princess who describes herself as a rakshasi (demoness), and Chitralekha an Anga princess already disappointed in her weak, 'mongrel' husband. Sharmishtha's partly sub-human or non-human identity accounts for her ungovernable behaviour and Yayati's fascination with her, as he explains to Devayani when she wants to know why he desires Sharmishtha:

Because I feel bewitched by her. Even now, at this moment, I want her. I have never felt so entranced by a woman. What is it? Is it some spell she has cast? Some secret sorcery? I can feel youth bursting out within me again. Her beauty, her intelligence, her wit, her abandon in love. Not to marry her is to lose her, don't you see? I must have her. I have to keep her with me. Please try to understand.[6]

What kinds of 'contemporary' meanings do these ancient, mythic markers of identity carry? Do they represent the dichotomy of culture and nature, mind and body, high and low birth? Or the erasure of individual identity in group-speak and group-think, a form of social and cultural determinism? The play invites these interpretations, but it is also worth noting that the social–cultural polarities represented by the two principal women are translated into their sexual natures, and absorbed into the sexual rivalry which becomes the engine of destruction. Similarly, Chitralekha's suicide follows her horrified reaction to the actual sight of Pooru's decrepit body, and her revulsion against the father-in-law who has become the logical stand-in for her husband. The 'ancient' identity categories estrange and de-familiarize these characters, while the triangulation of the relationships between Devayani–Yayati–Sharmishtha and Pooru–Chitralekha–Yayati re-familiarizes them. Karnad's revised text, designed for efficient staging, stays brilliantly suspended between the ancient and the contemporary.

III

The inside front cover of the 2009 paperback edition of *Wedding Album* identifies the subject of the play as,

an event so common in the life of the urban middle class in India today, and yet so fraught with anxiety, that it has provided the staple for innumerable tele-serials and commercial films: the impending 'arranged' marriage of a girl to a 'suitable', expat boy.... In one of the most penetrating intellectual explorations of the situation in modern Indian drama, Karnad ... create[s] a play which is funny, poignant, and deeply unsettling.[7]

To position the play in the popular cultural context of film and television in this way is not inappropriate; but it is equally appropriate, and far more challenging, to consider the complex dramatic, theatrical, and performative contexts in which it can and should be placed. *Wedding Album* is Karnad's first full-scale entry into the mode of urban proscenium realism and its quintessential setting, the middle-class family home, which have together defined an important and prominent strain in post-Independence theatre. The play also registers the evolution of Karnad's own thinking about the elements that make up realist domestic drama, and gives the urban Indian home a twenty-first-century identity in sociological, economic, and psychological terms.

In his 1985 essay 'In Search of a New Theatre', Karnad had commented on the efforts by a group of Indian playwrights in the 1930s and 1940s to deal seriously with domestic and social issues through the resources of realism, noting that they could succeed only partially because of the differences between Western and Indian conceptions of home, family, and the individual. Western realism is defined by its concern with the individual 'as an entity valuable in itself', whereas 'Indians define themselves in terms of their relationships to the other members of their family, caste, or class. They are defined by the role they have to play'. Equally important, the Indian realists had miscalculated the geography of the Indian home:

From Ibsen to Albee, the living room has symbolized all that is valuable to the Western bourgeoisie. It is one's refuge from the sociopolitical forces raging in the world outside, as well as the battleground where values essential to one's individuality are fought out and defended. But nothing of consequence ever happens or is supposed to happen in an Indian living room! It is the no-man's land, the empty, almost defensive front the family presents to the world outside.... [I]t is in the interior of the house, in the kitchen, in the room where the gods are kept, or in the backyard [that] family problems are tackled, or allowed to fester, and where the women can have a say. Thus the living room as the location of dramatic action made nonsense of the very social problems the playwright set out to analyze, by distorting the caste dimensions as well as the position of women in the family.[8]

It is fascinating to place these comments from 1985 alongside the stage directions at the beginning of Act 1, Scene 2 of *Wedding Album* (2009).

The living room of a house obviously modelled on the travellers' bungalows of the colonial period. Sprawling, dusty.

On one side, there is a huge cupboard with glass doors, packed with books, mostly recent paperbacks which seem ill-at-ease on the old-fashioned shelves, wedged in between some heavy leather-bound volumes. A grandfather clock hangs on the wall, and next to it, a portrait of the Swamiji, the spiritual monastic head of the Saraswat Brahmins.... Mother and Vidula are examining silk saris piled on the sofa.... Vidula picks up a sari.

Not only is this conventionally appointed living room now the space where things of consequence happen, family problems are tackled, and women have their say—as the setting also for Scenes 3, 4, 7, and 9, it is in fact the *only* part of the home we are allowed to see, and women *dominate* the conversations that take place there (the kitchen and an adjoining room are referred to, but never shown). The old-but-new face of home complements the other modernized urban spaces in the play—a software production office in Scenes 1 and 5, an Internet café in Scene 6, and a restaurant in Scene 8—where individuals pursue professional lives, exercise their freedom, and negotiate relationships. In a move that seems especially appropriate in the medium of English, Karnad has also given an unusually prominent role to the transnational dimension of contemporary life, with Australia and the United States appearing constantly as the diasporic locations to which marriage has connected the two daughters, Hema and Vidula. For the same reason, the diaspora has played a significant role in the brief stage history of the play—Lillette Dubey's production for Primetime Theatre Company (2008) has had a 'world tour', and there have been well-publicized productions in Rochester, New York (directed by Baal Bhagat for Kalidas, 2011), Sydney, Australia (directed by Saba Abdi for Adakar, 2016), and Sunnyvale, California (directed by Sindhu Singh for the Bay Area Drama Company, 2017).

The form and content of *Wedding Album* suggest, then, that it is both a late and a distinctive entry into the substantial tradition of post-Independence urban realist drama created by such playwrights as Vijay Tendulkar, Mohan Rakesh, the early Badal Sircar, Mahasweta Devi, Madhu Rye, Jaywant Dalvi, Govind Deshpande, Mahesh Elkunchwar, Mahesh Dattani, and Manjula Padmanabhan, among others. In many respects, these authors are part of the larger trajectory of modern drama (defined most influentially by Ibsen, Strindberg, Chekhov, O'Neill, Arthur Miller, and Tennessee Williams) which portrays home as a place of victimage, and departure from home as the decisive assertion of the protagonist's autonomy and individuality. In other respects, the Indian playwrights have created culture-specific portraits of patriarchal oppression, failed relationships, emotional exploitation, economic decline, social antagonisms, misplaced idealism, hypocrisy, dishonesty, greed, and betrayal. Instead of being directed at one unique protagonist, the condition of victimage often extends to the entire cast of characters in a play, and departure is usually not a choice available to those who are suffering. These conditions account for the atmosphere of mounting crisis in realist classics such as Rakesh's *Adhe Adhure* (Incomplete, Unfinished, 1969), Tendulkar's *Gidhade* (Vultures, 1970), Elkunchwar's *Wada Chirebandi* (Old Stone Mansion, 1985), and Dattani's *Bravely Fought the Queen* (1991), which culminate in the real and/or symbolic destruction of the entire edifice of home.

In comparison with these precursors, *Wedding Album* appears clearly as a play characterized not by agonistic filial relationships and intense moments of suffering, but by indeterminacy, amorality, and ambivalence. The Nadkarni family has its share of resentment and guilt running beneath the surface of daily life, but the 'problems of place' are not overwhelming, and they are deferred if not resolved within the space of home. Expediency and compromise diffuse a series of crises before they become unmanageable.

The two generations of Saraswat brahmins portrayed in the play share these qualities equally. Late in their lives, the older Nadkarnis feel no particular sense of accomplishment, find their children rather disappointing, and complain about being under-appreciated, but continue to fulfil their parental and social obligations in the conventional way. Mr Nadkarni's fond memories of his dead brother Ramdas sit awkwardly beside the brother's decision to name himself as the father on his niece Vidula's birth certificate, and we never learn with certainty whether this was an act of malice or an acknowledgement of adultery within the family. Heightening the ambiguity is Mrs Nadkarni's suggestion that the family leave the mistake uncorrected, because 'all the bother' would probably not be worthwhile, and could upset her husband. Other uncertain events, not resolved until the last moments of the play, involve the old servant Radhabai, who (we are told) has had to deal with the trauma of losing touch with an adult daughter after she was cast away by the family of her dead keeper. Radhabai's grief seems to be a more intense version of Mrs Nadkarni's guilt over Hema's deprived childhood and lacklustre wedding, until we learn the real cost of servitude in a middle-class home: that Radhabai deliberately abandoned her destitute daughter to safeguard her own position in the Nadkarni family.

These qualities of ambivalence deepen with the younger generation. Hema is unable to enjoy her visits home from Australia because of lingering resentment over her wedding, but she also has a problematic preference for her teenage son over her husband and daughter. Her conservative views about 'marrying within the community', surprising to her siblings, reflect the increased parochialism about region, language, and caste that often marks Indian communities, especially first-generation expatriates, in the diaspora. For Rohit, the middle child, Vidula's marriage and Radhabai's unhappiness are equal opportunity professional fodder for the prime-time television narratives he helps to develop. His life-altering act of moral cowardice takes place off-stage—there are conflicting explanations for why he broke away from his Christian girlfriend Isabel and married Tapasya, a Saraswat girl whose affluent parents were annoyingly persistent in their pursuit of him—but the pragmatic advantages of the match have become self-evident. While his pregnant wife is away for the delivery, he does not hesitate to try and rekindle his relationship with Isabel. Vidula is an even greater conundrum. Described by her family as 'innocent' and 'timid', and describing herself on video as a girl who is 'not exceptional in any way' and not really interested in a career, she engages regularly in anonymous cyber sex at an Internet café. And while she rebukes young Hindu vigilantes for trying to police her activities, she willingly marries Ashwin, a self-regarding expatriate who has taken a lifelong vow to 'save' the unregenerate West through the power of Hindu spirituality. In the play's opening scene, we learn that she has not visited India since her marriage three years earlier, and has no plans to do so either.

This adds up to the portrait of a family that is neither happy nor unhappy—or, to put it differently, a family that has moments of happiness, togetherness, and empathy alongside moments of disaffection and distance. Karnad also evokes a culture that is being gradually hollowed out in a neo-liberal environment. The inventive structure of the play, in which the two office scenes take place three years later than the other seven, and video images mix in with live dialogue, is one prominent sign that new forces are taking over the older constructs. As in real-life Indian cities, the artefacts and spaces of globalization are everywhere—cameras, television screens, mobile phones, cyber cafés, Internet pornography, email, skype conversations. Separated into scenes rather than acts, the play creates the impression of offering a fast-paced and panoramic montage of urban life rather than moments of stasis and reflection. The intersection of provincial Indian home with metropolitan Western diaspora dissipates the sense of cultural cohesion further. Indian men like Ashwin and Hema's nameless husband are said to be conquering the world, yet Vidula's siblings feel compelled to let her know before she leaves for the United States that they would understand her decision if she chose to divorce Ashwin because of his cold and indifferent temperament. The most chilling scene of disconnection in the play is therefore Ashwin's self-congratulatory monologue in the restaurant (Scene 8), where he offers marriage to Vidula, but in terms that leave her expressionless and silent. More than any other moment in the play, this one-sided proposal indicates why *Wedding Album* is not primarily a play about 'the impending "arranged" marriage of a girl to a "suitable", expat boy', but a darkly comic portrait of individuals who lack interiority and are trying to make the best of their day-to-day lives of compromise.

IV

Boiled Beans on Toast is, if anything, even more deeply ambivalent than *Wedding Album*, because its partial focus on the privileged Padabidri family (mother, son, and grandmother) is diffused by the presence of a second woman of privilege (Dolly), two female servants (Vimala and Muttu), and a range of male characters in varying states of crisis. Karnad notes that the play's title 'relates to the founding myth of the city of Bengaluru or Bangalore, which is today admired as the "Silicon Valley of India" and is the subject of this play'. Juxtaposing the founding myth against the twenty-first century present brings out the full irony of the contrast—between an old woman's life-giving act of kindness towards a stranger that gave the city its name in the eleventh century, and the place of exploitation, casual cruelty, and destruction it has now become. Shanta Gokhale's Foreword to the 2014 edition of the play complements Karnad's view by suggesting that 'the chief protagonist of *Boiled Beans on Toast* is the city of Bangalore, a throbbing organism spawned by globalization', and the play's structure evokes a 'prose symphony' of long and short movements arranged around particular themes: 'village versus city; human relations guided by family and community versus human relations guided by pragmatic principles; the idea of home, ancestral versus self-made'.[9] Gokhale adds that Karnad observes the organism, with its 'multiple misalignments', without nostalgia and judgement.

Like *Wedding Album*, *Boiled Beans on Toast* also has a modern genealogy. If the first play participates in the tradition of urban realism eventually traceable to Ibsen, the second joins the line of modernist fiction, non-fiction, and cinema which takes the industrial or post-industrial city as its subject, from Chicago in Theodore Dreiser's *Sister Carrie* and Dublin in all of James Joyce's works to Calcutta/Kolkata in Satyajit Ray's *Mahanagar* (1963) and Dominique Lapierre's *City of Joy* (1985), and Bombay/Mumbai in Mira Nair's *Salaam Bombay* (1988), Rohinton Mistry's *Family Matters* (2002), and Suketu Mehta's *Maximum City* (2005). In the genre of drama, the collection of three *City Plays* (2004) edited by Mahesh Dattani brings together Mahesh Elkunchwar's *Party*, Shanta Gokhale's *Avinash*, and Manjula Padmanabhan's *Lights Out*, the last two plays having been written originally in English. The stage premiere of *Boiled Beans on Toast* (in Mohit Takalkar's Marathi adaptation titled *Uney Pure Shahar Ek* [One City, More or Less]) also coincided with Dattani's own theatrical take on Mumbai, *The Big Fat City*, in 2013. Karnad's intervention in the unfolding narrative of the Indian city suggests that neo-liberalism and globalization have given class privilege a commonplace quality, but their larger effect has been to harden class divisions and resentments, amplify greed, and make survival a more contingent condition.

The subject matter of *Boiled Beans on Toast* has novelty even in comparison with the content of *Wedding Album*, and the cast of characters is surprising. The role of the female servant, which was not especially notable in Karnad's earlier work, has gained increasing prominence in the plays included in this volume. Swarnalata is part of the outspoken quartet of women in *Yayati*, a poignant figure with a lost past who feels such loyalty towards her royal mistresses that Devayani's departure and Chitralekha's suicide push her over the edge, into madness. Radhabai in *Wedding Album* appears to have all the prerogatives of a long-time, loyal 'family servant'. She participates in family conversations and quarrels with her mistress like an equal—and yet only her abject dependence as a servant can explain the act of abandonment that is now consuming her. In *Boiled Beans on Toast*, one servant figure splits into two, and the stories of the two women receive as much attention as those of their employers (there is only one scene in the Padabidri home, between Anusuya and her grandson Kunaal, which does not involve the servants). Muttu is younger, more docile and honest, and grounded in the city because of the presence of husband, child, and mother; Vimala is unmoored, defiant, unscrupulous, and determined to exploit every money-making opportunity within her limited sphere of action. Muttu's backstory in the village of Karimangala also makes her the unexpected vehicle of a familiar thematic in contemporary narratives—the resentment those in the village feel towards those in the city, however much the latter may complain about their own struggles for survival. Vimala begins as a surrogate (sometimes parodic) figure of power and condescension in the Padabidri household, someone who is described as 'indispensable' until she is exposed as a thief and a compulsive liar. We might say that Muttu's star rises as Vimala's declines, because the younger woman quietly seizes the opportunity to replace her rival without any blatant manipulation. But as in Radhabai's case, the sphere of action and freedom among the servants is strictly limited by the determinism of class, in a hierarchy that will not allow them upward mobility beyond a certain point.

The three upper-class women who counterpoint the servants project the instinctive easy presumption of those who have become accustomed to privilege. Anjana struggled as a young wife, but because of her (nameless and absent) husband's corporate success she can now devote herself to volunteer work with terminally ill patients, and treat intruders like Prabhakar Telang with amused indifference. Dolly is a schoolteacher 'for want of anything better to do', but the driving force in her life are the fantasies of social access which lead her to interfere at will in the lives of others, without any regard to the consequences. Significantly, as she goes about destroying Prabhakar's professional and family life, she is the main propagandist for the importance of seizing opportunities in the 'modern business world', and taking full advantage of the 'age of globalization'. Dolly is the morally vacuous upper-class counterpart of Vimala, but while the servant lies to preserve herself, the Brigadier's wife lies to feed her pathological need for control, and her husband's rage at her behaviour is not likely to prevent future victims. Anusuya, the grandmother, is yet another amoral presence who borrows money secretly to gamble at the race course because that is where she has had visions of God. Perhaps the only poignant moment in the representation of these women appear when Anusuya talks to Kunaal about his mother's musical talents, and Anjana tells him the story of her attempted suicide as a young mother, which put an end to the music in her life.

As the place that contains these overlapping stories and misalignments, the city of Bengaluru displays the qualities of a dystopia, through several reversals that counteract nature and instinct. Prabhakar's nuclear family is destroyed in the course of the play, and Muttu's bond with the village and her extended family suffers irreversible damage, because for her brother Shankara she has become the infuriating image of 'what happens when people move to the city'. As Shankara lies injured in a Bengaluru hospital at the end, Muttu has no evident means of locating him. Anjana prefers to have both her husband and son away from home, and Vimala's troubles with the police are more important to her than talking about Kunaal's activities with the absent husband. The second reversal is ecological. In Anjana's consciousness the rain tree outside her house is so intimately connected with the idea of home that its loss for the sake of 'development' is a symbolic loss of home, although the scale of destruction is too large for any one person's emotions to carry much weight. Prabhakar complicates the ecological thematic, however, by offering an opposite viewpoint: after the suffocation of small-town life, the cement and concrete jungle of the city signifies 'solidity', the polluted environment is like an 'oxygen-chamber', and the waves of traffic are like waves in the sea. These perceptions seem dystopian because they suggest the evolution (or devolution) of a new kind of urban subject who sees life-affirming qualities in what is really inert and sterile. The third site of reversal is the city itself, which has metamorphosed from a place celebrated for its gardens and wholesome climate into an uncontainable, inhospitable organism with a will of its own. As an information technology hub, Bengaluru witnessed a 50 per cent increase in population within a single decade, from 6.3 million in 2001 to 9.6 million in 2011, so that the play's recurring image of people 'pouring' unstoppably into the city has a literal dimension. As a member of the generation that will fully inherit the new reality, Kunaal gets the last word on the subject: the 'new residential extension in Uttarahalli' was 'an absolute nightmare from which there was no way of waking up', and 'Big Bang Bangalore is a Big Black Hole!'

Uncontrolled urban development and economic growth have become such widespread symptoms of neo-liberal expansion and globalization in India that, as viewers and critics have stressed, Karnad's fiction about the transformation of Bengaluru can apply equally well to a large number of emerging metropolises around the nation. This analogical potential was demonstrated brilliantly in the first major production of *Boiled Beans on Toast*—not in Kannada, but in the Marathi adaptation by Pradeep Vaidya, titled *Uney Pure Shahar Ek*, which Mohit Takalkar of Pune's Aasakta group directed for the Vinod Doshi Festival in 2013. With Karnad's active encouragement and input, the adaptation replaced the city of Bangalore with Pune, and the state of Karnataka with Maharashtra. Pune's prominence in the IT boom, its proximity to the megapolis of Mumbai, and its long-standing position as a magnet for rural populations made the substitution very plausible. At the same time, the city's rich and complicated history as a stronghold of Hindu nationalism and brahmin culture as well as British colonial power made its assimilation to a new globalized identity even more intriguing. Because the director wanted to preserve Karnad's allusions to the Kannada poetic and musical heritage, the Padabidris remained a family from Karnataka who had settled in

Pune for professional reasons, Anusuya was a visitor from Dharwad, and there was even some dialogue in Kannada between these family members. But the other characters were connected to towns and rural areas around Kolhapur, Sholapur, and Amravati in Maharashtra, and locations were found in Pune to correspond to the contrast between Anjana's affluent home and the nightmare of Uttarahalli.

Takalkar's production was exceptionally well-received, not only in Pune and Mumbai, but by non-Marathi-speaking audiences in Bengaluru, smaller towns in northern Karnataka, and Delhi, where it was part of the NSD's Bharat Rang Mahotsav. According to the director, it has also played well before rural audiences in Maharashtra, who identified particularly with the two female servants. This is not the first time that a play by Karnad has had its first success on stage in a language other than the original medium of composition. The same had happened with *Hayavadana*, which had three major productions in Hindi in 1972, directed respectively by Satyadev Dubey, Rajinder Nath, and B.V. Karanth, before Karanth's first Kannada production of 1973. In Kannada, *Benda Kaalu* on Toast has been performed at the Ranga Shankara Theatre in Bengaluru, and by an amateur theatre group in Mangaluru. The play's other notable staging has been in English, by Lillette Dubey's Primetime Theatre Company, which had also produced *Wedding Album*.

V

In the concluding section of my Introduction to Volume 2 of Karnad's *Collected Plays*,[10] I had discussed some important extra-textual dimensions of his career: his place in a multilingual theatre culture; the relation of playwriting to his work in the media of film and television; and his presence as an engaged intellectual in the volatile Indian public sphere. All these facets continued to be more or less visible and relevant in the intervening decade, but with twelve plays now available in the uniform medium of English in the three-volume *Collected Plays*, Karnad's active bilingualism and lifelong role as translator of his own work demand more detailed attention. As a dazzling example of linguistic *and* cultural 'translatability', *Boiled Beans on Toast*, the last play in this volume, also provides an apt segway to this subject.

Over the course of nearly two hundred years, modern Indian theatre has produced only two fully bilingual playwrights—Michael Madhusudan Dutt (1824–1873) in the 1850s, and Karnad more than a century later. Both playwrights also use their bilingualism in more or less the same manner—to create plays in a major 'regional' language and translate them into English, to create plays in English and translate them into the regional language, and to create plays in either the regional language or English without translation. An unpublished note by Karnad, titled 'On Translating My Own Plays', offers important information and makes observations about bilingualism in practice that are worth summarizing.[11]

The first play of his own that Karnad translated from Kannada into English was *Tughlaq*, for a production by Alyque Padamsee's Theatre Group in 1970. He felt confident about the process because he had already translated Badal Sircar's *Ebong Indrajit*, working with Pratibha Agrawal's Hindi version in consultation with Sircar himself. There were two basic reasons for Karnad's decision to be his own translator, one theatrical and the other authorial. Theatrically, Karnad wanted to produce dialogue in the target language that could be *spoken* successfully on stage, keeping in mind the rhythms of conversational English. Achieving this quality was so important to him as a playwright-director-actor that he even turned down an offer from his mentor A.K. Ramanujan, the most accomplished Indian translator of his generation. Authorially, the process of translation gave Karnad an unusual opportunity to revisit his work: since he had control over both texts, he could 'improve' the original in translation, and then also alter the original in light of the improvements. Translation thus became a process of reciprocal, mutually beneficial movement between the two versions of a play in two different languages.

Karnad was also keenly aware of the mobility of the English text as a print commodity, nationally and internationally. When plays such as Tendulkar's *Silence! The Court Is in Session*, Sircar's *Indrajit*, and his own *Tughlaq* became available in the classroom, Indian students had the option to move away from the remoteness of Euro-American drama, and engage with dramatic texts that spoke powerfully to them.

In a process that had a large impact on both readers and viewers, the English versions of Karnad's plays also became accessible and reliable source-texts for translations into other Indian languages, expanding the total body of available works considerably. This has been especially important because Karnad's plays have been translated into almost all the other major regional languages, as well as the pan-Indian media of Hindi and English. Indeed, the scale of multilingual circulation in India made the playwright more ambivalent in his later years about the additional access that English provides to international audiences: '[T]here was a time ... when I thought the ultimate destination of my play in English would be the British or the American stage, but not anymore.... There is much more English spoken and understood today in India itself than half a century ago, there is much more theatre in English.' He also came to believe that a play carried with it a cultural and emotional context that had greatest resonance for audiences who are 'insiders' to that culture. The crucial audience for his plays is therefore in India, regardless of the particular language in which they are published and performed.

Karnad's final statement on the subject of translation is also a conclusive one: 'I translate my own plays,' he notes, 'because I don't know a more reliable translator for my plays in English.' The same statement would, of course, be true of the plays he wrote originally in English and translated into Kannada (such as *The Dreams of Tipu Sultan* and *Broken Images*). The oscillating relationships between the two languages throughout his career are complex enough, and pervasive enough, for his comments on some of the later plays to be quoted in full, with the relevant dates of composition added in square brackets.

Nāga-Mandala was jotted down in a rough draft in Kannada which I then shaped into an English text for the students of the University of Chicago. [1987–8]

The Dreams of Tipu Sultan was commissioned by BBC Radio, and since the resource material was available only in English, there seemed to be no point in contorting one's way through Kannada first. [1996–7]

The Fire and the Rain was commissioned for a theatre workshop organized by the Guthrie Theatre, Minneapolis, with American actors, and therefore, although I started with a very rough draft in Kannada, the work evolved as

I worked along with them and my excellent Dramaturge Barbara Field in English, almost from scratch. [1994]

Bali: The Sacrifice was commissioned by the Leicester Haymarket Theatre for a British cast and audience. I discarded an earlier Kannada draft and wrote the play afresh in English. [2002]

Flowers was written in English, for an actor who knew no Kannada. [2004]

So having started as a translator of my plays, I have slowly morphed myself into a playwright in English.

The chronology of the plays mentioned in this list indicates that the reciprocal roles of Kannada and English began shifting seriously with *Nāga-Mandala* in 1988, and continued along that trajectory, because although Karnad's list stops with *Flowers*, the three plays included in the present volume are also part of the same processes. To take the full measure of any one play by Karnad, therefore, you have to take into account its position within his own bilingual oeuvre, as well as the output of his contemporaries. Any one of the major features of his work—myth or history or folklore or contemporary life as subjects, realism, or anti-realism as modes, English or Kannada as source languages, theatre or film or television as creative mediums—would have sustained a lifelong career in drama, theatre, and performance. The singularity of Girish Karnad's larger-than-life presence in post-Independence drama is that he engaged with *all* of them, enriching contemporary Indian and world theatre in immeasurable ways.

APARNA BHARGAVA DHARWADKER
PROFESSOR OF ENGLISH AND INTERDISCIPLINARY
THEATRE STUDIES
UNIVERSITY OF WISCONSIN-MADISON, USA

Notes and References

1. 'Performance, Meaning, and the Materials of Modern Indian Theatre', *New Theatre Quarterly*, 44 (1995): 355–70.

2. A few examples can demonstrate the significance of this institutional support for leading practitioners. The NSD and its Repertory Company were major creative arenas for the directing work of Ebrahim Alkazi (1962–77) and B.V. Karanth (1977–81). The NSD also produced a succession of national-level directors and actors during this period, including Ratan Thiyam, Prasanna, Amal Allana, Bansi Kaul, M.K. Raina, Neelam Mansingh Chowdhry, Om Shivpuri, Sudha Shivpuri, Manohar Singh, Surekha Sikri, Rohini Hattangady, Naseeruddin Shah, Amrish Puri, and Om Puri, among others. Rajinder Nath headed the Shri Ram Centre Repertory Company during the 1980s, and Marathi playwright P.L. Deshpande had a long-standing association with the National Centre for Performing Arts in Mumbai. Karnad personally considers the role of the central Sangeet Natak Akademi especially important. Its administrators included influential cultural figures such as Kamaladevi Chattopadhyay, Keshav Kothari, Suresh Awasthi, and Karnad himself (he chaired the Akademi from 1988 to 1993). Karnad recalls that in 1968 the Akademi funded a trip to Calcutta which enabled him to meet Mohan Rakesh, Shyamanand Jalan, Badal Sircar, Pratibha Agrawal, Sombhu Mitra, and Utpal Dutt for the first time. He was also an active participant in the landmark Roundtable on the Contemporary Relevance of Traditional Theatre that Awasthi organized in 1971.

3. Girish Karnad, *Collected Plays of Girish Karnad*, vol. 1 (New Delhi: Oxford University Press, 2005), p. xvi.

4. *Collected Plays*, vol. 1, pp. xiv–xviii.

5. It is an interesting detail in the history of modern Indian theatre that the blending of myth (and especially episodes from the Mahabharata) and a multi-act modern structure began in the 1850s, and was evident in Michael Madhusudan Dutt's first full-length Bengali prose play (also based on the Yayati myth), *Sharmishtha* (1858), which he translated into English as *Sermista* the following year. Separated by a century, these two 'Yayati plays' make fascinating objects of comparison, because Dutt uses the Sanskrit dramaturgical elements more extensively. The play opens with the conventional banter between the sutradhar and the *nati* (actress), and the cast of characters include a *vidushak* (jester) and a symmetrical pair of female servants borrowed from Sanskrit drama. Karnad's modernist imagination is caught by the same narrative, but with entirely different effects in terms of form, structure, character, theme, and message.

6. Girish Karnad, *Yayati* (New Delhi: Oxford University Press, 2008), p. 30.

7. Girish Karnad, *Wedding Album* (New Delhi: Oxford University Press, 2009).

8. Girish Karnad, 'In Search of New Theatre', in Carla M. Borden (ed.), *Contemporary Indian Tradition* (Washington, D.C.: Smithsonian, 1985), p. 100.

9. Girish Karnad, *Boiled Beans on Toast* (New Delhi: Oxford University Press, 2014), p. viii.

10. Girish Karnad, *Collected Plays of Girish Karnad*, vol. 2 (New Delhi: Oxford University Press, 2005), pp. xxxiii–xxxix.

11. This note was made available to me by the author in February 2017.

YAYATI

Preface

Yayati is my first play. I wrote it in 1960 in Kannada. The play was published by G.B. Joshi in his *Manohara Grantha Mala*, Dharwad, on the advice of his editor, Kirtinath Kurtkoti, at a time when published texts of plays had no hope of selling and no theatre person would touch it. It lay there gathering dust for six years until I accidentally met Satyadev Dubey, who listened to me read it directly from the Kannada original and told me he would stage it. After a three-year struggle to get the right budget and cast, Dubey presented the play in Hindi for the Indian National Theatre, a magnificent production with Amrish Puri in the eponymous role.

However, I have continued to feel dissatisfied with the original text. When I wrote it, I was twenty-two and had no experience of theatre (nor I might add, of life). Over the years I have been fortunate enough to receive critical comments from professionals, who have actually staged it, and have rewritten the play incorporating many of their insights and suggestions. I hope the present revision, produced half-a-century later, has benefitted by the rewriting, but retains the vision and excitement of the first draft.

Girish Karnad
8 June 2007
Bengaluru

Yayati was first presented in Hindi by the Indian National Theatre at the Tejpal Auditorium in Bombay in 1967, with the following cast:

GURUNAM SINGH	The Sutradhara
SUNILA PRADHAN	Devayani
TARLA MEHTA	Sharmishtha
ASHA DANDAVATE	Chitralekha
SULABHA DESHPANDE	Swarnalata
AMRISH PURI	Yayati
SATYADEV DUBEY	Pooru
Directed by	SATYADEV DUBEY

This translation of *Yayati* was first performed by Artistes Repertory Theatre at the Ravindra Kalakshetra in Bangalore on 24 October 2006 as part of the Karnataka Nataka Academy's Kannada Rangabhoomi Festival, with the following cast:

APORUP ACHARYA	The Sutradhara
VEENA APPIAH	Devayani
SUKHITA AIYAR	Sharmishtha
ANJALIKA KAPUR	Chitralekha
MYTHRI SURENDRA	Swarnalata
APORUP ACHARYA	Yayati
KARTIK KUMAR	Pooru
Directed by	ARUNDHATI RAJA
Designed by	M.S. SATHYU
Costume by	JAYANTHI
Lighting by	PRADEEP BELAWADI
Music by	SANKARSHAN KINI
Vocalists	DIPTI RAO & SANKARSHAN KINI

Music genre: Hindustani Classical—*Khayal*
Theme raga: *Darbari Kanada*   Foil raga: *Tilak Kamod*

Prologue

The Sutradhara enters and addresses the audience.

SUTRADHARA: Good evening. I am the Sutradhara, which literally means 'the holder of strings'. It has been argued by some scholars that this title establishes my lineage back to the puppeteer, the manipulator of marionettes. But others, equally eminent, have said the string, being an instrument of measurement, actually points to my descent from the carpenter, the prop-maker or the architect. In effect, I am the person who has conceived the structures here, whether of brick and mortar or of words. I have designed and consecrated the stage. I am responsible for the choice of the text. And here I am now, to introduce the performance and to ensure that it takes place without any hindrance.

Our play this evening deals with an ancient myth. But, let me rush to explain, it is not a 'mythological'. Heaven forbid! A mythological aims to plunge us into the sentiment of devotion. It sets out to prove that the sole reason for our suffering in this world is that we have forsaken our gods. The mythological is fiercely convinced that all suffering is merely a calculated test, devised by the gods, to check out our willingness to submit to their will. If we crush our egos and give ourselves up in surrender, divine grace will descend upon us and redeem us. There are no deaths in mythologicals, for no matter how hard you try, death cannot give meaning to anything that has gone before. It merely empties life of meaning.

Our play has no gods. And it deals with death. A key element in its plot is the 'Sanjeevani' vidya—the art of reviving the dead, which promises release from the limitations of the fleeting life this self is trapped in. The gods and the rakshasas have been killing each other from the beginning of time for the possession of this art. Humans have been struggling to master it. Sadly, we aspire to become immortal but cannot achieve the lucidity necessary to understand eternity. Death eludes definition. Time coils into a loop, reversing the order of youth and old age. Our certainties crumble in front of the stark demands of the heart.

We turn to ancient lore not because it offers any blinding revelation or hope of consolation, but because it provides fleeting glimpses of the fears and desires sleepless within us. It is a good way to get introduced to ourselves.

Enough however of circumlocution! Let us get on with the play.

What is represented here on stage is an inner chamber on the first floor of King Yayati's palace. The King's son, Prince Pooru, is returning home today after many years of absence. He has successfully completed his education in the hermitage under renowned gurus, and is bringing home with him his bride, Chitralekha, the Princess of Anga.

Crowds have started collecting in the grounds around the palace, eager to see the royal couple. The two must enter this space and on this bed they must create for themselves the magic kingdom of love, ambition, and power. He must sow his seed here and then launch forth on a campaign of victory and death. She must proudly bear on her breasts the toothmarks incised by their offspring. Must. Nothing, however, ever happens as it must. What we have in front of us is not a well-charted map but a network of paths, many of which plunge into the shrubbery and disappear before we have even registered them.

But we must trust the narrative we have chosen for ourselves. Invent bits if necessary, but go on. We must relive, not a saga embedded in books, but a tale orally handed down by our grandmothers in lamplit corners.

Act One

An inner chamber in King Yayati's palace. Devayani is sitting on a large ornately carved bed in the chamber. Swarnalata is sitting on the floor, leaning against it, evidently upset.

DEVAYANI: Enough, Swarna. How often do I have to tell you not to pay her any attention? Get up now. There is so much to attend to yet—

SWARNALATA: That spiteful whore—I would have torn her hair out if you hadn't stopped me. Taught that fiend a proper lesson. The rakshasi. You heard us, madam. Did I say a word against her? All those dirty insinuations. The nasty jibes. They are too horrible to think. She didn't even spare His Majesty. I ... I can't bear it.

DEVAYANI: She has a foul tongue. I know. Just ignore her.

SWARNALATA: What have I done to her? What has she got against me?

DEVAYANI: Nothing. It is all my fault. I didn't realize she would tear into you like that. I'll see that you don't have to deal with her from now on.

SWARNALATA: But why do you tolerate her? Why don't you send her back to her tribe?

DEVAYANI: Enough, I say. Just get back to your work. There is still a lot left to do. Remember, it is an important day in my life.

SWARNALATA: Two years of it! I can't take it any longer. How she lashed out at His Majesty yesterday. She was so vicious it took our breath away and yet you tried to reason with her. Why? Why do you put up with her? I know she was your friend once. But today she is your slave. You mustn't let her forget that. And *you* mustn't forget it either.

DEVAYANI: All right. All right. No need to go on.

SWARNALATA: Forgive me! May I say something? I am older than you. I have seen more of life. So if you will permit me ...

DEVAYANI (*impatient*): What is it now?

SWARNALATA: Take care, madam. Not about what she is doing to you, but about what you are doing to yourself. Someone like her, she can become an addiction. You may begin to need her more than she needs you.

DEVAYANI (*surprised*): I must say! I didn't expect that from you.

SWARNALATA: I know. No one expects that from Swarnalata. I am expected to be jolly, keep everyone's spirits up, be the life and soul of the palace. But madam, I can't tell you how scared I am of the shadows that curl around my jokes. I can feel them seeping in like slow fumes of poison. Alone, I am forever fighting them, struggling to block them.

DEVAYANI: We all have them, Swarna.

SWARNALATA: She is satanic. She can barge into the poisonous fumes and watch me choke while she remains untouched. She can creep into the hidden corners of my mind, claw those shadows out and set them dancing. I am terrified of her.

DEVAYANI: Don't be insane.

SWARNALATA: Not yet, but I am halfway there. So please listen to me. It is not Sharmishtha's nastiness that one has to be wary of. It is her uncanny ability to cut close to the bone.

DEVAYANI: Come on. Enough. You don't need to tell me about her. I have known her for years. Don't let us waste any more time on her. The young couple should be arriving any minute and this chamber is nowhere near ready. Go, see if the florists have come. Ask them to hurry up. Go.

SWARNALATA: Yes, madam.

(*Swarnalata exits. Devayani leans against a bed-post, exhausted, depressed. Sharmishtha enters noiselessly. Watches Devayani from a distance.*)

SHARMISHTHA: Your Majesty ...

(*Devayani almost jumps out of her skin.*)

Forgive me for disturbing, madam. But I saw that darling maid of yours leave and rushed in here. It wouldn't do to have madam suffer for lack of distraction.

DEVAYANI (*calmly*): Why do you try so hard at being nasty? I feel sorry for you sometimes. It won't help to ...

SHARMISHTHA: Help? I am afraid I don't know what 'help' madam can possibly mean. I may not be able to provide all that Swarnalata so freely provides, but ...

DEVAYANI: I feel sorry for you. I have often thought of sending you back home. But there is no way you can force me to do so. And this, certainly, is no way.

SHARMISHTHA: I promise you, madam, I was not being deliberately nasty. It is just that I am an uncouth rakshasi. And the situation here ... a kshatriya palace, ruled over by a brahmin queen! Confusing isn't the word.

DEVAYANI: Don't you ever tire? The same old stings, the blunted barbs. They don't even hurt anymore. But what have you got against that poor Swarnalata? Or His Majesty? Attack me. Do your worst. I don't care. This is between us. Leave the others out of it.

SHARMISHTHA: Others? There are no others. There is only the two of us here. You, my respected mistress, and me, your favourite slave. Entwined, lacerating each other, gouging each other's eyes out. The 'others' are there because they happen to be there. I didn't ask them in. Incidentally, I am told—actually I wasn't told, since no one talks to me here, but I gather—that your Prince is expected to arrive this evening with his new bride. I can barely wait. ...

DEVAYANI: Don't you dare touch them.

(*Sharmishtha shrugs, casually. Devayani goes on, frustrated.*)

Can't you see that you are only hurting yourself? Can't you see the futility of it all? Why don't you just open your eyes and see?

(*Sharmishtha suddenly drops her mocking smile.*)

SHARMISHTHA: I opened my eyes, two years ago. Don't you remember? *I* do. The precise moment. When I closed my eyes, I was the princess of the rakshasas. You were the offspring of a destitute brahmin, dependent upon my father. I had everything. Beauty, education, wealth. Everything except birth—an Arya pedigree. What was your worth? That your father knew the 'sanjeevani' spell. That is all. Yet I worshipped you. No, I loved you. To me, the most wondrous power I possessed seemed to be my ability to shower gifts upon you—things you hadn't asked for but which you so gracefully accepted. My personal jewellery, my mother's diamonds, precious stones from the treasury. Some even stolen.

(*Devayani has heard all this before. But she lets Sharmishtha go on since the spiel gives her a sense of power which she makes no attempt to hide.*)

I opened my eyes. You had become the Queen of the Arya race. Wife of King Yayati. And I was your slave. My eyes have no lids now. I live staring at you, unflinchingly. Like the fish. No, like the gods. No, more a corpse, its eyes wide open. As the King crawls into your bed night after night, I want you to remember I am there, hovering around ...

DEVAYANI: You make me sick.

SHARMISHTHA: ... waiting, peeling back your lids, looking into your eyeballs. Waiting.

DEVAYANI: For what?

SHARMISHTHA (*smiles*): I don't know. But when the moment arrives, I shall recognize it and seize it. And you will know too. You won't be able to shut your eyes to it.

DEVAYANI: And you would see only one thing in my eyes. The reflection of His Majesty's face ...

SHARMISHTHA: Really? And what would you see in His Majesty's eyes? Have you tried to find out? Have you ever dared examine those eyes and acknowledge the lust burning there?

DEVAYANI: And why not? That's what I am here for. To be lusted for by His Majesty.

SHARMISHTHA: Except that he is not lusting for you, you poor darling, he lusts for immortality. Your father's art of 'sanjeevani'.

DEVAYANI: Shut up!

SHARMISHTHA: Yayati. The scion of the Bharata dynasty. He is not short of women, is he? Women of his own kind. Sensuous kshatriya maidens. Virgins reared for him. But he chooses you. Why? You know the answer. You, only you, could lead him to the ultimate goal: a sanctuary beyond the reach of death. Ah! The joy of turning the funeral pyres of one's kinsmen into altars for one's own fire sacrifice. The timeless thrill of it.

DEVAYANI: Like your father, you mean, who has been fawning on mine for his favours?

SHARMISHTHA: Precisely. Like my father. So I know that kind intimately, you see. From the inside. (*Pointing to the window.*) Those crowds there. To have the power to look upon them from a distance, supreme and untouched by the fear of mortality, to sigh wearily and wait as they crumble into dust and the next generation takes their place. I have seen my father drugged on that ambition, panting for that supreme privilege. And now I see him in Yayati, who has the world in his palm. And your father, the great Shukracharya, has the means to keep it there. For eternity. That is what he lusts for.

DEVAYANI: I could have had your tongue slashed. But I won't. I want to see how long you can go on abusing it before it wears out.

SHARMISHTHA: Just think of when Yayati saw you first. You were in a well—covered in mud and filth. Scratched. Bleeding. Your clothes in tatters. You think he fell in love with that spectacle? Fool! He would have gone away without a second thought—except that he learnt that you were Devayani. Devayani! Daughter of Shukracharya! And Yayati's manhood raised its head. And all he had to do to keep his banner flying over the world was to plant his flag pole into you.

DEVAYANI: Go on. Go on if it makes you feel better.

(*Pause.*)

That's not how it happened. And you know that. I was in the well, crying out for help. Frightened. Distraught. And I heard someone call. A face peered into the well. An arm stretched out and pulled me up. I recognized him instantly. I had seen him from far—dreamt of him—and now he was there in flesh and blood. I stared, spellbound.

SHARMISHTHA: I know how it goes after that. You forgot that you despised men. You forgot the oath you had taken after Kacha's betrayal, never to love a man. It was love at first sight. Once again.

DEVAYANI (*triumphantly*): Yes. And, as it transpired, for him too. We stared at each other. And then I spoke: 'Sir, I am a maiden. And you have held me by my right hand.' That's it. Only two sentences. Fourteen words. I should know. How often have I counted them, coercing myself to believe that mere fourteen words could actually so completely change a life. It was only later, when I tore away the blouse, that he asked why.

(*Pause.*)

He didn't even know who I was when he accepted me.

SHARMISHTHA: Very nice. Actually, I was discussing that story with one of the palace concubines the other day. And you know what she said? 'The King was no doubt in a hurry to have some quick fun and go,' she said. 'Even with prostitutes picked off the street, the first thing a man does is ask her name.' And you say with you, the King dispensed with even that formality? You knew what would happen if you didn't act quickly. I mean, you didn't want the Kacha experience again! So while he was locked in your embrace, you quickly told him you were Devayani, daughter of et cetera et cetera.

DEVAYANI (*flaring up*): Bitch! I'll kill you. I'll feed you to the ...

(*She is about to hit Sharmishtha when Yayati enters. The three stand frozen, staring at each other.*)

SHARMISHTHA: Hail, immortal King.

YAYATI: What is going on here? I mean why isn't this chamber ready yet?

SHARMISHTHA: The Queen was in need of some entertainment. Now that His Majesty is here to take over, I hope I may be excused.

(*Exits.*)

YAYATI: What is this, darling? What is going on? I mean, it is an auspicious day today. Such an important occasion for us. The

Prince is meeting you for the first time! He is bringing home his bride! Their entourage is at the city gates. They should be here any moment. And nothing is ready. The room hasn't been decorated. Look at you. You aren't ...

DEVAYANI: That's all you are worried about, aren't you? Celebrations. Revelries. Festivities. That's all you care about. What I am going through means nothing to you. You are so wrapped up ...

YAYATI: Oh, ho! What's wrong? Tell me. What has upset my little pet?

DEVAYANI: I am the daughter of a brahmin teacher. A pet is the one thing I have never had the chance to be.

YAYATI: If you can tell me what you are so upset about, perhaps ...

DEVAYANI: Why did you marry me?

Yayati (*surprised*): Listen, is that a question for now? We have been married two years.

DEVAYANI: If you had deserted me after we first made love, left me on the bed of leaves, no one would have blamed you. Kings are used to women throwing themselves at them. I too would have kept silent from fear and shame. Why then did you marry me?

YAYATI: Because you are the most beautiful woman I know. And at that moment you were an apparition of the kind I had never seen before: dirty, dishevelled, ravishing. All at once.

DEVAYANI: Don't play the fool, please. I must know.

YAYATI: And fortunately, I had pulled you up by your right hand. I was enchanted by you and you were not exactly disinclined. So.

DEVAYANI: But they say ...

YAYATI: What? (*Pause.*) What do *they* say?

DEVAYANI: They say even a prostitute is asked her name first when she is picked off the street. And you didn't ask mine.

YAYATI: Didn't I? I can't remember. (*Annoyed.*) Then how did I discover your name? Perhaps it was written in my horoscope that, lost in the jungle after a hunt and riding along a god-forsaken track, I would hear a voice call out from a well and there I would see a woman caked in mud, a wood nymph, and according to the stars, the first two letters of her name would be ...

DEVAYANI: Stop that.

YAYATI: How can I? I am amazed. I am amazed to learn that there is a traditional order of questions, meticulously followed by the lechers haunting the debauched quarters. I am amazed at how my wife, sitting in one of the best guarded women's quarters in the world, suddenly comes to know the questions with which whore-mongers accost stray women ...

DEVAYANI: I am sorry. I am stupid. Let us forget it.

YAYATI: Dare I ask who is behind all this? Will you permit me a guess? Surely it is that accursed creature, the deranged witch rampaging around in the palace grounds.

DEVAYANI: *You* are delaying things now. Go away. Let me get this chamber done up.

YAYATI: No, I won't go. I have had enough of this ghoul sucking blood from our married life. I am sick of hearing every living soul in the palace complain against her. And I am scared lest she defile today's festivities. I have had enough. I must talk to her. (*Calls out.*) Who is there?

SWARNALATA (*enters*): Sir.

YAYATI: Send that Sharmishtha in here.

SWARNALATA (*to Devayani*): The florists are waiting, madam.

YAYATI: Let them wait. I must have a word with that woman first.

(*Swarnalata leaves.*)

DEVAYANI: What are you going to say to her?

YAYATI: I'll give her a month. If she behaves herself, I shall send her home. And I mean it.

DEVAYANI: It's no use. She will not listen.

YAYATI: Devi, look. I had come to tell you that the head priest is waiting for us. He wants to go over the details of the pooja with us. And I forgot. Go to him. I'll have a word with this woman and follow you.

DEVAYANI: No, please. Let her be.

YAYATI (laughs): Are you afraid to leave me alone with her? You can stay if you wish. But I have a feeling she will be easier to deal without you around.

DEVAYANI: It's not that. It is ...

YAYATI: I am no stranger to women, darling.

DEVAYANI: Ohho! You and your ...

(Sharmishtha enters. An uncomfortable silence ensues. She stands in a corner, docile and obedient, without looking up at either the King or Devayani. Yayati waits for Devayani to leave. After a pause, Devayani exits. The silence continues.)

YAYATI: Well, let me not beat around the bush. It is not proper that I am seen conversing with—someone like you. So let me come to the point.

My son, Pooru, arrives today with his new bride. On this auspicious day, with my family deity as my witness, let me give you my word. If you behave yourself for one more month, just till the next full moon, I shall see that you are sent home.

SHARMISHTHA: Home? Whose home?

YAYATI: Yours. Who else? You aren't happy here. You can't be. Fair enough. Different manners, customs. An unfamiliar way of life.

I can imagine how excruciating it must be to live amongst strangers against your will.

SHARMISHTHA: Against my will? Who said so? No, sir. I agreed to this arrangement. This is my life now. My home. Devayani has her father's word that I shall be her slave. My father has given her father his word that I shall be her slave. And I have given my father my word that it shall be so. We can't go back on all those words. Too many words to break.

YAYATI: Look, when Devayani demanded that you come with her to my palace as her companion ...

SHARMISHTHA: ... as her slave. You don't have to be kind, sir.

YAYATI: ... as her companion, it was meant to be a formal punishment for your offence. But she is a friend of yours. She loves you. Two years have passed. You have served your term. I shall arrange to have you freed.

SHARMISHTHA: Oh! But I love it here.

YAYATI (*defeated*): Are you happy even in this hell you are creating?

SHARMISHTHA: I could have spewed out nectar. But we leave those things to namby-pamby brahmin girls. I am a rakshasa woman. We have our code.

YAYATI: What code? You are from a royal family. Where is your self-respect? Your dignity—the obligation to be a princess that you owe your family? You behave like a cheap harridan.

SHARMISHTHA: You own hundreds of slaves. But have you ever wondered what it does to a person to be made a slave? It turns that person into an animal. A domesticated animal. One's will to act is destroyed. One's selfhood humbled into grateful submission. 'Accept that crumb, wait for a pat on the back.' To be a good slave is to have all your vileness extracted from you.

(*Pause.*)

I snarl because I want to retain a particle of my original self. I abuse and rave to retrieve an iota of it. It's all useless of course. Scream as I may, I know there is no escape from the degradation. The louder I scream, the more I declare myself a slave. That is the point. I have decided to turn myself into a performing freak.

YAYATI: You are a very intelligent woman. I didn't allow for that.

SHARMISHTHA: You Aryas have sorted out things so neatly for yourselves that we must seem confused. And confusing. Why does she behave like that? Why can't she see what is good for her? The answer, sir, is because we rakshasas have chosen to live in chaos, proud that it is a chaos of our own creation. And yet of course we also despise ourselves for not being lucid and rational, like you Aryas.

(*Pause.*)

To be thus convoluted is our prerogative.

YAYATI: I have said all that I wished to say. I must now go.

SHARMISHTHA: Please, wait. It is true I am your wife's slave. You may dismiss me as you wish. But you asked to see me. And as you said yourself, I am a princess by birth. I have a right to be heard.

YAYATI: Then answer my question first. Is pushing a friend into a well an act worthy of a princess? That is where it all began, didn't it?

SHARMISHTHA: Yes, it did. But she has never explained to you why?

YAYATI: Oh, yes. Something about your blouses getting mixed up and you flying into a wild temper ...

SHARMISHTHA (*smiles*): Yes, of course.

YAYATI: You started the chain of events. You can't now blame her for it.

SHARMISHTHA: Of course I don't. I accept the responsibility for every act, including the first, which was, actually, to love Devayani. Until she stepped into my life, I was a perfect rakshasa princess. Spoilt. Proud. But not too much. I liked being with other rakshasa girls and boys. Go singing and dancing with them under the bright moon. Weave garlands of wild flowers for our festive games. Prance around in the river naked on dark nights, aware of the naked boys sensing us from the distance. But outside that world, conscious every moment that we were rakshasas, held in contempt.

Then Devayani came into my life. Devayani. She was unlike any woman I had met. She seemed completely unconscious of the fact that she belonged to a superior race. Actually let me confess, sir. She was equally affectionate to everyone in our tribe. It was I, as the princess, who claimed her for myself. I wallowed in the privilege her equality endowed me with. I gloated. I flaunted her company in the face of other rakshasa girls. And she accepted all that with such easy grace. If she had mocked me as a rakshasi even by suggestion, we might have been happier today.

YAYATI: I am captivated. But I must go. It is ...

SHARMISHTHA: One day we went for a swim in the lake. We two had grown closer since her brahmin lover, Kacha, had spurned her. I liked to think I was nursing her bruised self back to health, guarding her against further hurt. I wanted to be like her. I even dressed like her.

We finished our swim and stretched out on the grass, our hair spread out to dry in the sun. I could feel myself being sucked languidly into a stupor, when Devayani woke me up. 'We have exchanged our blouses, I think,' she said.

I felt a sudden stab of anger that the delicacy of the moment had been so needlessly disturbed. 'I was on the brink of a beautiful dream,' I replied, 'You've ruined it.' I was smiling, of course, but the suggestion of bitterness in my words must have stung her. I suddenly felt alarmed at my thoughtlessness and wanted to make up for it ... when the world fell into shivers around me.

YAYATI: Why? What happened?

SHARMISHTHA: 'You poor people,' she said. And I realized with rising panic that she had never ever used that phrase before. Never talked of us in plural. 'You poor people. You only have to get into a piece of Arya attire. And you start fantasizing.'

(*Pause.*)

Please, sir, bear with me. If those words had come from anyone else, I would have brushed them aside. I was used to worse. But Devayani—*my* Devayani—Devayani to whom I had dedicated myself! My mind froze. I watched myself, like in a dream, straining to stop myself but powerless to do so, as I got up and grabbed her long loose hair. I twisted the strands round my hand and pulled her up. And as she screamed and thrashed about, I dragged her to a well nearby and pushed her in. And I stood there and watched, as she crashed through the brambles that filled the well. The world knows I threw her into a well. But not that I was sitting there, for I don't know how long, racked with sobs. Does that surprise you, sir? I do have tears in my eyes. But the world only cares for the embers there.

(*Long pause.*)

YAYATI: I came here to reprimand you. But now I am lost for words.

SHARMISHTHA: You don't have to believe my story. It must simplify your life to believe that I acted as a savage would be expected to.

YAYATI: Let me say I feel benefitted by our little chat in at least one small way. I know there is nothing I can do. I stand disabused of my belief that I have the ability to solve the problem.

SHARMISHTHA (*calmly*): No, sir, but you have helped. Perhaps during these two years all I needed was someone to listen to me. You have done that and that is enough for me. I am grateful. I shall not torment you any further.

YAYATI: What do you mean? You agree to go home?

SHARMISHTHA (*takes out a vial from her inside her blouse*): Home is just a blank spot, sir, erased from my life. This is the dowry my father gave me when I left home. A vial of lethal poison. The purest extract of wild mushrooms.

(*Smiles.*)

'Instantly effective,' my father has assured me. I meant to use it, first on Devayani and then on myself. But now I have no desire left to kill her.

YAYATI: Killing her would have solved nothing.

SHARMISHTHA: Perhaps. But that is immaterial now. At this moment I am in a position to bring the game to an end.

(*Sharmishtha calmly lifts the vial to her lips.*)

YAYATI: Don't be stupid, Sharmishtha. You pushed Devayani into a well. And now you are plunging down a crueller abyss.

SHARMISHTHA: But you turned up in time to pull her out. I am a barbarian. My arms have thorns.

(*She is about to drink the contents of the vial when Yayati jumps forward and grabs her right hand.*)

YAYATI: Drop it, Sharmishtha. Instantly.

(*They both stand frozen. Sharmishtha drops the vial, which falls on the bed.*)

SHARMISHTHA (*without any emotion*): Sir, you are holding my right hand. And I am a princess.

(*Yayati instantly lets go of her hand and withdraws. Sharmishtha sits down on the bed.*)

Forgive me, sir. I did not mean to trap you in my words. I know I have no life but of a slave. But please, sir. I can't go on living, floundering around in this hell hole.

(*Swarnalata enters.*)

SWARNALATA: Your Majesty, the floral decorators are outside awaiting orders.

YAYATI: Send them away. I shall ask for them. And listen, I don't want anyone to be admitted until I say so.

(*Swarnalata exits, expressionless.*)

So you see, Sharmishtha, I too am joining in.

(*The stage darkens.*)

Act Two

Yayati on the bed. Sharmishtha is adjusting her dress. Her hair is cascading down her shoulders. She deftly gathers it in her hand and ties it up in a knot. Turns and looks at him. He sees the vial of poison lying on the bed and picks it up.

SHARMISHTHA: You should have let me drink the poison.

YAYATI: Would you have, if I had let you?

SHARMISHTHA: Yes.

YAYATI: So it wasn't just a threat then—a theatrical gesture?

SHARMISHTHA: No.

YAYATI: Rakshasas are known for their histrionics.

SHARMISHTHA: I didn't plot it. I wanted to die.

YAYATI: I can never understand that. The fascination with suicide. The flirtation with death.

SHARMISHTHA: You talk of death as though it was another woman ready to succumb to your charms. It isn't. You cannot flirt with one death and then pass on to taste the next one. There is no next one.

YAYATI: Tsk! Don't try to teach me about death. I deal with it everyday.

SHARMISHTHA: Other people's death. I am not talking about that.

YAYATI: The only death real to me is that of someone else. Not mine. I never think of my own death. That is not for me a possibility at all. When I ride out into combat, I know I shall return alive.

SHARMISHTHA: To what? More women?

YAYATI: Among other things. Women, music, dance, celebrations, my subjects. I love life. I love my subjects. I like those around me to be happy and cheerful. I would like you to remember that.

(*Pause. He waits to see if she has caught the import of his remark. She has.*)

SHARMISHTHA: Me? It doesn't apply to me. (*Pause.*) I am not going to be around here. Devayani will not allow that. Not after all this. This is going to make her very angry.

YAYATI: Why should she mind? She knows she is married to the King. She can't afford to be jealous.

SHARMISHTHA: I don't know whether she will be jealous. But she will most certainly be livid. And along with her, her father. I should tread warily there if I were you.

YAYATI: Oh! But surely, he can't be such a prude. He is a guru in your father's court. He must be used to worse.

SHARMISHTHA: Let us not get into that, sir. Let me just warn you that by spending this half an hour with me, you have already lit the fire. Better douse it before it explodes into a conflagration.

YAYATI: Let it. I don't care.

(*Sharmishtha coolly stares at him.*)

SHARMISHTHA: You are amazing.

YAYATI (*smiling*): I have heard that said before.

SHARMISHTHA: But not, I am sure, in the sense I mean.

YAYATI: How do you mean?

SHARMISHTHA: You see yourself as awesome and powerful, a figure towering over your vast possessions, a demi-god if not god himself. You are so busy visualizing the grand design of life, you have no sense of the traps and snares waiting in the grass. You have no sense of how illogical suffering can be and therefore how terrible.

(*Pause.*)

You don't know what a disaster you could be.

YAYATI: No one has dared say that to me.

SHARMISHTHA: There you see! A simple statement like that and they have to 'dare' to utter it. I wish more people had said such things to you. You are a good man, I am sure. But you are naive, which is dangerous for a powerful man to be.

YAYATI: You are insolent. That is dangerous for a slave.

SHARMISHTHA: I am not your slave, Your Majesty. I am hers. I have absolutely no need to be scared of you, for she will not let me into your vicinity again. She will send me away. If she doesn't, I shall run away.

YAYATI: How?

SHARMISHTHA: That is between her and me. I will not betray my mistress' trust ... a second time.

YAYATI: You leave me no choice then.

SHARMISHTHA: I beg your pardon, sir. A King, by definition, has every choice. It is the slave who is deprived of it.

YAYATI: Quite. And Devayani will deprive me of my choice if she takes you away. So I shall have to take measures to prevent that from happening.

(*Pause.*)

I am making you my queen.

SHARMISHTHA (*stunned*): Me? Your queen? Nonsense!

YAYATI: Mind your words, lady. When I say something, I mean it. I shall make you my queen.

SHARMISHTHA: What absolute rubbish! Don't ... Stop uttering such ...

(*She suddenly bursts into tears. He watches, pleased with the effect he has had on her. She cries for a while and then controls herself.*)

There. You should be ashamed of yourself. You have made me cry.

YAYATI: I didn't intend to.

SHARMISHTHA (*wiping her tears*): It is not fair. Going round offering to marry every woman you have slept with.

YAYATI: I do not offer to marry every woman I sleep with.

SHARMISHTHA: Oh, bother! I have forgotten what I started out to say. Oh, yes. Sharing this palace with her has been unpleasant enough. I am not going to start sharing a bed.

YAYATI: You have already.

SHARMISHTHA: I know. I should have had more sense. Well, it is too late to regret that now. No, thanks. I must turn down your kind offer.

YAYATI: What are you afraid of?

SHARMISHTHA: Of her. Of you. The two of you are nice enough apart. But together you would make a deadly combination. And then there are the crowds outside.

YAYATI (*suddenly remembering*): Oh my god! It completely slipped my mind. The crowds. This chamber has to be done up for my son.

SHARMISHTHA: I shouldn't worry too much about that. They were getting another one ready. Just in case. Your maids are adept at handling crises.

YAYATI (*calls out*): Who is there?

SWARNALATA (*enters*): Your Majesty.

YAYATI: Send the florists in.

SWARNALATA: The florists have gone away, sir. The Queen asked them to leave.

YAYATI: Devayani? Is she here?

SWARNALATA: She has been waiting outside for a while, Your Majesty.

YAYATI (*taken aback*): Has she? Send her in. Send her in.

(*Swarnalata bows and goes out.*)

You go now, Sharmishtha. I'll handle her.

SHARMISHTHA: It won't help. Let me be here. Please. I know her better than you.

YAYATI: Go.

SHARMISHTHA (*pleading*): Don't annoy her further, sir. Please be careful. Treat her gently.

(*Sharmishtha exits left. Devayani enters from the right.*)

YAYATI: Come, devi.

DEVAYANI: Very nice. An auspicious reopening of your son's bed chamber. Where is she gone?

YAYATI: Listen, devi. It is no use getting excited ...

(*Devayani goes and pulls open some curtains on the left. Sharmishtha is hiding behind one of them.*)

DEVAYANI: There you are! You see, Your Majesty. She is my childhood friend. There is nothing we don't know about each other.

SHARMISHTHA (*with a smile*): My words. Precisely.

DEVAYANI: Shut up! You, you treacherous hyena ...

YAYATI: Listen to me, devi. Let us just forget ...

DEVAYANI: There is only one way to forget. She must go. Treachery runs in her veins. I shall send her home.

SHARMISHTHA: Home? I have no home. I have promised my father that I shall be your servant for life.

DEVAYANI: I treated you with compassion. Kept you here with me and this is how you return my trust. You are evil beyond redemption. You are ... you are ... I don't want you here. Go. I grant you your freedom. Go and hang yourself with it. I shall arrange for you to be sent home instantly.

YAYATI: Don't be foolhardy, devi.

DEVAYANI: These are royal orders, Sharmishtha. Go. Get out.

(*Sharmishtha seems about to challenge her but suddenly controls herself. Softly, with a smile,*)

SHARMISHTHA: Thank you. Now that I have forfeited my shackles, I can die in a ditch of my choice.

YAYATI: Wait, Sharmishtha. I forbid you to go.

SHARMISHTHA: Thank you, Your Majesty. But I am under no obligation to obey you. I am not your subject.

YAYATI: Who is there?

(*Swarnalata enters.*)

Tell the guards this lady may go anywhere she likes in the kingdom but she is to be kept under strict surveillance.

DEVAYANI: What do you want? You have had her. All right. That is over and done with. I now want her out of our sight.

YAYATI (*to Swarnalata*): You heard me. I want her kept under watch. If she disappears, someone will pay for it with his life.

(*Swarnalata exits.*)

DEVAYANI: Let her go! Don't you have enough concubines to keep you occupied?

SHARMISHTHA: Me his concubine? You must be joking. Yes, I got him into bed with me. That was my revenge on you. After all, as a slave, what weapon did I have but my body? Well, I am even with you now. And I am free. I shall go where I please.

YAYATI (*to Sharmishtha*): You are not fooling anyone. (*To Devayani*) I am not out to make her my concubine. She will be my queen.

DEVAYANI (*horrified*): Your queen? Your royal consort?

YAYATI: Yes, but you don't need to worry, devi. Your position will not be touched. You will remain the Senior Queen. You will share my throne. You will be at my side in all public celebrations. That goes without saying. She can never be a threat to your position, you know that, because of her race.

DEVAYANI: Oh god! This slave of mine is to be ... No. That is not possible.

YAYATI: She is not a slave any more; you have just freed her.

SHARMISHTHA: So I am free to spurn your proposition.

YAYATI: Very nice. Exquisite.

(*Grabs her by her arm.*)

Now speak the truth. Aren't you desperate to be my queen? Aren't you?

SHARMISHTHA: Let go of me. Let go. Please.

DEVAYANI: Let go of her, sir. Does my being here mean nothing to you?

YAYATI: What is the point of all these theatrics, Sharmishtha?

(*Lets go of her.*)

Devi, what are you upset about? She will be lodged in a separate residence. I shall ensure that she does not impinge on your life for one fleeting moment.

DEVAYANI: Please, take as many wives as you want. I don't care. But not this reptile. Not her.

YAYATI: But why not?

DEVAYANI: Just send her away. I beg of you.

SHARMISHTHA: Let me go, sir. She doesn't want me here. And I don't want to be here. For once, Devayani and I are in perfect accord.

YAYATI (*genuinely surprised*): Why are you being so difficult? Are you afraid of her? Or are you being nice to her? (*Firmly*) My answer to both of you is sorry, my mind is made up.

SHARMISHTHA (*calmly*): Well then. I know I am doomed. If you are so keen to join me, so be it. But don't blame me later.

(*The beating of drums is heard. And the tumult of the crowds.*)

Where is this guard who is supposed to keep an eye on me? I suppose Swarna will point him out.

(*Exits.*)

YAYATI: Come, devi. You have to welcome the Prince. He must be nearing the palace.

DEVAYANI: Sir, I have never asked any favour of you in these two years. I implore you now. I too can bare my fangs. I too can draw blood. Don't provoke me on account of this woman.

(*Suddenly, with vehemence,*)

Why? Why do you want her?

YAYATI (*calmly*): Because I feel bewitched by her. Even now, at this moment, I want her. I have never felt so entranced by a woman. What is it? Is it some spell she has cast? Some secret sorcery? I can feel youth bursting out within me again. Her beauty, her intelligence, her wit, her abandon in love. Not to marry her is to lose her, don't you see? I must have her. I have to keep her with me. Please try to understand.

(*Swarnalata enters.*)

SWARNALATA: The Prince's entourage is at the palace gates.

YAYATI: Come, darling. We must go and welcome them.

(*No response from Devayani.*)

You can't not.

(*Sees the futility of further persuasion.*)

All right then. Wait here. I shall greet them and bring them in here.

(*He leaves. Devayani stares after him. Then, as Swarnalata watches horrified, she tears the marriage thread from around her neck and flings it on the floor.*)

SWARNALATA: Madam ...

(*Devayani snatches out other pieces of jewellery she is wearing and throws them down.*)

Please, madam. Your son is here. You can't ... Madam ...

DEVAYANI: I have nothing more to do with this lot. I am finished with them.

SWARNALATA: Don't say that. Your daughter-in-law—she is still a child. Think of her. Her happiness is your concern now.

DEVAYANI: I am no kshatriya queen to suffer relatives foisted on me. I am leaving ...

SWARNALATA: No, please. His Majesty is ... he is like a child. He will forget that woman once he finds another toy. But if you go away now—in front of all those crowds—the damage will be for ever. You will never be able to undo it. And they will blame it all on the young bride.

DEVAYANI: Do you expect me to worry about them when I have enough worries to drown me?

SWARNALATA: The Prince can't even remember his mother. He lost her when he was a baby. He is your son. And she is your daughter-in-law. You accepted that pledge the moment you became the Queen.

DEVAYANI: It's all my fault, I know. I am to blame for everything. It is just that I am unworthy of this palace ...

SWARNALATA: Madam, Let me say one more thing. I have seen more of the world than you ...

DEVAYANI: Enough, menial.

(*Swarnalata recoils.*)

Don't over-reach yourself. (*Taking off her last bangle*) I came here without these trinkets. I shall go back without them.

SWARNALATA: Forgive me. But won't you at least talk to your father before you decide ...

DEVAYANI: I don't need you to tell me that. I am going home. Go, tell them to summon my carriage.

SWARNALATA: But, madam, your father is here. He has come to the city to greet the Prince.

DEVAYANI (*surprised*): Has he? When did he come?

(*The deafening sound of drums erupt again. Panegyrics. Hosannas by the crowds fill the air. Swarnalata gets excited.*)

SWARNALATA: The Prince has entered the palace. The welcome rites are about to start. Please ...

DEVAYANI: Tell me. Where is my father?

SWARNALATA: I was told he was resting in the Shambhu shrine.

DEVAYANI: Good. That saves me a lot of trouble.

(*Sharmishtha comes rushing in.*)

Well, well. Guess who is here. The new queen herself. Aren't you going to welcome the Prince? What are you doing in here?

SHARMISHTHA: I don't know. I don't know what I am doing here. But Devayani, don't do anything rash. Your temper ...

DEVAYANI: You are a fine one to talk. Do you think I don't know why you have come to me now? You have heard about Father. And you are here to prevent me from seeing him. You want to keep me trapped in here till the Prince arrives.

SHARMISHTHA: Yes, perhaps you are right. I don't know what to do. But Devayani, I can sense disaster, I can feel it looming. And only you can avert it. At least wait till you have met the Prince and his bride. Talk to them. That may lead to some way out of this terrible mess ...

DEVAYANI: I will. But only if you get out of here. I want you out of my life.

SHARMISHTHA: And go where? My father will not accept me. And the King has me under watch.

DEVAYANI: I will not be able to sleep a wink while his hands caress your body.

(*Sharmishtha makes a helpless gesture.*)

Well then.

(*Devayani exits. Sharmishtha looks around, lost. While the above conversation is going on, Swarnalata is collecting the pieces of jewellery flung around by Devayani.*

Music is played outside the door. Sharmishtha runs out following Devayani as Yayati, Pooru, and Chitralekha enter. Swarnalata moves to a corner and awaits orders. Pooru looks around the room.)

YAYATI: Where is Her Majesty?

(*Swarnalata does not reply.*)

Did she say where she is going?

SWARNALATA: The revered Shukracharya was in town. She ...

POORU: She must be eager to see her father. Fair enough. We can finish the remaining formalities.

YAYATI: The priests will take care of that. You two go and rest. Swarnalata, lead them to their chamber.

POORU: Rest? We have been hanging around outside the city gates for two days. Waiting for the right conjunction of stars. (*To Chitralekha*) Devi, would you please go ahead with your entourage?

SWARNALATA: This way, please ...

(*Swarnalata leads Chitralekha out.*)

YAYATI: If you are feeling that energetic, shall we move to the assembly hall? The ministers will be waiting. They will bring you up to date on the affairs of the state. There is some disturbing news from the frontiers.

POORU: Oh, I am sure you can take care of it. Why don't we just sit here for a while? Perhaps the Queen will return soon.

YAYATI: If you say so. This has always been your favourite chamber.

POORU: Yes. Something haunting about it, something beautiful. You know they say walls have ears. I wish these walls had vocal chords, to sing to me. The few moments in my life I could really call happy—they are all associated with this room.

YAYATI: Your life isn't over yet. There is plenty of time to enjoy happiness.

(*Pooru smiles sardonically.*)

So how did the wedding ceremony go? I am told your father-in-law spared no pains.

POORU: A ceremony befitting the scion of the Bharata family, I would say. The messengers must have given you the official description.

YAYATI: What do you mean the 'official description'?

POORU: I mean the version agreed upon by their court poet and ours.

YAYATI: Was there an unofficial version?

POORU: A personal one. Yes.

YAYATI: There is a personal angle to everything, usually not very pleasant. But you are Prince Pooru, the next Sovereign of the land of the Aryas. What matters in our case—yours as well as mine—is the public memory of the events.

POORU: So what a person is going through—within himself—doesn't matter?

YAYATI: It is our duty to make sure that what we 'go through' is the experience of our dynasty. It is a dynasty that has produced some of the greatest rulers in the history of the world.

POORU (*smiles*): The great mystery then surely is how this glorious bloodline produced a specimen like me.

YAYATI: Don't, Pooru. Don't start on that again. And don't tell me you are still striking those adolescent postures. Don't you know what our forefathers achieved in their ...

POORU: I do. I do indeed. How could I not? The hermitage resonated with tales of their wonderful deeds—and most of these feats were performed, it was carefully pointed out to me, 'when they were so much younger than you'. That was the refrain. It was not that I was backward. I was stunted.

YAYATI (*enraged*): Who said so?

POORU: I did. I agreed with them. I had not the slightest inclination to follow in the steps of my illustrious forefathers. I found their deeds pompous. I was bored by the hermitage, unembarrassedly. I wanted to run away from all that it represented: that history, those triumphs, those glorious ideals.

(*Pause.*)

I wanted to be back here—in this palace—in this room.

YAYATI: Pooru, what do you want? Why ...

POORU: Here in this room there was something to look for. Something to brood over. My mother's memory. The memory of her face. Floating bodyless like the moon. Was she beautiful?

YAYATI: Yes, she was. I have told you that a hundred times.

POORU: Of course. And you added, 'A Bharata prince would not have married a woman not beautiful'. Stupid of me to keep asking. But I can only sense the face. I keep feeling the need to fill in the details.

YAYATI: Do you put on this act as a special favour for your father? Or has it become your general style? What does your bride think of all this?

POORU: Oh yes. You were asking me about my wedding and I never answered the question.

(*Pause.*)

You know Chitralekha's father had invited princes from all over the country and organized an archery contest for them. (*Pause.*) The contest had to be cancelled at the last moment.

YAYATI: Did it? Why?

POORU: Even I didn't pay attention to the cancellation. If I had, I wouldn't have accepted the invitation. The pretence of course was that Chitralekha would choose her own mate—the most gifted of the princes. But it had been decided long in advance that she should marry the Bharata prince, that she was destined to become the Empress of Aryavarta. They thought: Ah, well, a simple archery contest. It should be child's play for someone from the great dynasty. Then they received reports about my skills and quietly dropped the requirement. There was an uproar among the invited princes, of course. But the family had made up its mind. Actually, they didn't need me. They needed some male figure from this palace. A door-keeper's statue would have done just as well.

YAYATI: Who has stuffed your head with such nonsense?

POORU: Chitralekha.

(*Yayati stares at him, aghast.*)

Yes, she told me. Who else? And why do you call it nonsense? That is the truth. From her birth, she has been groomed for this moment and when it arrives, what does she find? Me. Gormless me.

YAYATI: Surely she didn't say that?

POORU: No, she did not. Actually, when she was recounting all the confusion I had managed to create in their plans, she was laughing. Not at me. But at her own family. At their pretensions. Their eagerness to snare me. That is what I like about her: she is intelligent, loving, full of fun; but also honest and practical. She accepts me as I am, a fact to live with.

(*Pause.*)

But deep down, I can sense her disenchantment. She deserved someone worthy of her. Under the circumstances, *I* couldn't have made a more felicitous choice. She wants a son. And so do I.

YAYATI: Good. It is gratifying to know you realize you owe the family something.

POORU: I want to have a son so she will have no grumble against me. Nor will anyone else. I can place him in her arms, under your tender care and leave. He can take after his ancestors.

YAYATI: And you?

POORU: How shall I put it? My forefathers were the great eagles, keen-eyed, hovering regally in the clouds. I shall seek to be a worm.

YAYATI: And do you think that is easy?

POORU: I would have to find out, wouldn't I?

YAYATI: I had a charioteer. He was married to this maid, Swarnalata. One day, suddenly, he decided to become a worm. Went berserk—women, drinks, asceticism, opiates. Nothing brought him peace of mind. Finally he committed suicide.

POORU: This Swarna's husband?

(*Yayati nods.*)

I remember him. He used to play with us. But she is dressed as a married woman.

YAYATI: She probably hasn't been told.

POORU: Another lie?

YAYATI: Or perhaps she was told and would not accept it. I don't know. I leave these things to my officers. But you, where will you go?

POORU: I don't know: that is the most exciting part of it.

YAYATI: But surely you must. If you want to go away, where do you want to go?

POORU: There you are. You think everyone has a readymade answer. I just want to go somewhere where I can sit quietly and ask myself questions. Just ask questions. Not seek answers. Ask questions of myself. I should be quite content if I found the right question. Just one.

(*A longer pause.*)

I could do it in this room, I know. But in this palace I'll never be left alone.

YAYATI: So?

POORU: Nothing. (*Smiles.*) We seem to have reached our usual point of silence—faster than usual.

YAYATI: Shall we move to the assembly hall?

POORU (*ignoring him*): I love this room. I want to live in this room. Actually, I had asked for it to be our chamber.

YAYATI:. That was the plan. But things went wrong. I'm sorry. We have got another room ready for you. But if you insist, we can have this room done up for you.

POORU: No, no. What I wanted to know was: can Chitralekha use that other room while I use this one—for just one evening?

YAYATI (*scandalized*):What are you talking about? Do you want to keep your bride away from you?

POORU: No, I don't. But just now—when she stepped in here—suddenly it was like a violation of this air. Desecration. This room is mine. It is a sanctum that belongs to me—only me—and my memories. I don't want a third person to come in. At least, not today.

YAYATI: Will you explain that to her? No one else can.

POORU: I will. There is so much I haven't told her. About my mother's face. About the deathly silence which surrounds that face. I haven't warned her that no one talks about my mother in this palace: she is a conundrum. Untouchable.

YAYATI: Not untouchable. It was ... well, a little distasteful.

POORU: Distasteful? My mother?

YAYATI: All right. You are a man now. You might as well know.

(*Pause. Pooru waits expectantly.*)

I met her on one of my military campaigns. I had never seen anyone so beautiful—ethereal. She seemed one of the gentlest, most loving creatures one could imagine. Everyone loved her and I married her. She gave me a son and I made her my Senior Queen. And then, suddenly she changed. She started to scream and curse as though she had gone mad, when actually she hadn't.

Very lucidly, she would explain to me her plan—which was to make life intolerable for everyone in the palace.

POORU (*smiling*): Lovely. And then?

YAYATI: Her last days were not happy. She was bed-ridden and even from there she continued to spew out her virulence. It was only in her last few moments that she told me the truth. She was a rakshasa woman and the Aryas had destroyed her home and hearth. She was bent on vengeance and the inferno she had created was her way of celebrating her success. She had made sure that the Crown prince of the Bharatas had rakshasa blood in him. The Aryas would be ruled by a ...

(*Fumbles for a word.*)

POORU: Say it. A half-caste. A mongrel. And that is me?

YAYATI: We were silly about these things in those days. Mean. I can see it now. Today I would not hold a person's rakshasa origins against her. And yet ...

POORU: And yet even today no one knows that the Prince of the Aryas has polluted blood in his veins. How absolutely terrible! How excruciatingly thrilling!

(*He bursts into laughter. And then as suddenly he turns on his father.*)

But why didn't you tell me all this before? Why did you hide the truth while my need for it festered and suppurated? You didn't mind destroying my life for the sake of a lie? God! I despise you all. I loathe you and your hypocrisy ...

(*Sharmishtha comes running in. She falls at Pooru's feet.*)

SHARMISHTHA: Please, please, Prince. Only you can save His Majesty now. Please, hurry up and go. You mustn't waste time.

POORU: Who are you?

YAYATI: What is this, Sharmishtha? What has happened to you?

(*Pooru reacts to her name.*)

SHARMISHTHA: There is no time to explain, sir. Please go. Before they leave town.

YAYATI: They? Who is 'they'? Have you gone mad?

SHARMISHTHA: The revered Shukracharya and Devayani. They are about to ...

POORU: But why are they leaving? What has happened, Father?

SHARMISHTHA: Shukracharya is so incensed he has cursed His Majesty. Only you can save the situation now.

POORU-YAYATI: Curse?

YAYATI: What did you say? Curse? What curse? Why? Come on. Speak up.

SHARMISHTHA: Go, Prince. Hurry up and go.

YAYATI (*angry*): Sharmishtha.

SHARMISHTHA: He has placed a curse on His Majesty—that he will lose his youth and become decrepit by nightfall. I fell to his feet. I begged him to remember that His Majesty had saved Devayani's life. But he wouldn't listen.

YAYATI (*genuinely baffled*): Curse? Why? What have I done? Why should he curse me?

SHARMISHTHA: Please, hurry.

POORU (*lost*): Me? Me?

SHARMISHTHA: Only you can save the situation now. Please. Go.

(*Pooru, baffled, goes out.*)

YAYATI: Is this true? Or is this another one of your tricks? Why?

SHARMISHTHA: It is Devayani, sir. He is angry that you have humiliated her.

YAYATI: But I have not. She is my queen. Where have I humiliated her?

SHARMISHTHA: I tried to warn you ...

YAYATI: This is outrageous. I shall go and catch that wizened old fool by his beard and demand ...

SHARMISHTHA: No, please don't. That will only make things worse.

YAYATI (*in a daze*): Old age! Decrepitude! By nightfall! And then? Then what? Sharmishtha. You she-devil! You are the cause of all this. You are responsible. You trapped me with your wiles.

SHARMISHTHA: Please, don't lose heart. I am sure the prince will succeed in appeasing Shukracharya. He will get the curse annulled. He is his grandson after all.

YAYATI: And I wait here, helplessly, till he gets that done? A dessicated fool on the one side, who can't see beyond his silly offspring. And on the other, a youth still wet behind the ears, who despises his father. No, I had better go and ...

SHARMISHTHA: Please, sir. Listen to me at least now. Have patience.

YAYATI: Patience? Patience of a man falling into a bottomless pit. Patience? The deafening rush of emptiness. What can be more terrible than that? And suppose Pooru fails? Suppose that shrivelled mendicant refuses to listen to reason?

SHARMISHTHA: So what?

YAYATI: What do you mean by that 'so what'?

SHARMISHTHA: No one can escape old age. You have just hastened its arrival. Let us accept it. Let us go away from the city. I'll come with you. I'll share the wilderness with you.

YAYATI: No, no, you cannot possibly imagine the horror of it. You will always be an outsider. An outsider to my anguish, to my grief, to my nightmare. You can only watch. With such care, with such pride, I had gathered the rarest moments of my life in my palm like precious stones. So I could play with them. Relive them.

Juggle them. And suddenly, they explode, each moment hurtling through my muscle and bones like a meteorite.

SHARMISHTHA: Everything has been a game for you so far. An object of diversion, to be used and discarded. But there are things far more important. Let us go and seek them in solitude.

YAYATI: Solitude? What are you talking about? I don't want solitude. I can't bear it. I want people around me. Queens, ministers, armies, enemies, the populace. I love them all. Solitude? The very thought is repulsive. If I have to know myself, Sharmishtha, I have to be young. I must have my youth.

(*He sits down on the bed and starts feeling the mattress, like a blind man searching for a lost object.*)

SHARMISHTHA: Sir, what are you doing?

YAYATI: I am trying to recapture my youth. Moments when I handed out pain, moments when I slaughtered enemies, razed hostile cities to the ground, made my queens writhe in pain and demanded that they laugh and make love to me in gratitude. Why do I think of those moments now, Sharmishtha? Why do moments of tears and torture and blood seem priceless?

SHARMISHTHA: So it was my tears that attracted you.

YAYATI: Have I upset you? You won't hold it against me, will you? I blurted it out because I hunger for them again. But you won't let me go, will you? You won't abandon me?

SHARMISHTHA: I have given myself to you. There is no going back.

YAYATI: Sharmishtha, where is Pooru? Why isn't he back? He must be celebrating his youth, his chance to rule the world. He has rakshasa blood in his veins, do you know? How could we have trusted him? The sight of me fills him with repugnance.

SHARMISHTHA: Calm yourself, please. Shall I go and look for him?

YAYATI: No, please. No. Don't leave me alone.

SHARMISHTHA: Who is there? Swarna!

SWARNALATA (*enters*): Yes, madam?

YAYATI: Where is the Prince? Have you seen him?

SWARNALATA: He is in the outer courtyard, sir. He seems to be on his way here.

YAYATI: What is he waiting for? Does he expect to be welcomed with conch shells and drums? (*To Sharmishtha*) I told you. He must be exulting at the turn of events, indulging in his fantasies of the future.

SWARNALATA: Pardon me, Your Majesty. The Prince seemed very agitated. He was in consultation with the Chief Minister.

YAYATI: Here I am on a bed of burning coals and he hangs around confabulating. Ask him to come in. Immediately. Tell him I order him to come.

(*Swarnalata exits.*)

But so soon? How is it that he is back so soon? And why is he talking to the ministers? Sharmishtha, didn't he get to see Shukracharya? Has he come back empty handed? What then, Sharmishtha? What do I do then? What do I do?

(*The stage darkens.*)

Act Three

Only a short time later. Yayati and Sharmishtha. Pooru enters.

YAYATI: What happened, Pooru? Why are you late?

POORU: By the time I reached the Shambhu shrine, the revered Shukracharya had left with his daughter. A disciple was waiting for me. He gave me the message.

YAYATI: What message? Has the curse been lifted?

POORU: In recognition of the fact that you saved Devayani from starving to death in the well, Shukracharya has relented and said that the curse of instant decrepitude will not have its effect on you—

YAYATI (*triumphant*): It will not? He has withdrawn the curse then?

POORU: —the curse will not have its effect on you if a young man agrees to take it upon himself and offers his youth to you in exchange.

(*Pause. Yayati heaves a sigh of immense relief. Slowly but gleefully he rubs his palms.*)

YAYATI: That is good news. That is good news indeed. So I don't lose my youth, thank god. What a relief! So you see, Sharmishtha. You were asking me to accept the curse as though that was the end of everything. You wanted me to turn my back on life. But even a dotard like Shukracharya can see reason.

(*Looks at them and sees no sign of joy in them.*)

Why do you look so gloomy? Aren't you happy that I have escaped a fate worse than death? Don't you feel any happiness, any joy at my escape from the blight? Why are you silent? Am I doing something wrong?

POORU: The question, Father, is who will accept the curse from you.

YAYATI: Oh that! Surely that is not a serious question. Surely there is no shortage of men who will come out to take over their king's burden. They are my people. They love me. Surely they will not hesitate to step forward.

SHARMISHTHA: Why should they? Why should they take upon themselves the scourge you have brought upon yourself? Please, sir. Let us not look around for the fool or the yogi who is seeking holy martyrdom. Let us go ...

YAYATI: Go? You are out of your mind. You want me to spurn the hand Shukracharya has extended and crawl into the funeral pyre? You want me to be dependent on you, don't you? You trapped me once and you want me to stay trapped, clinging to you for survival. Woman, will you never give up your demonic machinations? Get out of my sight. Out.

POORU: Father—

YAYATI: You be quiet. This conniving barbarian ...

POORU: Could you please leave us, madam—

SHARMISHTHA: Let me be here—

POORU (*to Sharmishtha*): Please, do me a favour. Please.

(*Sharmishtha exits.*)

YAYATI: Yes? What do you want to say?

POORU: It is not a question of what I want to say. It is a question of fact.

YAYATI: What fact?

POORU: No one is willing to accept the curse. *Your* curse.

YAYATI: No one? What do you mean by no one? My dear subjects for whose sake I have faced a thousand deaths?

POORU: They say they have seen you enjoy the glory you thereby earned.

(*Pause.*)

Actually, some even pointed out that they had paid taxes and tributes for your services.

YAYATI: Someone actually dared say that? And you didn't have them lashed publicly for their insolence? Ask the soldiers.

(*No reply.*)

They are trained to lay down their lives for me.

POORU: I suppose it would have been easier if I were offering them death, rather than decrepitude.

YAYATI: Their kith and kin will be looked after. They will live like the royalty. Not just riches, Pooru. Let them think of the glory and the fame. The world will look up to them with reverence.

POORU: Or perhaps laugh behind their backs?

YAYATI: Why? Are deeds of glory dead in this world? Has the world become so cynical, so corrupted that there is no place for ... for ...

(*He is lost for words. Pooru waits patiently.*)

I am not trying to shun old age, Pooru. I am not that foolish. I know it is inevitable. Let me have my normal term of youth. I shall take back the curse and whatever comes with it after a few years.

POORU: I offered all that.

YAYATI: And they didn't trust your word?

POORU: Trust? Glory? Sacrifice? Who was there to discuss the big words with? They refused to talk to me. Or even to listen, as though mere listening would fetter them to some unknown commitment. They retreated even as I approached them. As if I was offering them plague.

YAYATI: I don't believe it! They are here to welcome you, their next sovereign.

POORU: All that was before Devayani met her father. The drama was acted out before the thousands assembled outside. The weeping and the cursing was there for everyone to see, but not many could have heard what was said. You know how it is. As I stepped out, I could almost see whispers snaking through the crowds. And then they see me rushing about, in desperate search of Shukracharya. That must have confirmed their worst fears. For all you know, by now the malediction may have transformed itself into the curse of death.

YAYATI: What shall I do, Pooru? What am I to do? Go. Go and talk to Shukracharya. Try to convince him ...

(*Pause.*)

POORU: Why don't you do ...

YAYATI: Why don't I do what?

POORU: Do as Mother suggests.

YAYATI: Mother? What Mother?

POORU: Sharmishtha. Take her advice. Accept the inevitable.

YAYATI: Don't. Don't please go on as though you cannot understand. It is the crushing suddenness of it—not being given a chance. Don't you see the arbitrariness of it all? To be hurled into an unchangeable future—without warning, without a chance to redeem one's pledges to life? You can stumble down a road without lights, Pooru. But to go on where there is no hope. That's unthinkable.

(*He bursts into sobs. Pooru watches him with immense compassion. Then in a matter-of-fact voice*)

POORU: There is one person who is willing to take on the curse.

YAYATI: There is? Why didn't you say so? Who is it?

POORU: A worm, aspiring to outdo the eagles.

(*For a moment, Yayati stares uncomprehending. Then as the import of Pooru's remark strikes home*)

YAYATI: Shut up, fool. I ... I refuse to talk to you.

(*Rushes out. Pooru stands, staring in his direction. Sharmishtha comes in.*)

SHARMISHTHA: Where is he gone? What happened, Pooru?

POORU: Before I answer that question, may I ask you something?

SHARMISHTHA: Yes.

POORU: Before I came here, I had heard a lot of unkind tales about you. How you had turned this palace into a noxious pit for those living in it. And I came rearing to meet you, to join in your rebellion against this stuffy palace. And what do I see? You love him. You actually love Father. I had never imagined a person could be capable of that. You are offering to share his wretched fate. I can't understand it.

SHARMISHTHA (*laughs*): I suppose it is a little bizarre. I suspect even your father finds it so. But I don't know whether I'll make sense ...

POORU: I could try.

SHARMISHTHA: All he has to do, to get out of this situation, is to let go of me. Send me away. But he won't think of it.

POORU (*laughs*): This is what moulting must feel like. Everything has suddenly started making sense. And can I ask a favour of you?

SHARMISHTHA: Yes?

POORU: Could you please ask Chitralekha to come here to this chamber? I ... need her here.

SHARMISHTHA: Of course, I will. But tell me what happened with your father. He wouldn't even look at me—

POORU (*slowly*): There is a person willing—indeed keen—to accept his curse. But Father was not ready to hear the name. In point of fact, I didn't even need to mention the name.

SHARMISHTHA: Who is it?

POORU: Me.

SHARMISHTHA: No, no, no, you can't. That is utter stupidity! Pooru, the desire for self-sacrifice is a rank perversion.

POORU: I want to root myself back in my family. I want to realize the vision that drove my ancestors.

SHARMISHTHA: What about Chitralekha?

POORU: I am like an infant on the brink of birth. Please don't shove me back with that name.

(*Suddenly collapses and tries to hold himself up. Sharmishtha rushes to his help.*)

SHARMISHTHA: What is it, Pooru?

POORU (*laughs*): The curse, Mother. The spasms of imminent birth.

(*The stage darkens.*)

Act Four

Night. There are only a few clay lamps burning; the room is therefore very dimly lit.

Chitralekha is standing near the window looking out. She is obviously bored and plays with a little object in her hand. Swarnalata enters.

SWARNALATA: Madam—

CHITRALEKHA (*startled out of her reverie*): Yes?

SWARNALATA: I just came to check the oil in the lamps. I thought you might be asleep.

CHITRALEKHA: I dozed off when the drums were thundering. They suddenly fell silent and woke me up.

SWARNALATA: Thousands have gathered out there ...

CHITRALEKHA: Yes. And they are all so silent! In my city, only ten have to come together and there is a riot. You can't imagine what it would be like with this many.

SWARNALATA: Our crowds can be boisterous too.

CHITRALEKHA: Then why are they so quiet? I was wondering ... I mean ... Well, let us forget it. Customs can be so varied. But do you know what I found in this chamber?

(*She holds out the object in her palm. Swarnalata reacts.*)

SWARNALATA: Where did you find that?

CHITRALEKHA: Here, beside the leg of the bed. Isn't this the pendant from the marriage thread of the Bharata queens?

(*Swarnalata nods.*)

> I had seen so many paintings of it. Heard so many descriptions. Had always wanted to possess it. But I never thought it would come my way in this fashion.

(*Smiles.*)

SWARNALATA (*upset*): Please don't ask me about it, Madam. I don't know how to ...

CHITRALEKHA: That's all right. What is your name?

SWARNALATA: Swarnalata.

CHITRALEKHA: I had a maid of that name back home. A very nice person. Witty, alert. And active.

SWARNALATA: Well, then, the name is obviously the only thing we have in common.

CHITRALEKHA: I am sure not. But it is a comfort to have someone with a familiar name. Makes one feel at home. Would you mind if I called you Swaru?

SWARNALATA (*agitated*): Please don't, madam. Please. Anything but that.

(*Pause.*)

CHITRALEKHA: Sorry. I have upset you. I didn't mean to.

SWARNALATA: It's just ... just ...

CHITRALEKHA: This stillness. So many thousands. Standing in frozen silence. Waiting for something. For what? It has something to do with the curse of Shukracharya, doesn't it?

SWARNALATA (*taken aback*): Oh, you have heard about it, madam? I wasn't informed. Yes, it has.

CHITRALEKHA: Pushpa, my personal maid from my mother's house, found out and told me about it. I was distressed, of course. But not for long. After all, I belong to the Bharata family now. Their problems are mine too.

SWARNALATA: I wish the problems had waited a little longer.

CHITRALEKHA (*pointing to the crowds outside*): I suppose everyone out there has come to know of these problems too? And therefore this silence?

SWARNALATA: Why don't you rest, madam? I'll come again a little later.

CHITRALEKHA: More rest? If you go away now, I shall have no company. Except of course for this pendant. Tell me, is it true that Pushpa and my other maids have been sent out to see the illuminations in the city?

(*Pause.*)

SWARNALATA: No, madam. They have been housed in the eastern wing of the palace.

CHITRALEKHA: How far is it? Would they hear me if I called out?

SWARNALATA: No. They won't.

CHITRALEKHA: I thought so.

SWARNALATA: I shouldn't worry about them, madam. If you come and stand in this corner, I could point out to you the famous landmarks of the city.

CHITRALEKHA: No, thanks. I tried that earlier. But my eyes kept returning to the faces. They look so eerie in the flickering light of the torches.

(*Laughs.*)

Sit down. Let us talk. Yes, why don't you tell me a story instead?

SWARNALATA: Story? What story is there to narrate? It is all being acted out, right in front of our eyes.

CHITRALEKHA: No, no. I meant a tale of some distant land.

SWARNALATA: Forgive me. But this is probably not the right time for it.

CHITRALEKHA: Why not?

SWARNALATA: Because it is your nuptial evening.

CHITRALEKHA: What is the connection?

SWARNALATA: After a point, every story that matters has something to do with nuptials.

(*Chitralekha laughs. But not Swarnalata.*)

CHITRALEKHA: Then let us talk of something else. You know about me. Probably more than I do. So tell me about yourself.

SWARNALATA: Me? My story has only two lines.

CHITRALEKHA: You got married. And then lived happily ever after?

SWARNALATA: The first line is correct. And the second ... well, perhaps. But so far as I know, I got married. Then my husband left me and went away.

CHITRALEKHA: Oh, I am sorry.

SWARNALATA (*laughs*): Nothing apocalyptic. He left me after ten years of marriage.

CHITRALEKHA: Where did he go?

SWARNALATA: He got tired of life. Not that he was ever at home very much. He was His Majesty's charioteer. Used to accompany His Majesty on his expeditions.

CHITRALEKHA: And?

(*There is a thunderous eruption of the drums and conch shells. Startled by its suddenness and ferocity, Chitralekha runs to the window. Swarnalata bursts out crying.*)

CHITRALEKHA: What's that? What's that for?

SWARNALATA: I shouldn't have agreed to this. I should have sent someone else. I didn't have the courage to face you, but I wanted to see you. I couldn't tell you what I came here to tell. I should never have agreed. I should have sent someone who had faith in all this. ...

CHITRALEKHA (*irritated*): What is wrong with you? Stop wailing, I tell you. Stop it, instantly. What were you supposed to tell me?

SWARNALATA: I will, madam. I will. But ...

CHITRALEKHA: Stop whining, you silly woman. You are getting on my nerves.

SWARNALATA: Curse me, madam. I don't mind. Not a soul offered to accept the King's curse. Then ...

CHITRALEKHA: Yes? Go on.

SWARNALATA: One person.

CHITRALEKHA: Who was it?

SWARNALATA: The Prince, madam. Young Pooru. Your husband. He has agreed to take on his father's old age. That's why these revelries, madam, this flourish and fanfare ... these, these ...

(*Chitralekha stands, stunned.*)

Cry, madam, please. Don't hold back your tears. Nothing is more harmful than suppressed tears.

(*Long silence.*)

CHITRALEKHA: Cry? Why should I cry? I should laugh. I should cheer ... except that I have been so unfair to him. So cruelly unjust. I thought he was an ordinary man. What a fool I have been! How utterly blind! I am the chosen one and I ... Which other woman has been so blessed? Why should I shed tears?

SWARNALATA: Perhaps I meant tears of joy. But why now? Why ...

CHITRALEKHA: No, it is just as well. I don't know how long I would have gone on being unfair to him. Now I only have my idiocy to blame. I am so happy.

SWARNALATA: May that happiness last for ever. Madam, I forgot ... I had come to inform you ... The drums were to announce that the Prince is on his way here.

CHITRALEKHA: Is he? How stupid you are! If you hadn't made such a song and dance about it, I would have rushed to him and thrown myself at his feet. Is he on his way? Be off now.

SWARNALATA: Yes, madam.

(*She starts extinguishing the lamps one by one.*)

CHITRALEKHA: What are you doing?

SWARNALATA: There should be no lights on the first night in the nuptial chamber.

CHITRALEKHA: Leave a couple of them burning. I want to dazzle my eyes with his glory.

(*Music outside. Excited*)

Here he is! Off you go.

(*Swarnalata leaves a couple of lamps burning in a corner and moves out.*)

SWARNALATA: I shall be outside. Please call me if you need me.

(*Pooru comes in. His face cannot be seen in the dark but he is bent double. When he speaks, his voice is feeble and quivers with exhaustion. Swarnalata is about to help him when Chitralekha takes him over, almost possessively. Swarnalata exits. Chitralekha seats him on the bed.*)

POORU: Chitra ...

CHITRALEKHA: Please relax, sir. The silly maid has plunged the room into darkness.

POORU: Chitra ...

CHITRALEKHA: Yes, I am here.

POORU: Forgive me, please.

CHITRALEKHA: But why?

POORU: I didn't consult you.

CHITRALEKHA: Hush now. I was a fool, blind to your greatness. I didn't realize my good fortune.

POORU: This is no ordinary old age, devi. This is decrepitude. The sum total of Father's transgressions. The burden of the whole dynasty, perhaps. I couldn't take it on without your help.

CHITRALEKHA: Of course I am there with you. I have no life apart from you. I want none.

POORU: I feel empty. Shrivelled.

CHITRALEKHA: You don't have to explain anything to me. I am so privileged.

(*She goes and picks up a lamp and brings it to him.*)

POORU: No light, please. It hurts my eyes. I can't ...

CHITRALEKHA: I want to perform the arati. May I? Just once? Only for a moment. Please. To welcome you into my heart ...

POORU: All right ... Make it quick, please.

(*Heaves an exhausted sigh. Chitralekha takes the lamp to his face and moves it in a circle in front of it, performing an arati. The flame casts its light upon his face. His withered features look even more terrifying in the dim light. Chitralekha screams and drops the lamp to the floor.*)

POORU: Devi, devi ...

CHITRALEKHA (*screaming*): Please don't come near me. Go out. Please, please. Don't touch me ...

POORU: But you said ...

CHITRALEKHA: I don't know anything. Don't ask me. Forgive me, but please ... please, get out of here. At once. Swaru ...

(*Swarnalata comes in running. Pooru gets up slowly.*)

SWARNALATA: Madam ...

CHITRALEKHA: Take him out. Right now. Please.

(*Swarnalata leads Pooru out. Pooru lets her, without a word. Chitralekha collapses on to the bed and bursts into a crying fit. Swarnalata comes, sits by her and gently pats her on her head. Chitralekha reacts.*)

CHITRALEKHA: Don't touch me. I am a sinner. Kill me please. But leave me alone. Go out and ...

SWARNALATA: Now, now. Don't blame yourself.

CHITRALEKHA: I don't deserve the Prince. I am unworthy of him. But ... but what am I to do, Swaru? I couldn't help myself. I can't take it. I can't.

SWARNALATA: Go on. Cry. Don't stop yourself now. It's all right. Don't blame yourself. Just let go ...

(*Chitralekha bursts into renewed sobs as Swarnalata goes and shuts the window and comes and sits next to her. Takes Chitralekha in her arms and caresses her like a child.*)

CHITRALEKHA: Please. Say something. Scold me. Punish me. Say anything. I can't bear the silence.

SWARNALATA: I know. I know the terror of silence.

(*Pause.*)

I started to tell you about myself, but didn't. Couldn't bring myself to. But even my story is not as terrifying as ... as your situation.

I was my father's only child. He was not very well-to-do. Didn't have enough money to engage a proper teacher for me. So he persuaded a poor brahmin to teach me in return for a free meal a day. My teacher was naturally anxious that the news of this arrangement should not get around. So he would come to our house after dark, teach me, stay the night with us, and leave early next morning. I was a keen student. I learnt well and when I came of age, I was married off.

I couldn't have prayed for a nicer husband. All he wanted was for me to be happy. He showered me with endearments, with love, with gifts. It was 'My Swaru—', 'My darling Swaru—' every minute.

Then, one day, he came to know about my teacher. Misgivings sprouted in his mind. I told him there was no basis for his doubts. I begged and pleaded. If there was the slightest evidence for his apprehension, he would have forgiven me. But there was none. Doubt grew into suspicion and then slowly twisted itself into an obsession, a laceration he had no means of controlling.

As months passed and the disease spread, I could see him tossing and turning in his bed. And yet there was not the slightest abatement in his love for me. There was also his conviction that I was innocent. He began to look for solutions to his torment. To revenge himself on me by indulging in women, in drinks, in the campaigns. And he hated himself for inflicting this torture on me. And the more I loved him, the more venomously he hated me and himself.

At last I decided I had to help him out. I still shudder when I think of it. One night as he was moaning in his sleep, I woke him up and admitted that my teacher had seduced me.

CHITRALEKHA: You lied?

SWARNALATA: I described the scene in convincing detail. My husband smiled at me, turned on his side and for the first time in many years, fell into deep sleep. With that, Swarnalata's story too ended. But not Swaru's private hell. He disappeared next morning. I haven't seen him since. I still deck myself up as a married woman. Our house awaits his return: every one of his possessions in its place, exactly as he left it. But if he doesn't return, I hope he at least found peace in death. That is the great thing about death, isn't it? The assurance of peace, the deliverance from uncertainty?

(*She takes out Sharmishtha's vial of poison.*)

CHITRALEKHA: What is it?

SWARNALATA: The vial of poison which Sharmishtha carried. I found it as I was cleaning the room this afternoon. It promises instant death—release from living hell. But I don't have the courage it takes.

CHITRALEKHA: Can I see it?

(*Swarnalata gives her the vial of poison.*)

SWARNALATA: I have been churning out this old tale, for I can't think of another tale with which to divert you. We are alone in our unhappiness, devi. Sometimes a distant cry from another unhappy soul—it helps.

(*Yayati and Sharmishtha call out from outside.*)

YAYATI: Who is there?

SHARMISHTHA: Swarna ...

SWARNALATA (*leaping up*): The King!

CHITRALEKHA: Now?

SWARNALATA (*shouts*): Sir ...

CHITRALEKHA: Tell them I don't want to see anyone now.

SWARNALATA: You will have to face them some time. Later won't make it any better.

CHITRALEKHA: Yes. You are right. I must thank God that I met you, Swaru.

SWARNALATA: There is nothing to fear. It cannot get much worse than this.

(*Yayati enters. Swarnalata exits. A pause.*)

YAYATI (*kindly*): What have you done, child?

CHITRALEKHA: Forgive me ...

YAYATI: This is no time for recriminations. My heart goes out to you. But you are an educated woman, versed in the arts, trained in warfare. You could have displayed more self-control. Now act in a manner worthy of an Anga princess and Bharata queen. Act so that generations to come may sing your glory and Pooru's.

(*No reply.*)

My blood froze when I heard your scream. I was panic-stricken lest you bring the names of both our families into disrepute. But nothing is beyond repair. Go, welcome Prince Pooru back. You don't know how grateful the people will be to you. Go. Escort him back.

(*No reaction.*)

Chitralekha—

CHITRALEKHA: No.

YAYATI: What do you mean?

CHITRALEKHA: I will not let my husband step back into my bedroom unless he returns a young man.

YAYATI (*calmly*): I hope you realize where you are. This is the palace of the Bharata's. I can order you—not as your father-in-law, but as your ruler—to take him in and you will have to obey. But I am not doing that. I request you—I plead with you—not to act in a manner that will bring ignominy on us all.

CHITRALEKHA: Let him come. I shall leave the kingdom.

YAYATI: Do you remember the vow you took not so long ago—with the gods as your witnesses, in the presence of the holy fire? That you would walk in the path marked by his footprints: whether home or into the wilderness ...

CHITRALEKHA: Or into the funeral pyre?

YAYATI (*horrified*): Hold your tongue! You dare indulge in levity about your husband's death?

CHITRALEKHA (*flaring up*): I did not push him to the edge of the pyre, sir. You did. You hold forth on my wifely duties. What about your duty to your son? Did you think twice before foisting your troubles on a pliant son?

YAYATI (*shouts*): Chitra! Take care ...

CHITRALEKHA: Sir! This is my chamber. Only my husband has the right to come in here without my permission. Or to shout out my name when he pleases. I am not aware I have allowed anyone else that freedom.

YAYATI: I apologize. I ...

CHITRALEKHA: Yes, I was keen to become your daughter-in-law. But so were you to accept me as one. Even apart from my family, because of my accomplishments, because of what I am. And now you want me to meekly yield to your demands?

YAYATI: I am sorry. I shouldn't have raised my voice. But please, try and understand. I know I have caused you grief. But I am confused, lost. The last few hours have been so traumatic, I feel myself on the brink of insanity. Let me explain.

CHITRALEKHA: I came here today as your new daughter-in-law. And do you know what gifts welcomed me in my chamber? First, this—from the mother-in-law who has discarded me. A pendant from her marriage necklace.

(*Shows him the pendant.*)

And this from the mother-in-law to be. A vial of poison.

(*She tosses the two objects on the bed. Yayati stares at her, lost for words. Then, almost to himself*)

YAYATI: Please try to understand. I am whatever I am. I am the king. There is no me if there are no subjects, no people. I cannot forget my duty by them and at this moment my duty is to ensure that the forces of chaos will not overwhelm them.

CHITRALEKHA: Is that the choice now—the forces of chaos on the one side and my husband's youth on the other?

YAYATI (*genuinely anguished*): I swear to you it never occurred to me that he would accept the curse. I was dumbfounded when he told me. Even now I am willing to take it back on my shoulders. What father would wish such a fate on his son? Pooru took it on of his own free will. Without a word from me. Without saying a word to me.

(*She listens transfixed.*)

I had looked forward to presenting you and Pooru with a peaceful, prosperous kingdom. Unfortunately, recently, unexpected troubles have started brewing in corners of my realm. Enemies on the border, rebellious forest tribes, the prospect of a famine, the danger of rakshasa depredation. I tried discussing these problems with him. But he is not interested. That is where I need your help.

CHITRALEKHA: My help?

YAYATI: Pooru lacks the experience to tackle these problems.

(*Pause.*)

Actually, more than the experience, he lacks the will, the desire. Instead of welcoming the responsibilities of a king—and of a householder—he has welcomed senility. Within a fortnight of his marriage. Why?

CHITRALEKHA (*with her head bowed, quietly*): Modesty requires that I claim not to understand the question. But since it has been asked and since it is now the most important question in my life, let me state that I consider myself immensely fortunate in having found such a husband. The last fifteen days have been among the happiest in my life. He is warm, considerate, and loving. I have grown up amidst kshatriya arrogance. His gentleness is like a waft of cool breeze.

(*Pause.*)

As a wife I am happy—indeed blessed.

YAYATI: What then is he trying to run away from?

CHITRALEKHA: Has my husband been complaining against me? Some lapse on my part ...

YAYATI: No, no, no. He admires you. That is why I am here. In the hope that perhaps you—his mate—you can help him. He has taken the curse upon himself to come to grips with some inner turmoil of his own. He needs time to think. Time to recover. Perhaps time to heal. And only you can give it to him.

(*Pause.*)

Once Pooru regains his health, it is you who will share that future with him.

(*A slight pause.*)

Give him a little more time. Give me a little time. Let him find himself. By then, I shall settle the affairs of the state. I shall present you and Pooru with a future that shall be secure and yours to keep. Please think.

CHITRALEKHA: Think. And will Your Majesty also think about how old I shall be by the time that future is attained?

YAYATI: Only a few years. Say a decade. Or even just four or five.

(*Chitralekha laughs.*)

CHITRALEKHA: Four or five! Do you think it would make a difference if it were only one or two? This morning I was the mistress of all that I had yearned for. But within half a day—no, within half an hour actually—half a century has driven across my bed and crushed the dreams on my pillows. And you would like me to wait ...

YAYATI: This is not merely a question of an individual. We are talking of the future of our entire people.

CHITRALEKHA: I am here, this minute, sir. And I cannot interest myself in your unborn future.

YAYATI: This is a time when we are all being put to test. Not just the time to come but even our past is watching us. Judging us. There has never been a crisis like this before. Nor is there ever likely to be one again. Rise above trivialities, Chitralekha. Be superhuman.

(*Pause.*)

CHITRALEKHA: All right, Your Majesty, I shall try. But when I do so, please don't try to dodge behind your own logic.

YAYATI: Beware. No one has ever accused me of cowardice.

CHITRALEKHA (*scared but persistent*): Yes, this is the moment. No one has ever faced such a situation before. No one is likely to again in future. So do you have the courage to accept the challenge?

YAYATI: What are you blathering?

CHITRALEKHA: I did not know Prince Pooru when I married him. I married him for his youth. For his potential to plant the seed of the Bharatas in my womb. He has lost that potency now. He doesn't possess any of the qualities for which I married him. But you do.

YAYATI (*flabbergast*): Chitralekha!

CHITRALEKHA: You have taken over your son's youth. It follows that you should accept everything that comes attached to it.

YAYATI: Whore! Are you inviting me to fornication?

CHITRALEKHA: Oh, come, sir. These are trite considerations. We have to rise above such trivialities. We have to be superhuman. Nothing like this has ever happened before. Nothing like this is likely to ...

YAYATI: Where did you learn such filth, you beast?

CHITRALEKHA: It's the price I have paid for my education.

(*Yayati stands, speechless.*)

So, sir, you refuse to return my youthful husband to me. Nor will you accept my logic. I know. It is part of the sacrifice we all have to make. Your Majesty, would you say this sacrifice measures up to the demand?

(*She picks the vial of poison from the bed, walks up to him, and holds it up to him.*)

YAYATI (*terrified*): Chitralekha, don't be foolish!

CHITRALEKHA: Foolish? What else is there for me to do? You have your youth. Prince Pooru has his old age. Where do I fit in?

(*She lifts the vial to her lips.*)

YAYATI: Chitralekha, wait. Listen to me.

(*He rushes forward and grabs her hand. Then recoils in horror.*)

CHITRALEKHA: There you are. You say I shouldn't be foolish but you can't even bring yourself to stop me.

YAYATI: No, no! It is not that. Wait ... Listen ...

(*Calls out.*)

Sharmishtha, maid ...

(*Chitralekha smiles defiantly and swallows the poison. Suddenly she crumples up with pain. Sharmishtha and Swarnalata rush in. Chitralekha collapses, writhing, in their arms.*)

SWARNALATA: Devi, devi ...

CHITRALEKHA (*screaming*): Help me. Please. Don't let me die. I don't want to die. Swaru, Swaru, help.

(*Dies.*)

SWARNALATA: No, oh my god, no ...

(*Falls on her and weeps.*)

SHARMISHTHA: Where did she find this vial?

YAYATI: Call the doctors, Sharmishtha. Send for help!

SHARMISHTHA: Nothing is going to help now. There is no antidote for it.

YAYATI: I couldn't catch hold of her hand. She was like my daughter and yet, I didn't dare ...

SHARMISHTHA (*erupting*): What does it matter who she was. You destroyed her life. I pleaded with you but you were drunk with your future ...

YAYATI: Please, Sharmishtha!

(*Swarnalata starts laughing to herself. Bursts into small spasms of laughter in between moans and sighs.*)

SWARNALATA: But I wanted to help her. She was in such pain, I only wanted to release her.

SHARMISHTHA: What is that, Swarna?

SWARNALATA: But she found no peace. 'Save me, Swaru.' There is no release in death. Poor darling ...

(*Sharmishtha shakes Swarnalata, trying to wake her up, but she is in her own fog. She keeps stroking Chitralekha and moaning.*)

Poor thing. There was no peace.

SHARMISHTHA: So here is the foundation of your glorious future, Your Majesty. A woman dead, another gone mad, and a third in danger of her life. Goodbye, sir.

YAYATI: Where are you going?

SHARMISHTHA: I must escape before the news reaches the mob outside. I know one thing for certain. They will all take it out on me.

YAYATI: Will you send Pooru in, please?

SHARMISHTHA: Don't worry about him. He is dozing happily outside—afloat his grand sacrifice.

YAYATI: Send him in, please. And wait for me.

SHARMISHTHA: For you?

YAYATI: Yes.

(*Sharmishtha looks at him and exits. Yayati stands staring at the dead Chitralekha and the demented Swarnalata. He speaks almost to himself.*)

I thought there were two options—life and death. No, it is living and dying we have to choose between. And you have shown me that dying can go on for all eternity. Suddenly, I see myself, my animal body frozen in youth, decaying, deliquescing, turning rancid. You are lying on your pyre, child, burning for life, while I sink slowly in this quagmire, my body wrinkleless and grasping, but unable to grasp anything.

(*Sharmishtha leads Pooru in, still in his decrepitude.*)

POORU: Father, you sent for me?

YAYATI: Please help me, Pooru. Take back your youth. Let me turn my decrepitude into a beginning.

POORU: But ... why? There is so much you have to ... Oh, this crushing exhaustion! No, I don't want my youth. But may I sit down? I ... I ...

(*Goes to the bed and sees Chitralekha there.*)

What? What's this? Chitra ...

YAYATI: She killed herself, Pooru.

SHARMISHTHA: The first martyr to His Majesty's glorious vision.

POORU: She killed herself? But why? Let her go. I am ready for any ...

SHARMISHTHA: That was no self-sacrifice. She was slaughtered. And now there is no one except a demented maid left to mourn her.

YAYATI: Take back your youth, Pooru. Rule well. Let me go and face my destiny in the wilds.

(*He embraces Pooru. When they part, Pooru has become young again and Yayati is bent with age.*)

POORU (*looks around*): It is still dark, Father. Why don't you wait till dawn to leave?

YAYATI: We have a long way to go, Pooru. Come, Sharmishtha ...

(*Pooru touches the feet of Yayati and Sharmishtha. Sharmishtha embraces him as she might a son. They leave. Pooru goes to where Chitralekha is lying.*)

POORU: We brought you here only to die. But our senses are blighted and we shall never grasp the meaning of all that you taught us.

(*Suddenly calls out to the heavens.*)

What does all this mean, O God? What does it mean?

(*Long pause. The Sutradhara enters. While he speaks, Pooru lifts Chitralekha up and exits, followed by Swarnalata.*)

SUTRADHARA: So perhaps Pooru at last found the courage to ask a question. But was it really a meaningful question or was it a cry of despair that he could hope for no meaning? Well, conventions of Sanskrit drama require that a play have a happy ending. So let us assume that this question led to many more and that finally Pooru found the question he was seeking.

　　For we have it on the authority of the epics that Pooru ruled long and wisely and was hailed as a philosopher king.

　　Namaskara.

(*Exits.*)

Afterword*

My generation was the first to come of age after India became independent of British rule. It therefore had to face a situation in which tensions implicit until then had come out in the open and demanded to be resolved without apologies or self-justification: tensions between the cultural past of the country and its colonial past, between the attractions of Western modes of thought and our own traditions, and finally, between the various visions of the future that opened up once the common cause of political freedom was achieved. This is the historical context that gave rise to my plays and those of my contemporaries.

In my childhood, in a small town in Karnataka, I was exposed to two theatre forms that seemed to represent irreconcilably different worlds. Father took the entire family to see plays staged by troupes of professional actors called *natak companies* which toured the countryside throughout the year. The plays were staged in semi-permanent structures on proscenium stages, with wings and drop curtains, and were illuminated by petromax lamps.

Once the harvest was over, I went with the servants to sit up nights watching the more traditional *Yakshagana* performances. The stage,

* This is a considerably revised extract from my paper, 'In Search of a New Theatre', in Carla M. Borden, ed., *Contemporary India* (Delhi: Oxford University Press, 1989).

a platform with a back curtain, was erected in the open air and lit by torches.

By the time I was in my early teens, the natak companies had ceased to function and Yakshagana had begun to seem quaint, even silly, to me. Soon we moved to a big city. This city had a college and electricity, but no professional theatre.

I saw theatre again only when I went to Bombay for my postgraduate studies. One of the first things I did in Bombay was to go and see a play, which happened to be Strindberg's *Miss Julie* directed by the brilliant young Ebrahim Alkazi.

I have been told since then that it was one of Alkazi's less successful productions. The papers tore it to shreds the next day. But when I walked out of the theatre that evening, I felt as though I had been put through an emotionally, or even a physically, painful rite of passage. I had read some Western playwrights in college, but nothing had prepared me for the power and violence I experienced that day. By the norms I had been brought up on, the very notion of laying bare the inner recesses of the human psyche like this for public consumption seemed obscene. What impressed me as much as the psychological cannibalism of the play was the way lights faded in and out on stage. Until we moved to the city, we had lived in houses lit by hurricane lamps. Even in the city, electricity was something we switched on and off. The realization that there were instruments called dimmers that could gently fade the lights in or out opened up a whole new world of shifting nuances.

Most of my contemporaries went through some similar experience at some point in their lives. We stepped out of mythological plays lit by torches or petromax lamps straight into Strindberg and dimmers. The new technology could not be divorced from the new psychology. The two together defined a stage that was like nothing we had known or suspected. I have often wondered whether it wasn't that evening that, without being actually aware of it, I decided I wanted to be a playwright.

At the end of my stay in Bombay, I received a scholarship to go abroad for further studies. It is difficult to describe to a modern Indian audience the traumas created by this event. Going abroad was a much rarer occurrence in those days; besides, I came from a large, close-knit family, and was the first member of the family ever to go abroad. My parents were worried lest I decide to settle down outside India, and even for me, though there was no need for an immediate decision, the terrible choice was implicit in the very act of going away. Should I at the end of my studies return home for the sake of my family, my people, and my country, even at the risk of my abilities and training not being fully utilized in what seemed a stifling, claustrophobic atmosphere, or should I rise above such parochial considerations and go where the world drew me?

While still preparing for the trip, amidst the intense emotional turmoil, I found myself writing a play. This took me by surprise, for I had fancied myself a poet, had written poetry through my teens, and had trained myself to write in English, in preparation for the conquest of the West. But here I was writing a play, and in Kannada too, the language spoken by a few million people in South India, the language of my childhood. A greater surprise was the theme of the play, for it was taken from ancient Indian mythology from which I had believed myself alienated.

The story of King Yayati that I used occurs in the Mahabharata. The king, for a moral transgression he has committed, is cursed to old age in the prime of life. Distraught at losing his youth, he approaches his son, pleading with him to lend him his youth in exchange for old age. The son accepts the exchange and the curse, and thus becomes old, older than his father.* But the old age brings no knowledge, no self-realization, only the senselessness of a punishment meted out for an act in which he had not even participated. The father is left to face the consequences of shirking responsibility for his own actions.

While I was writing the play, I saw it only as an escape from my stressful situation. But looking back, I am amazed at how precisely the

---

* In the Mahabharata, King Yayati has five sons; after the elder four refuse their father, the youngest yields to his entreaties.

myth reflected my anxieties at that moment, my resentment with all those who seemed to demand that I sacrifice my future. By the time I had finished working on *Yayati*—during the three weeks it took the ship to reach England and in the lonely cloisters of the university—the myth had enabled me to articulate to myself a set of values that I had been unable to arrive at rationally. Whether to return home finally seemed the most minor of issues; the myth had nailed me to my past.

WEDDING ALBUM

Wedding Album was first produced by the Primetime Theatre
Company at the Tata Auditorium, National Centre for the
Performing Arts, Mumbai on 10 May 2008, with the following cast:

IRA DUBEY	Vidula Nadkarni
RAJEEV PAUL	Rohit
DEEPIKA AMIN	Pratibha Khan, Vatsala Sirur
NEENA KULKARNI	Mother
UTKARSH MAZUMDAR	Father
SUCHITRA PILLAI	Hema
SEEMA AZMI	Radhabai
ARMAAN SUNNY	Vivan Kaikini, Hindu vigilante youth 2
AMAR TALWAR	Gopal Sirur, Attendant at the Internet Café
RAGHAV CHANANA	Ashwin Panje, Hindu vigilante youth 1

Directed by	LILLETE DUBEY
Lighting by	INAAYAT SAMI
Set by	LILLETE DUBEY
	BHOLA SHARMA
Music by	MAHESH TINAIKAR

Note

The song, *I was a good little boy*, on pages 132–3 is based on a Konkani song, written, I believe, by Rev. Paul Lewis Bothello of Mangalore, in 1934.

Scene One

Scenes One and Five are continuous and take place about three years after the rest of the play.

A screen on which we see Vidula in close-up, speaking directly to the camera. She is extremely self-conscious and ill-at-ease. Every now and then she is interrupted by the person handling the camera, which happens to be Rohit. We only hear his voice, but do not see him on the screen.

VIDULA: I am Vidula. Vidula Nadkarni. I am twenty-two. Twenty-two and a half, actually. I have done my BA in Geography. Passed my exams last year. I am not doing anything at the moment. Worked for a travel agency for six months.

(Stops. Looks at Rohit.)

I got bored. If I come to the US, will I need to work? I am really not very good at it.

ROHIT *(offscreen)*: Why don't you smile a bit? Look cheerful.

VIDULA: Am I looking depressed?

ROHIT *(offscreen)*: No. No. But cheer up. Look happy. Shall we start again?

VIDULA *(aghast)*: Again? Absolutely not. This is the third time.

ROHIT *(offscreen)*: I know. But remember, you are trying to show your best face to him.

VIDULA: I am not. I just want him to know what I am like.

ROHIT *(offscreen)*: But don't go out of your way to make yourself unattractive.

(Pause.)

VIDULA *(visibly upset, speaks directly into the camera)*: I am not glamorous, as you can see. I am not exceptional in any way. I don't want you to be disappointed later.

(The camera swings away from her, showing a corner of the living room at some lopsided angle.)

ROHIT *(offscreen)*: Look, we can't possibly send this tape to him. He is ...

VIDULA *(offscreen, angry)*: I am not going to reshoot. Let's just continue. This is how I am. You know I won't be any better in the next take. I'll be worse. Make worse mistakes.

ROHIT *(offscreen)*: All right. It's your life.

(The camera comes back to Vidula. There has been no interruption in the shooting.)

VIDULA *(to Rohit)*: What do I talk about now?

ROHIT *(offscreen)*: Tell him about our family. He knows already, but you tell him.

VIDULA *(to the camera)*: My father was a doctor in the government service. We are three of us. Eldest sister Hema is married and lives in Australia. Then Rohit, who is shooting this film. He is a writer—writes stories and scripts for teleplays. Then there's me. Rohit is the smartest of us all.

(Looks at Rohit and giggles.)

At least he thinks so.

(Rohit tut-tuts.)

Of course, Hema and I don't agree.

(Giggles. Suddenly serious.)

> Apparently there was another brother between Hema and Rohit. He was retarded. Mentally. Don't know what he died of.

ROHIT *(offscreen)*: Listen! Are you trying to impress him or scare him off?

VIDULA *(to Rohit)*: Let him know the whole truth. Perhaps he is a believer in genetics. Heredity. *(To the camera)* You know how it is. There are some things no one talks about in the family.

ROHIT *(offscreen)*: Tell him about yourself.

VIDULA: But let me assure you I am not retarded.

(Laughs.)

> At least I don't think so. But my IQ is ... let's skip it. What else? Oh, yes. My cooking isn't great either. Fortunately no one has worked out a CQ yet—Cooking Quotient.

(Giggles.)

> That's my father's joke. I would grade about 80 on the CQ. But since I am no good at working in an office, I suppose I'll learn to be good in the kitchen. *(To Rohit)* Do we have to do this? I feel quite silly. *(To the camera)* You can see I am no good at this sort of thing. How did people get introduced before video cameras were invented? I feel like a goose. Well, I don't know what I mean by a 'goose' ... Really. What does a 'goose' feel like?

(Giggles.)

ROHIT *(offscreen)*: Please don't get into one of your giggly moods. You can't stop once you start.

VIDULA *(giggling)*: He should know about that too. Shouldn't he? *(To the camera, pointing to Rohit)* But he is right. I can't stop once I start giggling.

(Giggles.)

ROHIT *(offscreen)*: Control yourself.

(She goes into hysterics.)

> That's done it!

(The tape ends. Lights come on in a Software Production Office to reveal Pratibha and Rohit, watching the tape.

Pratibha is a woman of about forty, smartly dressed and with an obvious air of authority.

Rohit, around thirty-two now, is dressed in a suit but with the tie hanging stylishly loose and the jacket slung on the back of the chair. He was slim once, and proud of his graceful bearing, but has become a little portly and sports a fashionable moustache.)

PRATIBHA: I must say I like your sister.

ROHIT: That was her first tape. Gradually, she got over her shyness. Became quite good at it actually. Relaxed, funny.

PRATIBHA: I like her. Very much. But I don't think …

(Pause.)

ROHIT: Don't think what?

PRATIBHA: That anyone will swallow it today.

ROHIT: Pratibhaji, it actually happened. Just three years ago.

PRATIBHA: Rohit, we have an audience which is predominantly young. College going. Or young professionals. Westernized. At least potentially.

ROHIT: So?

PRATIBHA: Let me put it this way. They may believe it, but they won't like it. A girl from an educated middle-class family—a graduate—agrees to consider marrying a man whom she has never met. The boy turns up, all ready to jump on to the altar, without ever having seen her. In this day and age?

ROHIT: They were not total strangers. I mean, they had exchanged video tapes. SMSed. Talked on the phone. And he belonged to our caste.

PRATIBHA: She had no boyfriends? No affairs?

ROHIT: No, no. She was a nice girl.

PRATIBHA: Ah! That's your definition of a 'nice girl' then?

ROHIT: Why not? She was a genuine innocent. No one stopped her from having boyfriends. I had a girlfriend. Catholic. No one minded.

(Slight pause.)

PRATIBHA: How did the marriage pan out?

ROHIT: Okay, I guess. She hasn't come home in the three years since her marriage.

PRATIBHA: Not even to see your parents?

ROHIT: She became pregnant. *(Pause.)* Miscarried. He was worried about her frail health, so wouldn't send her home. She is expecting again.

PRATIBHA: But your parents didn't mind?

ROHIT: Of course, Mother was upset. Vidula keeps in touch with her. But I'm afraid, since moving to Bangalore, I ... you know, the pressures in our profession.

PRATIBHA: That's what I mean. How can you make a character interesting in a tele-serial when you are not interested in her in real life?

ROHIT *(annoyed)*: That's not fair, Pratibhaji. I am fond of my sister. I didn't say I wasn't ...

PRATIBHA: Sorry, Rohit. The story doesn't work for me. Can we take a look at that other line—Episode Ten? That seemed to have more meat.

ROHIT: Radhabai?

PRATIBHA: Yes.

(Rohit starts taking out his papers.)

Scene Two

The living room of a house obviously modelled on the travellers' bunga-
lows of the colonial period. Sprawling, dusty.

On one side, there is a huge cupboard with glass doors, packed
with books, mostly recent paperbacks which seem ill-at-ease on the
old-fashioned shelves, wedged in between some heavy leather-bound
volumes. A grandfather clock hangs on the wall, and next to it, a portrait
of the Swamiji, the spiritual monastic head of the Saraswat Brahmins.
The other walls have shelves filled with plastic bric-a-brac, miniature
Ganeshas, a sandalwood sculpture showing Lord Krishna preaching the
Bhagavad Gita to Arjuna, and snapshots of family members in frames
which vie for attention by their refusal to conform to any single taste.

A large sofa in the middle is flanked by two wooden chairs and
several cane chairs.

Mother and Vidula are examining silk saris piled on the sofa.

Father is sitting in a chair with a newspaper in hand on which he is
obviously not focussing. He puts the paper down now and then, looks at
the horizon, then goes back to the paper. He yawns now and then and
sighs, 'I am so bored,' or 'Time just won't move.'

Vidula picks up a sari.

VIDULA: This one for Indira Aunty, do you think? And that, perhaps
   for Mitrakka?

MOTHER: Such a fine sari for Indira? She has never bothered to invite us home for a meal. Not once in nine years.

VIDULA: She at least talks nicely.

MOTHER: Sweet talk, mostly. A smile like a toothpaste ad but pure tamarind inside.

(Picks up a silk sari.)

This Kanjeevaram, now. You think Hema will like it?

VIDULA: It isn't Hemakka's colour. At least I have never seen her wear that.

(Calls out.)

Hemakka, Hemakka …

HEMA *(from inside)*: Yes.

VIDULA: What are you doing in there? Chopra has sent saris. For selection. Come on out now.

HEMA *(from inside)*: I saw them. They are all nice. Very nice. But you don't need three to do the work of one, do you? You go ahead. Whatever you decide is all right by me.

(Mother gives Vidula an exasperated look as though to say she cannot understand Hema. She picks up two saris.)

MOTHER: These two should do for Shanti's daughters-in-law.

VIDULA *(bursts into laughter)*: These? Are you joking? Mukti uses more expensive ones for her daily wear. Hemakka, come out. Please. Just for five minutes.

MOTHER: Look, we don't have to play up to their vanity. We'll give what's within our means.

(Hema enters.)

Don't you know what sari I received at her daughter's wedding?

HEMA: Whose wedding?

MOTHER: Mukti's. I gave it away to Radhabai.

(Vidula bursts into laughter. Mother too giggles behind the corner of her pallu.)

VIDULA: Haven't you heard the saga?

HEMA: Which one?

VIDULA *(lowers her voice so it's not heard in the kitchen)*: Mukti gave Mother a sari for her daughter's wedding. Mother hated it. In fact, it annoyed her so much she gave it away *(pointing towards the kitchen)* to Radhabai. Two months later, we invite Mukti over for lunch. And when Radhabai comes out to serve food, what should she be wearing but …

HEMA *(joining in Vidula's laughter)*: Oh, god! You don't say!

(Radhabai comes to the door of the kitchen.)

RADHABAI: No use whispering, Vidula. My ears are still serviceable. But it wasn't my fault that it happened.

MOTHER *(laughing)*: I have given you half-a-dozen saris. How should I know you would pick just that one the day Mukti is here!

RADHABAI: No one told me. I wouldn't have touched it if I had known.

(Behind her effort to be casual, one can detect more than a trace of annoyance.)

VIDULA: Oh, come on. Don't get upset. No one is blaming you.

MOTHER: Serves that Mukti right anyway.

VIDULA: The point is, every time Radhabai came out to serve a dish, Mukti glared at the sari—like that—so fiercely that Radhabai was convinced there was something wrong. To make matters worse, Ma started signalling to her to go in and change. Finally, Radhabai just plonked the pot down, and started searching through the folds, saying, 'What's wrong? Is there some stain on the sari? Is it torn?'

(Mimics Radhabai.)

I tell you, I could have died.

(They all laugh, Radhabai joining in with slightly forced laughter.)

RADHABAI: Don't worry, Ma. I'll buy my own saris from now on. After all, you pay me enough.

(Goes in. Mother gestures to indicate that Radhabai is huffed. Vidula shrugs her shoulders good-humouredly.)

FATHER *(almost to himself)*: I wish Ramdas was here. He would have been such a help. I don't know how we are going to manage without him.

HEMA: Don't worry, Father. Rohit is there now.

FATHER: But will he manage? No experience. And you know what my situation is like. Like this. I can't run around. Ramdas would have been such an asset. At your wedding, he did all the running around.

HEMA *(half to herself)*: I can't remember anyone running around very much at *my* wedding.

VIDULA *(picking the Kanjeevaram sari up)*: How about this?

HEMA: For whom?

VIDULA: For you. Ma has chosen this for you. But I don't think this is your colour.

HEMA *(without enthusiasm)*: Why? It's nice. Very nice. Lovely.

VIDULA: So you see, Ma, she isn't too keen. Didn't I say? I'll choose another one for her myself.

MOTHER: If you don't like it, why don't you say so? Why all this …

HEMA: 'All this' what? What did I say?

MOTHER *(resigned)*: All right, Vidula. You sort that out with her. *(To Hema)* This dhoti is for your husband.

HEMA: What for? The sari is enough. Where is he going to wear a dhoti in Australia?

MOTHER: It's a wedding custom, Australia or no Australia. And along with the dhoti, this. *(Holding up a gold necklace)* For him. And one for the bridegroom.

HEMA *(putting the necklace aside)*: No, no. Such an expensive chain. What'll he do with it? He doesn't even wear a ring. *(Agitated)* Excuse me. With people just dropping in without warning, I haven't even begun unpacking.

(Goes into her room.)

VIDULA: I'm glad my wedding is giving everyone a chance to let off steam.

MOTHER: It has nothing to do with your wedding. She is always like that! It's the same story, every year. For the first few days after her arrival, she is normal. Happy. Laughing. Then I don't know what goes wrong.

(Vidula follows Hema into her room.)

One waits all year long, pining to see the daughter's face. But within four days, her mood changes, and after that, one word is too little, two are too many. I don't know.

FATHER: Well, she has left her husband and son back home. Bound to miss them.

(Vidula comes in holding Hema by her hand.)

VIDULA: Look, I don't know if this wedding will actually take place …

HEMA: Don't say such horrible things.

VIDULA: Well, it'll happen when it happens. But at least until then, can't we pretend and have some laughter around here?

HEMA *(as her eyes fill up)*: What did I say now? I don't want any money wasted on us, that's all. Who will wear that necklace in Sydney? It'll lie around in the bank vault.

MOTHER: Let it lie there, no harm done. If your husband doesn't want it, your son may, tomorrow. A wedding means expenses—there is no getting away from that.

(Hema doesn't reply. Just bites her lower lip. Mother sees it and explodes.)

Look, fifteen years have gone by. How long are you going to go on rubbing it in?

HEMA: Rubbing it in? *(To Vidula)* You see? That's why I said I'd rather stay inside.

MOTHER: I said we'll take a loan. We'll work out some arrangement. Give us time. But you couldn't even wait three months—you were in god's own hurry to get married and take off.

HEMA: Hurry? You think his Bank would have waited for him? For three months?

MOTHER: We couldn't come up with a big wedding overnight. All we asked for was a little time to …

HEMA: Big? Who had asked for a big wedding?

FATHER *(as though he has suddenly woken up)*: What is it now? What are we discussing?

VIDULA: Ma, Hemakka, please …

HEMA *(without raising her voice)*: Big! My poor husband. He said he would be quite content with a small fire altar and seven steps round it. That's all. And he was taken at his word. Literally. If he had made a fuss, wouldn't you have given him the whole caboodle?

MOTHER: Hema, you were a witness. You saw how I pleaded with your father. I almost fell at his feet. I said our daughter and son-in-law are going abroad, let's get some jewellery made for them. But has he ever listened to me? He just snarled at me: 'Our son-in-law isn't asking for anything. So what are you making such a fuss about?'

HEMA: Wasn't that convenient?

FATHER: Look, I grew up in poverty. My brother Ramdas and I—we struggled. We often had to share a plate of gruel between us. The only meal that day, quite often. We ran from house to house for free meals offered by relatives. If it wasn't for a scholarship from our Saraswat Education Society …

MOTHER: Yes, yes. Please. We know all that. We have heard every word a thousand times.

FATHER *(annoyed, gets up)*: I just shouldn't open my mouth. That's the mistake I make. I think I had better go in.

(Goes in.)

VIDULA: Ashwin hasn't asked for anything either. Poor chap! Says a simple registration would do. If Ma would only listen …

MOTHER: It's all very well for him to waive these things. He lives in the US, after all. But I have attended weddings in our neighbours' families. Accepted their hospitality. Gorged myself at their wedding feasts. And now, when it comes to my own daughter's wedding, you want me to pack the guests off with a betel leaf and a nut?

HEMA *(looks at her wrist watch)*: It isn't five yet. They won't be back from school yet.

MOTHER: You two had better decide about the saris. I have to attend to …

(Goes into the kitchen.)

VIDULA: Ma! That's done it. Now she won't emerge from the kitchen for another two hours. So much for the 'selection' of saris.

HEMA *(still worried about her own time schedule)*: Another half an hour should be okay. The school should get over by then.

VIDULA: What's this, Hemakka? How often do you need to check on them? Poor Brother-in-law is such a caring father. Why don't you just let him be?

HEMA: He is so absent-minded. But only when it comes to the kids, mind you. No problem with the affairs of the Bank.

VIDULA: But to be the Chief Commercial Officer! Wow! You don't know how proud we are of him. I mentioned it to Ashwin the other day and he said we Indians are about to take over the entire commercial world. These days most multinationals, international banks, corporations—they all have Indians in top positions.

HEMA: And do you know why? Because they are all transferable jobs and the white wife refuses to go trailing after her husband. We Indian women, on the other hand, are obedient Sati Savitris, ever willing to follow in our husbands' footsteps. Look at me— Melbourne, Johannesberg, Singapore, and now Sydney. Our men may get all the top jobs. But I am in no better position than Ma.

(Vivan, aged thirteen, comes in, carrying a book.)

VIDULA: Hello, Vivan. Come in.

VIVAN: Here, your book. I have come to return it. Hello, Hema Aunty.

HEMA: I'm sorry. But you are ...?

VIDULA: It's Vivan, son of Kaikini Chandrika.

HEMA: Gosh! How you have grown up! I would never have recognized you. *(To Vidula)* He is two years younger than my Ketan. And already so tall. You were this high when I saw you last. Really!

(The telephone rings. Vidula picks it up.)

VIDULA: Hello, yes? Yes, it's me.

VIVAN: I borrowed a book yesterday. I have come to return it.

(Gives her the book. Pause.)

I saw you yesterday.

HEMA: *Madame Bovary.* Oh, dear! Are you sure you should be reading this stuff at your age?

VIDULA *(speaking into the phone)*: But I can't wear it. It's too long. Almost two inches. Yes, of course. You will need to shorten it. No, no! I won't. Why couldn't you get your measurements right?

(The following dialogue is overlapped on Vidula's telephone conversation.)

VIVAN: I stand first in my class.

HEMA: I am sure you do. But you should wait another three or four years at least. I would never allow my Ketan to read this and he is older than you.

VIVAN: I have read *Lady Chatterley's Lover*.

HEMA *(scandalized)*: You should be ashamed of yourself.

VIVAN: There is a letter for you.

HEMA: Where?

VIVAN: In the book.

VIDULA *(in the phone)*: And the blouse. I mean. How *can* you? … The left shoulder is so tight I couldn't button up.

HEMA: A letter for me? In this book?

(Takes out the letter from the book and glances through it.)

VIVAN: I saw you yesterday. I immediately sat down and typed it out on my laptop. Very personal.

HEMA *(reading the letter, only half-interested)*: Personal? How odd.

(Suddenly her eyes widen in horror.)

Oh, god!

(Vivan deliberately turns his back to her and goes and picks another book from the shelf.)

VIDULA *(on the phone)*: You come tomorrow morning, please. Yes, at ten-thirty. Please, and don't for heaven's sake keep me waiting. I have got to get to the Internet Café. Before it gets too crowded.

(Vivan picks up a book from the shelf and takes it to Hema.)

HEMA (*still flabbergasted by the letter*): But ... but ... my god! This is
... you can't ...

VIVAN (*showing her the book*): I'll finish this by tomorrow.

(*Takes out another letter.*)

Until then, here. Another one. This one is even more personal.

(*Places the second letter on the sofa.*)

HEMA: This is ... you can't ... Oh, god!

(*Vivan goes out with his book. Hema, horrified, is still glued to the first
letter and doesn't notice the second letter on the sofa.*)

VIDULA: Have you stitched the fall? Please, Mister Ismail. Please, you
can't delay everything. I am getting married on—I know you
know—then why don't you hurry up? Please.

(*Puts the receiver down. Hema quickly folds the letter she is reading and
tucks it into her blouse.*)

God, he is so exasperating. Never on time. Never gets a thing
right. The senior Ismail Darzee was so good. So Ma feels loyal to
this ass.

(*She is about to collapse into the sofa when she sees Vivan's second letter.
Picks it up. The phone rings. As she speaks into the phone, Hema notices
the letter in her hand and is speechless with anxiety.*)

Hello. Ah, Isabel. No, I'm afraid not. He should be back any
moment. Say in half an hour? I'll tell him you called.

(*Puts the receiver down, casually looks into the letter and starts reading.*)

'Darling, you don't know how I desire to crush you in my arms ...'

HEMA (*snatches the letter from her hand*): Don't!

VIDULA: Sorry. Is that yours? I must say good for you both. Couldn't
help reading the next line also. He wants to ...

HEMA: Shut up!

VIDULA: After fifteen years of married life, you get letters like that from Brother-in-law. My fiancé hasn't even kissed me in a letter.

HEMA: I must ring Sydney.

(Starts dialling on her mobile.)

VIDULA: Brother-in-law's letters seem to have a powerful effect on you.

HEMA: No, no. It's … *(Listens)* It's ringing. Why isn't Ketan home yet? I hope he is all right.

VIDULA: Why shouldn't he be all right? Ketan is old enough. Older than this Vivan.

HEMA *(almost to herself)*: That's what worries me.

(Suddenly Radhabai starts shouting in the kitchen. Mother keeps her voice low initially, but as her temper rises, she too raises her voice and the two are soon quarrelling at the top of their voices.)

RADHABAI: There's nothing wrong with my hearing, Ma. I heard you. But can't you see how small these *triphala* nuts are? I have been cooking since I was ten. You don't think I know my measures …

MOTHER: Please don't start again on your cooking expertise. I don't have the time. I have told you clearly: show me the amount before you put in the masala. But that's simply too demeaning for you, isn't it? You are just too vain. Honestly …

HEMA: Again! This is the third time today.

VIDULA: We are used to it.

RADHABAI: Then why don't you take over the whole business of cooking, Ma? You've hired me to cook for you and I feel a fool being told every little detail. *(Mimicking)* This much *vagar*. This much salt. That much chilly powder. Like to a child.

MOTHER: If I am to come and slave in the kitchen, why do I need you here? Go, go and sit in that corner, just collect your salary while I do your chores.

RADHABAI (*at the top of her voice*): Yes, I'll do just that. We must have been arch enemies in some past life, so I'm paying for it now. God broke this forehead of mine and took away my husband. Even He has no pity on me. So I have got to live in your house and take whatever humiliations you pile on me.

(*The above fight goes parallelly with the following conversation between Hema and Vidula.*)

HEMA: What's this new *avatara*, Vidu? She was never like this before. I know Ma has a temper. But Radhabai! She used to be so docile, so quiet.

VIDULA: This has been going on for at least six months now.

MOTHER: Listen, if you're going to shout and scream like this, you pack your bags and go back to your brother's place. Go. I'll arrange for the tickets.

RADHABAI: What will I do there? The four paise I have saved here will go into his pocket and then he will throw me out again. I would rather lie down in a corner here and starve to death.

HEMA: What is wrong with Ma? Has she gone mad? Threatening to send Radhabai away a week before the big do? For a triphala nut?

VIDULA: Nothing will happen. Don't worry. Ma won't send her away. Radhabai won't leave. But the squabbling goes on every day.

HEMA: So surprising. I mean, all these seven years I've never heard her raise her voice. And this time, suddenly, I find her shouting and bashing her forehead like a harridan. What's gone wrong?

MOTHER: I don't want you whimpering in a corner. No, you had better go. Leave.

RADHABAI: If you say so, Ma. You are the mistress here. Who am I to …

(*Hema rushes into the kitchen.*)

HEMA: Enough, Ma. Radhabai, please stop it. Enough now.

RADHABAI: What have I done, Hema? What did I say?

(As Hema drags her out of the kitchen and takes her toward the backyard)

> She keeps asking me to go away. Go away, where? I can't go from house to house asking for a job now, not at my age.

HEMA: No one is asking you to leave. Now you go into the backyard and cool your top.

RADHABAI: That's all that remains for me to do now. Sit down, place a betel leaf on my head, and do penance under the jackfruit tree.

HEMA: All right. Do that. Sit there, doesn't matter.

RADHABAI: I'll tell you one thing. Ma has been an angel for me. Given me a roof over my head. Sat by my bedside all night when I was ill. But she has also done me harm. I'll say that.

(Frees herself.)

> I can't sit here. The food's almost cooked.

(Moves toward the kitchen at which point Mother emerges from the kitchen.)

MOTHER: I have done you harm, have I? Who is asking you to stay on then?

(Hema grabs Mother and takes her into the living room and pushes her on the sofa.)

HEMA: Ma, please …

MOTHER: I can't bear it any more. There's only one way out.

VIDULA *(giggles)*: Quite. Send her home!

MOTHER: You think this is a big joke. She eats my life up.

HEMA: But Ma, all this is so recent, this shouting and screaming ! I had never seen her do that before.

MOTHER: It's all that television rubbish. That's why going to her brother's village will do her good. They have no television there.

HEMA: The wedding is only a week away, Ma.

VIDULA: Or so we think.

MOTHER: So what? I'll manage …

HEMA: These sudden tantrums. Are you sure she is all right? Perhaps she should see a psychiatrist.

MOTHER: No need for any fancy treatment. You all have turned her head by praising her to heavens. '*Such* a marvellous cook. *Such* a nice person. Ma's *so* lucky!' I think *I* had better go away somewhere—far away—in search of mental peace.

(Mother gets up and heads for the kitchen.)

VIDULA: And she too heads for the kitchen!

MOTHER: There's enough to do there. This is what happens with female cooks, I tell you. Before she came, we had Nagappa. He worked with us for thirty years. But he never once raised his voice. Such a gentle soul. You can't get male cooks any longer, that's the problem.

(Goes into the kitchen, talking. Pause.)

VIDULA: True, Nagappa didn't raise his voice. But a lot of his energy went into raising skirts.

HEMA *(startled)*: What?

VIDULA *(embarrassed at having let that line slip)*: Well, he … used to put his hand up …

HEMA: What did you say?

(Shocked, they stare at each other and then both burst into peals of laughter.)

But you? You were so little. I never thought—

VIDULA *(shrugs)*: He would touch one in the oddest spots.

(Laughter again. The revelation has somehow cleared the air and brought them closer together.)

HEMA: And we left you home with him because we thought you were safe with him.

VIDULA: But you too? You were so much older.

HEMA: They leave their wives back at home. I suppose they have to get rid of the itch somehow.

(*Picks up her mobile. Sound of a motor-bike outside.*)

VIDULA (*excited*): Rohit!

HEMA: I think I'll ring later.

(*Puts the mobile away.*)

VIDULA: Time he was back.

(*Mother comes out of the kitchen.*)

MOTHER: That must be Rohit.

ROHIT (*entering*): Email!

HEMA: Anything for me?

VIDULA (*simultaneously*): For whom?

(*Father comes in and sits listening. He is all attention.*)

ROHIT (*to Hema*): You, absolutely. I mean, Brother-in-law must be sitting there, like a god, all his four hands continually busy. A mobile in this hand, the computer in that, the phone in the third, and a clutch of airmail letters in the fourth—all aimed at you.

(*Hands Hema the printouts. She anxiously glances through them. Rohit silently hands over an email printout to Vidula.*)

MOTHER (*sensing trouble*): What is that now?

ROHIT: He can't come on the thirteenth. He is arriving on the seventeenth.

MOTHER: Ayyo, the seventeenth. Why?

HEMA (*excited*): But that's absurd! That'll leave us no time! It'll give *them* no time. I mean, they need a week together at least, surely.

ROHIT: The US badminton team is travelling to Malaysia. Ashwin is their legal consultant. He will travel with them upto Chennai and then come to Dharwad from there. That way he feels he will have company till Chennai.

MOTHER: But that's—that's—how is that possible? It was all agreed. He has to meet Vidu. Spend some time together. And only if they liked each other, only then, we were to go ahead with the wedding. I mean, that's what *he* proposed. If he comes that late, when is all that going to happen? We have to print invitations, inform our relatives. I can't …

ROHIT: He has already said he doesn't want all that. No rituals, no wasteful *tamasha*, nothing. If he and Vidula like each other, they'll go to the Registrar and sign. If they don't, they'll shake hands and part. He proceeds to Malaysia. Catches up with his badminton team.

MOTHER *(enraged)*: Then why is he coming even a week in advance? Why not on the morning of the wedding? Tell him that. They have seen each other on the video. Talked on the mobile. Why meet at all beforehand? They can be introduced to each other in the Registrar's office.

ROHIT: I have assured our relatives that it'll take place. Ninety-nine per cent. We'll inform everyone by email the moment Vidu and he give the nod.

HEMA: My god, Rohit, this is the twenty-first century. And we call ourselves educated. How did we accept such a ludicrous arrangement? You didn't even bother to ring me before you agreed to this. I was informed at the tail end, like an outsider. I would have said let's not …

ROHIT: They seemed happy working out the arrangement between themselves. On the video, mobile … And according to him, there is still no firm commitment.

MOTHER: No, I tell you. Let's just call it off. Tell him. Right now. Our Vidu will get a hundred boys better than him. We didn't go to them begging for a bridegroom. They asked for her. They took all the initiative. And now at the last moment …

ROHIT: Mother, please. Let's be sensible.

MOTHER: He thinks we are so desperate for him? Just tell him the proposal is off.

VIDULA: No, we can't. We'll become the laughing stock of the town. We agreed to all this. Now to break off for no reason! I can't face it.

FATHER: No reason? I met your mother only a couple of times before we got married. But at least we had met.

HEMA: Let's go ahead and get the invitation cards printed anyway.

ROHIT: That doesn't take half an hour these days.

FATHER: We have given a hefty advance to the Wedding Hall.

ROHIT: Don't worry, Appa. We won't lose that.

VIDULA: Is that what we are worried about? For goodness' sake, I can't sleep at night. I sit up suddenly in the middle of the night, shivering. It's like having ice water poured into my entrails.

HEMA: I know. It must be dreadful. But look, if you have the slightest doubt after spending a couple of days with him …

VIDULA: Couple of days? You and Brother-in-law were going around for two years!

HEMA: It didn't help, let me tell you. A day before the wedding I started having a runny stomach. It just wouldn't stop. I cried on Chandrakant's shoulder and begged him, let's wait till my tummy rights itself. Let's postpone the date …

ROHIT: Did he agree?

MOTHER: To postpone? Ha. The daughter was born in exactly nine and a half months, to the day.

HEMA: Enough, Ma. We are not discussing my marriage here.

(Mother goes into the kitchen.)

FATHER: Let's face it. Marriage is a gamble.

ROHIT: Have you applied for your birth certificate yet?

VIDULA: Sorry. I forgot. Tomorrow.

ROHIT: Tomorrow. Tomorrow. When is that tomorrow going to happen? Every morning, you spend hours in that Internet Café and it is next to the Municipal Corporation. Why don't you just step in and hand in the application?

VIDULA *(curling up with embarrassment)*: I will. I promise you.

ROHIT: We have to get the birth certificate, then go to Bangalore, apply for the passport, and then to Chennai for the visa. When is all that going to happen? And you won't make the first move.

VIDULA: I will. I will. But it's so hard when I don't even know …

FATHER: If Ramdas were alive, he would have arranged for everything. He was so active.

ROHIT: Have you at least got yourselves photographed?

VIDULA: I had taken some. But they didn't come out right. So I tore them up.

ROHIT: They are only for the American Consulate, you know. Not for Ashwin's approval.

HEMA: Oh, be quiet. When we go shopping this evening, I'll attend to it.

ROHIT: Good luck. And don't let her enter that Internet Café.

HEMA: Stop nagging her! *(To Vidula)* What do you do in that Internet Café?

VIDULA: I listen to sermons by Swami Ananga Nath …

ROHIT: She plays video games. She is crazy about them.

VIDULA: … so I can forget about the wedding for a few hours.

ROHIT: It's your wedding. Not mine. Why should I care?

(Mother comes rushing out.)

MOTHER: Ayyo, I completely forgot. Mohan and Mira are coming this evening.

ROHIT: This evening? Why? They reserve their harassment for Saturday mornings.

MOTHER: Apparently the Sirurs have come from Hyderabad.

ROHIT: No! But I can't. I simply can't. Have to see Ashwin's uncle this evening. Can't miss that. You meet them.

HEMA: Not possible. The goldsmith has ordered some special jewellery samples from Belgaum for us. They have got to go back tonight.

ROHIT: Then let Appa meet them.

MOTHER: Look, when someone says, can we come and visit you, you can't say don't. Not when people have come all the way from Hyderabad.

ROHIT: Mother, you know why they are here.

MOTHER: Just see them for five minutes, will you?

FATHER: It's good of them to come from Hyderabad to see me.

MOTHER: I don't want them to think we are becoming uppity.

(Goes in.)

VIDULA (almost viciously): They have brought Tapasya along too.

ROHIT: This is unbelievable. Right in the middle of our own chaos.

HEMA (dialling a number on the phone): I agree with Rohit. We Indians have no sense of occasion.

VIDULA: I forgot to tell you, Rohit. Isabel rang. She wants you to call her back.

ROHIT: I am just about to go round the bend. I'll call her later. I want to sleep for half an hour.

(Storms into his room.)

HEMA: Who is this Isabel?

VIDULA: His girlfriend.

HEMA: A Christian?

VIDULA: With that name, what do you think?

HEMA: Weird.

VIDULA: This is a new thing he has started. Catnaps. Whenever there is a problem, he jumps into bed.

HEMA: Couldn't he find a suitable match within our caste?

VIDULA: Lucky him. He can actually fall asleep.

HEMA *(already on the phone)*: Hello. Ah! Ketan, you are home. So how was today, darling? … But why? I had told your father … . Now listen … . Doesn't your father listen when I … . Is he home? No, of course not. Call Imelda. She is probably busy on the mobile with one of her boyfriends. Yes, call her. Tell her I want to talk to her.

(Vidula watches wistfully as Hema talks to her son on the phone.)

Scene Three

The living room. Father, Rohit, Gopal Sirur, Vatsala Sirur, Mohan Hattangadi and Mira Hattangadi.

FATHER: It must be what—close to fifteen years, isn't it? Yes, it's fifteen. Isn't it, Mr Sirur? If I remember ...

GOPAL: No need to call me Mister, Doctor Uncle. Actually I am your nephew from my mother's side. Her mother was a Nadkarni.

VATSALA: Your daughter, Hema, was just about to get married.

FATHER: So Ramdas was still alive then.

GOPAL: Of course. We remember him vividly. Very active. Always on the go.

FATHER: And capable. Very. And affectionate. A genius. The only genius in our family. A gifted painter. Could have been a Ravi Verma. But he wanted to be rich. A successful businessman. Grow rich overnight.

ROHIT *(gently)*: Father ...

FATHER: Opened a grocery store. Couldn't run it. Then a restaurant. A bakery. A tailoring shop. Was cheated every time. Our community has no head for business, but he wouldn't face the fact. I had to bail him out every time. But I miss him. We would never have got through Hema's wedding without him. He saw to every detail. I don't really know how we are going to manage without him.

MIRA: Why, Doctor Uncle? We are here. I'm sure you have nothing to worry about. And we are told Hema too has come from Australia.

ROHIT: Father ...

FATHER: She is here. *(Suddenly formal.)* But my wife and my two daughters offer their apologies. They greatly regret they were unable to be here this evening to welcome you personally. *(Relaxes.)* They are out shopping. *(Guffaws.)* Shopping! A wedding is essentially an excuse for shopping. Everything else, as you know, is of secondary consequence.

MOHAN: Well, in the good old days, weddings would go on for weeks on end. Just preliminary discussions over exchange of gifts would take days.

FATHER: But Hema's husband didn't take a penny. And this boy who has come for Vidula—what's his name?

ROHIT: Ashwin.

FATHER: Ashwin. Ashwin Panje. He says the same thing: no dowry. Who says today's youth lacks values? Idealism? The first thing he said was: 'No, thanks. I don't want any dowry.'

ROHIT: Father, they are here ...

FATHER: Sorry. Sorry. I talk too much—a sure sign of senility.

MOHAN: Oh, but please! We are here to talk to you. Please don't stop.

ROHIT *(getting up)*: Well then. If you'll excuse me. I've an appointment to keep.

GOPAL *(to Rohit)*: Actually, it's for us to apologize. You are in the midst of your sister's wedding and we barge in. It's good of you to see us at all.

VATSALA: We realize we are being pests.

MOHAN: He understands the situation, Sister. *(To Rohit, gesturing to the Sirur couple)* You know, Rohit, they too have their compulsions.

ROHIT: The point is Ashwin is planning to stay with his uncle, Govinda Rao, when he is here. So I have to finalize the details with him.

GOPAL: We mustn't inconvenience you, Rohit. But …

MOHAN: … but it's golden, this *muhurta*. We were told: 'Whatever happens, do not miss this day.' He was insistent.

(Rohit looks up startled at the word, 'muhurta'.)

MIRA: We follow his instructions implicitly.

ROHIT *(baffled)*: He? I don't understand …

GOPAL: But you were right to say Tapasya shouldn't come along now. That was most sensitive of you. Very sensitive. We appreciate that.

ROHIT: I'm sorry I didn't even know you were coming to Dharwad. It was Hema who probably said that.

GOPAL: But she is right. I mean, it would have been most embarrassing for Tapasya to have us discussing her future right in front of her.

VATSALA *(smiling)*: Actually, I don't agree. Today's girls—they are not like us twenty-five years ago. It's *her* life we are discussing. I don't see why she couldn't be present. Poor thing! She is sitting there, all tensed up, waiting for us to call her and tell her it has all gone well.

MOHAN: No, no. Sister, that's not what Brother-in-law is talking about. Once Vidula's wedding's over, Rohit will be free—they will then have time to meet and chat at leisure. These are only preliminary matters.

ROHIT: I'm sorry, I don't know what you are talking about.

(A slight pause. Then Mohan gives an ingratiating laugh.)

MOHAN: You know, Mira and I have been coming here ...

FATHER *(suddenly wakes up)*: Oh yes! Every Saturday morning. At nine on the dot and without fail.

(Laughs.)

> If they were late by so much as five minutes, I would ask Rohit: 'Hasn't your weekly despatch arrived?'

ROHIT: Appa.

MOHAN *(unfazed)*: It's the most convenient hour for us to come. We have to come all the way from Hubli. Takes barely twenty-five minutes at that time of the day. Start ten minutes later and we have to allow for a good hour. The traffic. You know. Impossible.

MIRA: And from here, we can go on to the Someshwara temple, next door. They have their *arati* at ten, precisely. Very convenient.

FATHER: I would be sitting here dressed up to greet them, but they had no time for me.

(Rohit presses Father's hand. Father quietens down.)

MOHAN: Doctor Uncle, Doctor Uncle, how can you say that ...

MIRA: We respect elders. Everywhere ...

GOPAL: You see, the situation is like this. Our son, Sharad, is back from the States. On a six weeks' holiday. He must return next month. And then he can't get any leave for another three years. We thought if you said yes, we could have the wedding while he was still here.

(Rohit looks at them taken aback.)

VATSALA: That's why we are bothering you. We feel awful but ...

MIRA: If we miss this evening, there are no propitious stars for the talks for another three weeks. So we asked them to come right away ...

MOHAN: From Hyderabad. Don't worry, we said, come today itself.

MIRA: And bring Tapasya along.

ROHIT: But—but—I am not thinking of getting married. I haven't given it a thought.

(A slight embarrassed pause. Then Mohan plunges on.)

MOHAN: That's what you have been saying, of course. But how long are you going to go on waiting? Actually I had even proposed that they should get the nuptials done at the same time as your sister's—in the same *pandal*.

MIRA: You must think of your parents too. They are getting on—

FATHER: Don't worry about us. I'll look after my old age and you look after yours.

GOPAL: I said enough, Mira. Don't go on.

MIRA *(smoothly)*: Did I mention old age, Doctor Uncle? I was only talking of the concern you must feel. Please, don't …

(Radhabai comes in with a tray carrying six cups of tea and goes round. They all help themselves, excepting Father.)

GOPAL *(gently, to Rohit)*: Why don't you want to think of marriage?

ROHIT: I'm not in a position to get married. Not for another three years. *(Indicating Mohan and Mira)* I have already told them that.

GOPAL: Forgive me for being persistent. But may I know why?

ROHIT: I am thinking of resigning from my job. Planning to open my own office.

GOPAL: You should too. I always say, look, we Saraswat Brahmins are educated, artistic. But we have no sense of adventure. We are timid. A job, that's all we care for. A safe salary. But this is an age of opportunities. Go ahead. Take the plunge. We shall only be delighted.

MIRA: Tapasya *adores* you. She has seen all your documentaries.

ROHIT: Which ones?

MIRA: I suppose on the telly. *(To Gopal)* Hasn't she, Brother?

ROHIT: I don't make documentaries.

MOHAN: She is also very creative.

MIRA: Gifted. Sings. Classical music.

ROHIT: You have told me all that. But I can't.

(Father stands up to go.)

MIRA: You aren't leaving, are you, Doctor Uncle? Look, Rohit is refusing to consider. What do you say?

FATHER: What can I say? I have got a wife already.

(Forced laughter from everyone. Father goes into his room.)

MIRA: Doctor Uncle's joking. Ha! Ha!

MOHAN: God has been bountiful to Brother-in-law. They lack nothing. Only two children and the son lives in the States. He is doing very well, thank God. So everything Sister and Brother-in-law have in this world will go to Tapasya. You go ahead and take any risk you want to take.

MIRA: Go abroad for training, if you wish. They can give you …

ROHIT *(annoyed)*: Are you trying to bribe me?

MOHAN: No, no, no …

ROHIT: What else do you mean?

GOPAL: Rohit, let's be reasonable. You, today's youth, you are Americanized. You want to stand on your own feet. Which is admirable. For my generation, it was the duty of the parents to ensure that their childern had a comfortable life. Harmonious and comfortable. We really see no bribery there. We don't mean it.

MOHAN: We admire the drive in you. But we must place the facts before you.

ROHIT: No, I'm sorry. My answer is no. I am not interested.

(A long pause. Vatsala looks at her husband in bewilderment. Gopal looks dazed.)

GOPAL: You are not? But …

VATSALA: Our daughter …

ROHIT: That's what I want to know. Why have you brought her here, all the way down from Hyderabad, when I had very clearly—explicitly—said I don't want to get married? I am not interested.

GOPAL: You had said that? When?

VATSALA: We wouldn't have brought her here if you knew you were really not interested.

(Mohan and Mira become restive.)

ROHIT: You mean … do you mean to tell me … *(To Mohan and Mira)* You mean you didn't tell them what I told you? That I am not …

MOHAN: Listen, listen. No need to get upset. When someone does something it is always done with good intentions. So something good can come out of it.

ROHIT *(angry)*: I told you not once or twice—but twenty times—every time you came here, every Saturday morning, I said that—not once, but again and again—that I didn't want to get married. And you never conveyed it to them? You told them I was willing?

MOHAN: No, no. We didn't say that. But there is a difference—or at least we feel there is—between not being interested *at all* and not being ready for it *now*. We genuinely felt that although you were hesitant, you were bound to agree in the end. That is why—

ROHIT *(to the Sirurs)*: There you are! I said no in so many words. But they told you what *they* felt …

MIRA: Besides the Shastriji promised us the relationship couldn't *not* materialize. All the stars matched. 'Don't have any doubts,' he said. 'I have never seen two horoscopes match so perfectly.'

ROHIT: I can't believe it. Did you hear that? I tell them something and they tell you what their astrologer tells them.

(Rohit dials a number on the mobile.)

MIRA: The Shastri insisted the *guna*s matched hundred per cent.

(The number is busy.)

ROHIT: Tsk!

GOPAL: Rohit, let's forget whatever has happened.

ROHIT: Forget? Whatever I said—repeatedly—it didn't matter?

GOPAL: They were wrong. I'll accept that.

MIRA: It is said one shouldn't mind getting rebuked if it is for an auspicious cause.

GOPAL *(shutting them up with a vigorous wave of his hand and pleading)*: Tapasya is waiting for a word from us. She must be hanging on to the mobile. Will you talk to her?

ROHIT: Me? And say what? Ask them. *(Indicates the Hattangadis)* I have to leave. I am late.

(Speaks on the mobile.)

Hello. This is Rohit. May I speak to Mr Govind Rao? Hello, Govind Uncle. This is me. Rohit. I am starting right away. … Yes. Yes. I'll be there in ten minutes. Yes, ten minutes. Yes, please. Yes, you can get dressed and be ready and we'll go out together. I'm sorry I'm late.

(Puts the mobile in his pocket.)

Excuse me.

GOPAL: Rohit. Rohit. Please. Just let me finish what I was saying. What shall we tell Tapasya? What I suggest is this. Just say yes. A simple yes.

ROHIT: I must go. Please. You can wait here if you like. Mother'll be back …

GOPAL *(desperate)*: What shall I tell my daughter? I know you didn't agree to this match. But think of her. She has come here under the impression that you have. She has come from Hyderabad sure that everything will go well today and she will be engaged to you ...

ROHIT: This is awful. But what do you want me to do?

GOPAL: Just think of her position. She is not an uneducated girl. She has a First Class in MA in Sociology. She is a modern girl—educated and sensitive. How can you push her aside without a word? No, please, don't humiliate her like this.

ROHIT: Me? What have I done?

MOHAN: No one is blaming you. We accept the blame—my wife and I.

MIRA: We accept and apologize. What more can we do?

VATSALA: The girl has come here clutching her hopes to her heart.

(Rohit is about to say something when Gopal suddenly stands up and starts speaking at the top of his voice.)

GOPAL: You all—all of you—please be quiet. Don't say a word.

VATSALA *(stands up)*: Please, be careful. The doctor has warned you. He has said you shouldn't get excited ...

GOPAL *(screams at her)*: I said shut up. Shut up. Why don't you just shut up? *(To Rohit)* Rohit, first let me apologize. I don't know what transpired between you and these people. Perhaps they misunderstood you. Let's say they lied to us. But what could we—this wife of mine and I—what else could we have done? Could we have phoned you and asked you what you had decided? Could we have said to them, tell us on oath that you are telling the truth? We believed. We believed, you see. Because we wanted to believe. Why shouldn't we? It's for our only daughter. Why wouldn't we believe that everything would work out right for her?

MIRA: Brother …

GOPAL: I said quiet! Now, Rohit, we have told everyone in Hyderabad that this alliance has been finalized. Every one there thinks we are here for the engagement ceremony. And let me admit—we, in our confidence, may have encouraged that belief. Yes, we did. We shouldn't have, but we did. I admit it. But we too believed it.

VATSALA: Listen …

(While Gopal holds forth, Radhabai appears inside the other room and watches.)

GOPAL: Shut up. I don't care if I have a stroke for the sake of my daughter. To you, Rohit, it may seem a small matter. But we have told everyone in Hyderabad. Our relations have congratulated us on getting such an excellent son-in-law. Her classmates have actually thrown a party to celebrate the event. And now if we go back and say—can you imagine? She won't be able to show her face. She is our only child, Rohit. She is sensitive. Don't hurt her, please, don't wound her. We have brought her up like a flower. Don't insult her. Don't please. I'll fall to your feet …

(Gopal goes down on his knees and touches Rohit's feet. Rohit recoils in horror. The others pounce on Gopal and pull him back. They all speak together.)

MOHAN: Brother-in-law, what's this?

MIRA: No, no, Brother, you can't do this. This is madness.

VATSALA: You've got to be careful. Please …

GOPAL: I'll do anything for our daughter.

VATSALA: Your blood pressure. The doctor has warned us.

GOPAL *(slowly sinks into the chair and pants)*: I can't bear the thought, I tell you. It's too dreadful for words.

VATSALA: Quiet now. You have exerted yourself enough.

(Fans him with her pallu. Rohit nonplussed. The fire has gone out of his self-righteous tone.)

ROHIT: I'm late. I must go.

MOHAN: Can we ring you tomorrow?

ROHIT: No, not tomorrow. I'll be running around …

MOHAN: We'll ring after a couple of days then?

ROHIT: Perhaps. I have to go now. All right.

MOHAN *(pleased)*: That's all we want to hear. You said all right. That's enough. Why didn't you say so right at the start?

ROHIT *(puzzled and guilty)*: Sorry. But …

MOHAN: No need to apologize. We understand your position. If you had said right at the start that we could meet after two days, we would not have delayed you now.

MIRA: He has said all right. We can't trouble him more.

GOPAL: What shall we tell Tapasya? How can we face her with …

VATSALA *(firm)*: Let's go now. She is an adult. Not a child any more. She'll understand.

MOHAN: Brother-in-law, young men need time to consider. Let us give him time to consider. That is only right and proper.

VATSALA *(unsmiling)*: Let us go.

GOPAL: Rohit …

(Vatsala grabs Gopal's arm and leads him out. Before Mohan can say something Rohit starts dialling a number on his mobile.)

ROHIT: Hello, hello. This is Rohit. Is Govind Uncle … Oh! Oh! Has he left? But … I hope he isn't upset. I couldn't … I'm sorry. Where is he gone? Can I …

(The other party obviously rings off. Rohit sees Mohan and Mira waiting and rudely turns to go into his room.)

MIRA: Rohit, it's not for me to say. But was that Govinda Rao's daughter Usha?

ROHIT (*surly*): Yes.

MIRA: Govinda Rao wanted her to marry Ashwin. Now Ashwin is coming here to marry your sister. And you say he plans to stay with them?

ROHIT: Govinda Rao is his uncle, after all.

MIRA: That's precisely the point. Govinda Rao thinks his daughter has the prior claim. Take care, that's all. Just take care. Govinda Rao is … well … make sure he doesn't throw a spanner in the works.

VATSALA (*calls from outside*): Mira …

MIRA: Coming. Coming. Let's go.

MOHAN: You are young. You don't know the wickedness some people are capable of.

(*Mira and Mohan leave. The mobile rings. Rohit looks at the name on the mobile and speaks.*)

ROHIT: Isabel! Thank god for your voice. I can't tell you what hell I have been through. You see, the Sirurs were here. From Hyderabad.

(*But his caller doesn't let him speak and goes on. Rohit listens with increasing frustration and then with exasperation.*)

No, darling. I didn't agree to meet them. I didn't even know they were coming …

(*Listens.*)

But be reasonable. … No, darling, don't you realize what I'm in the middle of …?

(*He starts getting irritated.*)

No, I'm afraid I can't come for another two days. I just can't. Sorry.

(*While he is talking Vidula and Hema come in from the backdoor carrying several parcels.*)

Bye, love, I'll call you back later. Bye. (*Embarrassed whisper.*) Yes, I love you.

HEMA: Is that your Christian girlfriend?

ROHIT: Yes.

HEMA: Why should you take up with a Christian girl? Aren't there nice girls in our community?

ROHIT: Oh, please. You don't start getting at me too. I have been through hell.

HEMA: Yes, we saw some bits of the drama. I must say they went on a bit.

ROHIT: You mean, you were here when all that was going on? Couldn't you have come in and rescued me, for heaven's sake?

HEMA: We couldn't embarrass our guests. After all, we had said we wouldn't be home. Actually you should be grateful. If they had seen us, they would have switched on the replay.

(*Hema goes in, carrying a few packages.*)

VIDULA: But it gives you a sense of power, doesn't it? To have a girl waiting for you—her parents kneeling before you—begging and pleading. … It really must make you feel grand.

ROHIT (*angry*): I didn't ask them to come. I didn't want the scene.

(*Father comes out and sits on a chair.*)

VIDULA: Nonsense. Then why didn't you tell them you were going around with Isabel? You could have told them you two were as good as engaged.

ROHIT: Aw, come on. Why should I tell them about my personal life?

VIDULA (*getting upset*): Because if you had brought in Isabel, that scene would have ended right there. Not just today. A long time ago. I don't think you wanted it to. You were enjoying the grandstand—

ROHIT (*shouting*): Look, I've had enough.

MOTHER *(enters)*: So you didn't go to see Govinda Rao, after all.

ROHIT: Have a heart, Ma. These Sirurs—

MOTHER: Why can't you do even a small thing like that for your sister? Now that crotchety old fool will have one more reason to grumble.

HEMA *(back at the parcels)*: It doesn't seem to bother any of you that he is going out with a Christian girl.

ROHIT: Is this what going to Australia does to people? You are in the twenty-first century, you know.

HEMA: How did you citizens of the twenty-first century allow our Vidu to get into this mess?

MOTHER: I don't see any difference between Christian girls and Hindu girls these days. Take that Vidya and Sarika. Their blouses are open right down to their navels. Boys at least button up their collars properly.

FATHER: Naturally. Boys feel shy about the hair on their chests.

(Everyone, except Father, bursts out laughing.)

Scene Four

Vivan is alone in the living room and browsing through the books. He is tense and reacts to every little sound from outside the house.

An auto-rickshaw comes to a halt outside. He looks out, beams, takes out a book and pretends to be absorbed in it. Hema comes in, looking very distraught. She is about to rush in when she spots Vivan. Automatically, she drops her voice.

HEMA: You?

VIVAN: I have finished yesterday's book and kept it inside.

HEMA: Fine. Borrow any book you like.

(Opens the bag in her hand and takes out some files. Calls out.)

Rohit, Vidula … *(To Vivan)* Hurry up, please, Vivan. I'm sorry but the family is to have an important meeting here.

VIVAN *(takes out another letter from his pocket)*: Here.

HEMA: I don't want it.

VIVAN: I am leaving it here.

HEMA: Stop it, Vivan. I have got a son older than you.

VIVAN: I don't care who finds it.

(Places it on the table. She pounces on it.)

HEMA: What am I to do with you? If someone reads it …

VIVAN: Let them. It's all true. Every word.

HEMA: Such filth. Filth. I have no time now. But are you going to stop this nonsense or shall I tell your mother?

VIVAN: Go ahead. I'll also tell her I love you. The moment I saw you the other day, I fell desperately in love. I want to die kissing you. I want to die with my hand inside your blouse …

(Hema slaps him on his cheek. Not too hard. It is in fact a very helpless gesture. She then recoils scared by her own violence.)

HEMA: Such dirty stuff.

VIVAN: Hit me. The touch of your hand fills me with ecstasy. I'm crazy about you.

(He is about to take out another letter. Hema whips it off before he has even taken it out completely.)

HEMA: Do you think I have nothing else to do? Go now. Go.

VIVAN: Do you mind if I return this book tomorrow?

(She pushes him out. He marches out with a dignified adult tread. Hema hurriedly glances through the letter and a blush spreads on her cheeks. She smiles to herself as she shoves the two letters into her handbag, then takes them out, folds them carefully, and puts them inside her blouse. Suddenly remembers what she was about and calls out.)

Rohit, Rohit, Vidula …

VIDULA *(from inside)*: What's it, Hemakka?

HEMA: Where is Rohit?

VIDULA *(from inside)*: Sleeping, I think.

HEMA: Doesn't he have anything else to do? Call him …

VIDULA *(entering)*: He didn't want to be woken up unless …

HEMA: Call him. Please. Rohit!

VIDULA *(calls out)*: Rohit. Rohit. What is it? What are you so excited about?

HEMA *(shouts)*: Radhabai, tea, please. Three cups. *(To Vidula)* It's disaster. Call Mother. No. Actually don't call her. Not yet. Where is she?

VIDULA: In the store room, I think. She thinks she is clearing it up, but actually she is only piling the stuff out in the open. It will lie there for days. What is it?

ROHIT *(enters, rubbing his eyes)*: Why are you making such a racket?

HEMA: Here. Look at this.

(Takes out a paper from her file and gives it to Rohit. Vidula peers over his shoulder.)

VIDULA: Oh! So you got it.

HEMA: The clerk had seen me with you. He recognized me and gave it to me. Just read it.

VIDULA: Seems okay to me.

MOTHER *(from inside)*: Did you want me?

HEMA: No, it doesn't matter, Ma. I'll call you.

ROHIT *(as he is inspecting the paper, reacts)*: But … but … what …

(Hema shrugs helplessly.)

VIDULA: What is it? I don't see anything wrong.

RADHABAI *(inside)*: You go out, Ma. They want you. I'll get this sliced.

ROHIT *(testily to Vidula)*: Just learn to concentrate.

(Points. Vidula reacts.)

VIDULA: There has been a mistake.

ROHIT: I am glad you noticed.

(Mother comes out.)

MOTHER: What is it, Hema?

HEMA: A new problem.

MOTHER *(laughs)*: That's all?

HEMA: It's Vidula's birth certificate. Have a look.

MOTHER: I have forgotten my glasses somewhere.

VIDULA: You are wearing them.

MOTHER: Oh! Yes, of course. I never remember.

HEMA: Let me show you. Here. This is her birth certificate. I have just got it. All the other details are fine. But where it says 'Father's name', it says …

(Embarrassed pause.)

Ramdas Nadkarni. It mentions Uncle.

MOTHER *(uncomprehending)*: But why? Why should it say that?

HEMA: I don't know. All I know is, instead of Father's name, it records Uncle's.

MOTHER *(to Vidula)*: Didn't you fill in the application form properly? I mean, you are so absent-minded.

VIDULA: Of course, I filled it in correctly. Am I out of my mind to write Uncle's name …

HEMA: Ma, it has nothing to do with her.

ROHIT: The question is, when Vidu was born, who went to the Registrar's office to record her birth?

MOTHER: You should have asked the clerk. They are all lazy blackguards. Perhaps they have done it to extract a bribe.

HEMA: No, Ma. He showed me the original registration. It says Ramdas even there.

VIDULA: You mean someone goofed while registering my birth?

ROHIT: Some goof-up!

VIDULA: So who went to register my birth?

HEMA: Ramdas Uncle. There is his signature on the application.

(A sudden silence. Mother half-rises from her seat in consternation. She can't find words to utter and sits back again, half-stunned. Radhabai comes in with her tray of tea cups which she places in front of everyone. But no one touches the tea.)

MOTHER: Oh, god! How ... how ... horrible.

(Radhabai stands near the door and watches.)

I don't understand. How could he let such a thing happen? Why should he do such a thing? Why?

HEMA: It's no use our getting upset, Ma. We'll just have to get it sorted out.

MOTHER *(as the truth suddenly dawns on her)*: Oh, god! No. Shiva-Shiva.

HEMA: What is it, Ma?

MOTHER: Don't you see? This wasn't a mistake. That's not possible. This was deliberate. He knew we would need the certificate some day. He knew we would apply. So he put in his name, knowing sooner or later everyone would look at it. The rascal!

HEMA: It's all right, Ma. Don't ...

MOTHER: He meant to blacken our faces. But why? Every time he was in trouble, Appa bailed him out. He loved him. If he comes to know now, he'll die of shame—I can't bear it.

(Bursts into tears. Hema steps forward to console her but Vidula, who is nearer, hugs her, comforting her. Hema retreats. Mother lies down on the sofa, her eyes closed.)

ROHIT: Appa needn't know.

HEMA: How do you mean?

ROHIT: We'll have to apply for correction. But I can counterfeit his signature. I have to do it all the time.

HEMA: Don't you have to get that signature notarized?

(*Rohit shrugs.*)

Forgery and bribes? They are criminal offences, you know.

ROHIT: I have to have a shower.

(*As he goes in, over his shoulder*)

This is India, you know. Not Australia. We have a solution for everything.

(*Goes in.*)

RADHABAI: Mother …

HEMA: Let her rest.

RADHABAI: I have never seen her sleep during daytime. She is not the kind to bury her head in the palm of her hand.

HEMA: Let her be.

RADHABAI: If she's not well, let her lie down. I've nothing to say to that. But lying down because the mind is depressed is not a good thing. It only worsens the depression. My father-in-law used to say …

HEMA: Enough of your father-in-law.

RADHABAI: If you say so, Hema. But we have guests for lunch tomorrow.

VIDULA: Who is coming?

HEMA: Ashwin's uncle, that Govinda Rao, and his daughter Usha.

VIDULA: No one tells me. It could be someone else's wedding for all I'm told.

HEMA: Govinda Rao is sulking that Rohit didn't turn up that evening. So I invited them over. Might soothe their feathers a bit, I thought.

VIDULA: I never thought getting married would be such a hassle. Everything seems to …

HEMA: All weddings are like that, don't worry. I haven't told you …

RADHABAI: Hema, if Ma could tell me what I should cook for lunch tomorrow …

HEMA: Cook what you feel like. I'll tell Ma.

RADHABAI: Shall we have sour curry with sprouted *moong*?

HEMA *(trying to shut her up)*: Go ahead.

RADHABAI: Then I'll have to soak the *moong* right away. The guests aren't just any odd people, Hema. They are to be our in-laws soon. Everything must go just right. By the way, last time Usha was here she said she loved fish but that they didn't cook non-vegetarian stuff at home.

VIDULA: We could have hot-and-sour curry with pomfrets.

RADHABAI: In fact, if it is fish, please don't ask me to prepare it. Either you or Ma handle it.

MOTHER *(her eyes still shut)*: She won't let me be for a single minute.

RADHABAI: Ma, I didn't know what a fish looked like till I left my village.

MOTHER *(slowly gets up)*: All right, all right. We all know about your priestly pedigree. You have been with us for seven long years. There is no way we wouldn't know. I'll handle the fish. In any case, I had better be there to keep an eye on the salt.

RADHABAI: Ma, to hear you speak, no one would think I have been cooking for over fifty years.

MOTHER: How often have I told you to put a little bit of the curry in your mouth and judge the taste before adding salt? But you won't. You insist on judging by sight.

RADHABAI: All that about tasting a bit. That's not how I was taught. I trust my eyes.

(They both go in arguing.)

HEMA: Why are you sitting there all rolled up in a ball?

VIDULA: I feel so dirty. Filthy. Polluted.

HEMA: What has got into you now?

VIDULA: How could Ramdas Uncle do such a thing on Ma? It's such a mean thing to do … so vicious. Why do you think he did that?

HEMA: I don't know. But I don't see why you should get upset. He was probably settling some score with Appa.

VIDULA: But Appa loves him—talks of him with such affection!

(Hema shrugs.)

Do you think …

(Hesitates.)

HEMA: Do you think what?

VIDULA: Do you think—he had his eyes on Ma?

HEMA: Could be. She was very good-looking.

VIDULA: It doesn't bother you? Uncle used to stay here with them and him eying Ma like that? Doesn't it make you squirm?

HEMA: I'll tell you something. During our wedding, I caught my father-in-law looking at me and boy, was I glad I was leaving for Australia with Chandrakant! My mother-in-law must have learnt to live with that look.

VIDULA: I am sick and tired of these endless complications.

HEMA: You leave it to me: we'll sort it all out. Just stop moping.

(Radhabai appears at the door with three or four onions in her hand and says quite simply.)

RADHABAI: Now that she is on her feet, she'll be all right.

(Goes in, trying to pick the right onion.)

HEMA: What amazes me is Radhabai. I mean, you saw her just now. So affectionate. Warm. Caring. What gets into her when she starts ...

VIDULA: It's all that television.

HEMA: Don't be ridiculous.

VIDULA: Hasn't Ma told you the story?

HEMA: Has Ma ever given a direct answer to any question of mine?

VIDULA: All right. One day apparently Ma and Radhabai were watching television together. Some serial. A mother sacrifices her life to save her daughter. Some melodramatic situation like that. Ma said it was terribly banal. But Radhabai apparently suddenly stood up, switched off the telly and started railing against all the people who were hounding her. Why are these bastards after me? Why won't they leave me alone? And so on. In the foulest language.

HEMA: Really?

VIDULA: Ma had to give her a sedative and pack her off to bed. Anyway next day Radhabai told Ma her secret sorrow. She had a daughter ...

HEMA: Radhabai? She has never mentioned her.

VIDULA: Quite. Yamuna. They lived in a village. They were so poor that the daughter—Yamuna—came to Bangalore looking for a job. And found a good one. Used to send a fair amount back home. Then Radhabai's husband died and she too came to Bangalore. Took up a job as a cook with a family in Malleswaram. The day after her arrival, a messenger turned up and escorted her to her daughter's house and what does she find? Her daughter is being maintained by a rich trader.

HEMA: You mean she was his concubine? How terrible!

VIDULA: So the mother and daughter met. They continued to meet. But Radhabai wanted to keep her job, so she never mentioned her daughter to the family she worked for.

This went on for a couple of years. Then suddenly there was no communication from the daughter. No phone calls. No messages. So Radhabai went to her daughter's house and— and she found a lock on the door. The house was deserted. The neighbours told her that the trader had suddenly died and the young woman living there had been thrown out by his family. She was gone.

HEMA: Oh, god! I feel like crying. Then? Did she ever find out what happened to the daughter?

VIDULA: Wait. Wait. I am coming to that.

(Dramatically.)

One day Radhabai was on the terrace, working, and she heard kids shouting and cackling in the street. She looked down and she saw ...

HEMA: What?

VIDULA: Yamuna. She was standing there in the street calling out to her mother. Her sari was in tatters. He hair was loose and dirty. The kids were laughing and throwing stones at her. She was obviously out of her senses, calling out, Amma, Amma, asking passers-by, where's my Amma's house, and hurling abuses at her tormentors ...

HEMA: How heart-rending.

VIDULA: Radhabai called out. But her daughter couldn't hear her. You know the traffic in Bangalore. So she ran down to the street. But by the time she reached there, the daughter had disappeared. Vanished into thin air. Radhabai never saw her daughter again.

HEMA *(wipes away her tears)*: We knew nothing of this ... all these years.

VIDULA: Radhabai too had obviously put it away. Tried to forget it. But that episode in that serial must have brought it all back.

Since that day, she has been like this: sudden tantrums, sudden bouts of shouting.

HEMA: How terrible! I must talk to Samyukta.

(*Goes out dialing a number on the mobile. Rohit has entered while the above narration is going on and stands listening, buckling his belt on.*)

ROHIT: Well, that is one good thing to come out of your story.

VIDULA: What?

ROHIT: Haven't you noticed? She never talks about her daughter. Has never rung her since her arrival. It's always the darling sonny boy. Ketan. Ketan.

VIDULA: Really? I hadn't noticed.

ROHIT (*shouts out*): Ma, I am going to the market. Do you want me to bring anything? Don't send me out again later.

MOTHER (*from inside*): Oh, good you haven't left.

(*Enters.*)

Listen, I was kneading the dough and thinking. You have to buy the stamp paper, get Appa to write out an affidavit, then get it notarised—all those headaches. How long is it all going to take?

ROHIT: God alone knows.

MOTHER: That's why I am asking. Would it matter?

ROHIT: Would what matter?

MOTHER: If we left things as they are.

VIDULA: What do you mean, Ma?

MOTHER: All that extra running around. Talk of forgery and bribing. What for? All these days we didn't know what was in the Corporation files. So why can't we continue—with Ramdas's name on the certificate?

VIDULA: Ma!

(Hema enters and watches silently.)

ROHIT: We have to give the right details to the Passport Authorities.

MOTHER: Does the father's name appear on the passport?

HEMA: Yes, it does.

MOTHER: Oh, well then—I suppose we have to go through it all. I was wondering if all the bother was worth it.

VIDULA: You mean we apply with Ramdas Uncle's name as ... *(Revolted by the thought)* Issi! I won't. In my passport?

MOTHER: Well, I was hoping we could keep Appa out of it. I don't want him hurt. That's all. What does it matter what is in the files?

(She goes in.)

VIDULA: Did you hear that? Ma! Saying leave it as it is? Can you believe it?

ROHIT: Yes, I can. *(Lowering his voice)* Don't you know, Appa had a bad temper. And he was not averse to using his hand on Ma. Apparently Ramdas Uncle couldn't stand that. He never let Appa hit Ma when he was around.

HEMA: I know. Once Ramdas Uncle got so wild, he was about to beat up Appa.

VIDULA: But her saying we should live with a lie!

HEMA: Ma can be so strange. Cagey. Since coming here, I have been asking her at least twice every day about this sudden change in Radhabai. At least twice. But Ma never once told me.

ROHIT: She probably thought it was not worth mentioning.

HEMA *(grumbling)*: She has always been so distant with me. Since I was a child. Secretive even.

ROHIT: Listen, I think you should try and forget those old grouses.

HEMA: Why should I? When Appa was transferred to Sirsi, I had to stay with Bhavani Aunty in Dharwad for two years. Then he was transferred to Bagalkot and I was packed off to Amba Aunty's. But you two spent your entire childhood with them.

ROHIT: Look, Appa was transferred every year. If they had lugged you around like they did with us, you would have never finished your education. They had to keep you here in one place for your schooling.

HEMA *(testily)*: I never had a mother around me when I needed her. Try to understand that.

(Upset, she gets up to go in.)

ROHIT: I think I'll go and purchase the stamp paper.

VIDULA *(jumps up)*: No, not on that note. This is my wedding—my own if-at-all wedding. So I demand some joy. Some celebration. Let's just get together and sing and dance. At least once. Please. I insist.

ROHIT: Righty ho! Let's sing and dance. What song do you want? The future national anthem?

VIDULA: No, no, the one they taught us in the Convent school in Sirsi. *I was a good, little boy....*

(Vidula and Hema join him as he starts singing and hamming, and the three act out the characters in the song. Mother comes out followed by Father and then Radhabai. Mother too sings bits and pieces along with her children.)

I was a good little boy, I was Papa's pet,

Each day Papa fed me cheese and chocolate.

I started school when I was eleven,

And repeated every class, again and again—and AGAIN!

This drove the teacher wild and he swung his cane,

And I called out to Papa, but alas in vain:

'Papa, Papa, look how the teacher treats me.

'Papa, Papa, he is forever threatening to beat me.

"'I'll hit you on the palm," he says,

"'I'll rap you on your knuckles."

'And if I say, I'll tell Papa, he laughs,

"'DO!—and bring some pickles.'"

Papa! Papa!

(A happy family scene.)

Scene Five

This is a continuation of Scene One. Software Production office.
Pratibha and Rohit.

ROHIT: As the old woman runs down—imagine—one staircase after
    another—we could build up the suspense. She is aged. Arthritic.
    Finds it difficult to run, but it is her daughter.

PRATIBHA: There is no lift?

ROHIT: That's why I made it four floors. Old city regulations said you
    could build up to four floors without a lift.

PRATIBHA: I see. Actually, when you come to think of it, even if there
    were a lift there, it wouldn't matter. I mean, as she runs down,
    she stops on each landing and presses the button. But can't bring
    herself to wait till the lift arrives, so rushes on down the stairs.

ROHIT: True enough. That will also give us more footage on her run.
    A proper build-up.

PRATIBHA: So she reaches the gate and then?

ROHIT: She finds the daughter gone.

PRATIBHA: That's it? Bit of an anti-climax, isn't it?

ROHIT: But that's what happened in fact. What else can happen?

PRATIBHA: That's what you are here to tell me.

(Shakes her head.)

The scene has to be stronger. Much stronger.

ROHIT: All right. All right. So what we could do is …

(Gets up and moves about as though inspired by a new thought.)

When she reaches the gate, the daughter is still there. Mad. Raving. The kids throwing stones at her. Radhabai chases the kids away. And tries to take the daughter in. But the daughter doesn't recognize her mother. 'Where's my mother?' she raves. She pushes Radhabai away.

PRATIBHA: That's more like it. In fact, that is excellent.

ROHIT: Give me a minute. Pull me up if I become too melodramatic.

PRATIBHA: There is no such thing in a tele-serial. And we are Prime Time.

ROHIT: Let's go back to the start of the scene. Why is Radhabai on the terrace? Yes, it has started drizzling and she has come there to collect the clothes drying on the line. That's it. We start with the sky overcast. Ominous clouds. It begins to rain. Radhabai runs on to the terrace to collect the clothes. She is piling the clothes on her shoulder, that's when she hears the racket. Goes to the parapet. And looks down. Sees the daughter, recognizes her and runs down. It's pouring by the time she reaches the gate.

PRATIBHA: Very nice. The clothes keep falling off her shoulder as she races down. Superb.

ROHIT: So when she reaches her daughter, it is lashing with rain. All that struggle to take the daughter in—the daughter screaming and pushing her away—all that happens while the rain turns into a thunderstorm.

(Pratibha claps approvingly.)

Ultimately the daughter pushes her and runs away. Literally melts away in the rain.

PRATIBHA: A super shot to end the episode with. Her melting away.

ROHIT: Actually, we should probably end on Radhabai collapsing in the mud. Calling out and weeping. But the rain blinds her, chokes her calls.

PRATIBHA: Possibly. We can decide on that on the editing table. Either ending could be effective. You know, your great advantage is that you know the lower middle class inside out.

ROHIT: I told you. She worked for us.

PRATIBHA: Will the daughter simply disappear in our serial as she did in real life?

ROHIT: No, no. We could keep them both waiting in the wings.

PRATIBHA: Excellent. Well, I should be off. Incidentally, you and your wife must come and have dinner with us some time soon.

ROHIT: Thanks. That would be lovely. But I'm afraid Tapasya isn't in town. She has gone to her parents. Won't be returning to Bangalore for a couple of months. She is going to have a baby.

PRATIBHA: Oh, congratulations!

(Laughs. Shakes his hands.)

When did she leave?

ROHIT: She left for Hyderabad—let me see—yes, ten days ago. On the eighth.

PRATIBHA: So we just missed her. What a pity! Well …

(Pause. Rohit senses something.)

ROHIT: Yes?

PRATIBHA: Rohit, you mustn't mind this. But I want to clear the air. I like your work and if we are to work together I would like …

ROHIT: What is it?

PRATIBHA: I have a new girl on my staff. Isabel Pinto.

(Pause. Rohit tense.)

   She says she knows you.

ROHIT: Yes. We knew each other in Dharwad.

PRATIBHA: She told me. She is good. Intelligent. Immensely capable. But a bit fragile. *(Pause.)* Apparently, she went through a bad patch. Emotionally. Two years ago.

ROHIT *(defensive)*: I heard about that. I was in Germany when that happened. Training.

PRATIBHA: She came to Bangalore six months ago and joined me. I don't want to lose her. I certainly don't want her to have a breakdown. She lives on her own in Bangalore. I feel protective.

(Pause. Rohit watches warily.)

   She says you have rung her twice ... asked her out to dinner.

ROHIT: We were ... are good friends.

PRATIBHA: She says she has already made it clear she doesn't want to see you. But you are ... how shall I put it ... a bit persistent?

ROHIT *(getting annoyed)*: Pratibhaji, I could demand to know ...

PRATIBHA *(all sweetness)*: Please don't. I like you too. And I want to continue working with you. Which is why ...

ROHIT: All right. We were almost engaged. And suddenly she broke it off.

PRATIBHA: She seemed to think you had broken it off. When Tapasya's father financed your trip to Germany ...

ROHIT: Oh, that was much later. My sister Vidula was on her way to the US. I came with her to Bangalore and stayed in the guest house of Tapasya's father's firm. That was enough for Isabel. She screamed at me and ...

PRATIBHA: Rohit, I don't want to go into the past. That's none of my concern.

ROHIT: Then why this cross-examination?

PRATIBHA *(laughs)*: No, no. Just a plea, since you like legal terms. You telephoned her ten days ago?

ROHIT: I wanted to talk to her, you know, hopefully remove any bitterness she might harbour.

PRATIBHA: You know Isabel has been in Bangalore for the past six months. But you phoned her ten days ago. And invited her home. To dinner. On the day your wife left for Hyderabad! You didn't mention that you were alone at home. But she guessed. She knows you well, she says. Since then you have asked her again. Twice within ten days. In spite of her refusal. What's she to make of it? You know she is vulnerable.

ROHIT: You expect me to invite her home when my wife is there? To discuss our past relationship?

(Pratibha picks up her handbag.)

PRATIBHA: Rohit, I am forty. I am from Orissa. I came to Bangalore for reasons of my own and built up my business. Three years ago, I married a man ten years my senior. A Muslim. I married him when the anti-Muslim riots were at their worst. Because he offered me affection and security.

(Pause.)

There's nothing I don't know about harassment.

(Sudden smile.)

You must let me know when Tapasya is back. You two must come and have dinner with Irfan and me. Bye.

(Moves to the door and stops.)

And oh, yes, bring the baby along, please. We both love kids.

(Exits. A long pause.)

ROHIT: Bitch!

Scene Six

A tiny dark room which is a part of an Internet Café. It has a single computer with sophisticated acoustic attachments and is obviously meant for 'private' viewings.

Vidula enters, led by the Attendant.

ATTENDANT: Haven't seen you for a few days. Busy?

VIDULA: Yes.

ATTENDANT: Shopping, I suppose?

VIDULA: Yes. Endless.

ATTENDANT: You haven't sent me an invitation, madam?

VIDULA: It'll come. Don't worry. How could one forget you?

ATTENDANT: Oh, you would be surprised. You don't know how many people use our Internet Café to find life partners. And then, when it comes to the wedding, they clean forget us.

VIDULA: I won't, I promise you. The invitation cards are getting printed. Don't worry. You are among the first on my list.

(The Attendant has got the computer going.)

ATTENDANT: I'll wait for it. Right, there you are. All set. Anything more?

VIDULA: No, thanks. Just put out the lights, please, as you go out.

(The Attendant switches off the lights, leaving Vidula in virtual darkness and exits. She starts the equipment. A male voice comes on.)

VIDULA: The password, please.

VOICE: Ananga the Bodyless. And that's my darling, Kuchla …

VIDULA *(laughing)*: … the Jezebel. You should wait till I give my password.

VOICE: No need, love. I know the voice of my Indian pea-hen. I dream of you. I pine for you. Where have you been all these days? Why have you made me wait? Don't do that again.

VIDULA: Sorry, my darling, pining peacock. But there may be no 'again'. I have come to say bye.

VOICE *(groans)*: No! Don't say that, baby. I am addicted to you.

VIDULA: I have no choice. I am going away.

VOICE: They have computers even in Timbuktoo these days.

VIDULA: I know.

VOICE: Why are you saying bye then?

VIDULA: I have been sold off.

VOICE: You have been what, baby?

VIDULA: Sold off. I told you I am a kept woman. Kept by a trader. I am his concubine. Maintained by a man much older than me.

VOICE: Yes, you said something like that. I thought you were fibbing.

VIDULA: Not fibbing now.

VOICE: So?

VIDULA: He is dying. He has had a heart attack. Last night. He is in the ICU. Could be dead by tomorrow. His family is bound to throw me out. So I had to find a new master. A younger man. He lives in the US. He has paid a good price to my family.

VOICE: Sight unseen?

VIDULA: He can do whatever with me.

VOICE: Tell me your name and address and I'll come and buy you.

VIDULA: Thanks, mate. I knew you would say that. You are nice.

VOICE: Jeezus! These things still happen in India? What a country!

VIDULA *(laughs)*: Are we going to spend the whole of today discussing India?

VOICE: Oh, no. I want to do things to you. You have kept me waiting for three days. I am not going to let you go lightly.

VIDULA: Don't. That's why I am here, lover. What are you going to do today?

VOICE: First I'll strip you. Then I'll rape you.

VIDULA: I can't wait. I can't.

VOICE: But this time … I shan't stop there. I shall kill you and cut you up.

VIDULA: Oo! That sounds divine! I am yours.

VOICE: Into tiny pieces of meat.

VIDULA: Yes, love. Yes.

VOICE: God! This is going to be a wow. I am getting all excited.

VIDULA: Go ahead. I am yours. All yours.

VOICE: Good. Take off your shawl.

(During the following dialogue, Vidula does not remove any piece of her clothing.)

VIDULA: Okay. Done.

VOICE: Now unbutton your blouse.

VIDULA: Not blouse. It's called the *kameez*.

VOICE: I don't care. Just take it off.

VIDULA *(mimes the moves to get the timing right)*: I have.

VOICE: Now the bra.

VIDULA: Okay. Hold on.

VOICE *(more urgently)*: The bra.

(After a pause)

  Have you taken it off?

VIDULA *(in a strained voice)*: Wait. The hook's at the back and it's stuck.

VOICE: Hurry up, slut. Hurry up. I am all ...

VIDULA: Done. Done.

VOICE: Is it off? Is it?

VIDULA: Yes. Yes.

VOICE: You are bare-boobed, baby?

VIDULA: Yes.

VOICE: Caress them for me.

VIDULA *(without making any movement)*: Uhuh.

VOICE: The left one first. It is smaller than the right one. It shouldn't develop an inferiority complex.

VIDULA *(laughs)*: There is nothing you don't know about me.

VOICE: You bet. Are you caressing them?

VIDULA: Yes.

(She makes a moaning sound.)

  They are both so happy.

VOICE: Now take off your skirt.

VIDULA: Not skirt. Trousers. *Salwar.*

VOICE: Don't give me the details, darkie. Just take them off.

VIDULA: Done, master.

VOICE: Where are the trousers now?

VIDULA: Round my feet.

VOICE: What are you wearing inside? Your black-and-white lace mini?

VIDULA: Oh, no. Not today. Today I have brought something special for you.

VOICE: Really? What? Tell me. I am dying here.

VIDULA: Purple thongs. Just for you.

VOICE: Good. Now take them off.

VIDULA *(suddenly)*: Wait. Wait.

VOICE *(responding to her new tone)*: What's it, darling?

VIDULA: Wait. I am scared.

VOICE: Scared? Of what? This isn't your first …

VIDULA: Just scared. Suddenly. Please. Just wait. Suddenly I have the shivers. I am trembling. Wait till I tell you.

VOICE: As you say, love. I am your slave.

(Long pause.)

   Are you still there?

VIDULA: Yes, I am.

VOICE: Tell me. What's the matter?

VIDULA: Why are things so scary?

VOICE: They are what?

VIDULA: Scary. I feel …

VOICE: They are not.

VIDULA: They are. All this … we two … here together … this should be beautiful. Lovely and romantic. Why is it all so bleak … so …

(Sudden commotion outside the door. Loud banging.)

Hell! Hell!

VOICE: What's it, darling?

VIDULA: Shit!

(Switches off the computer as the Assistant comes in arguing with two young men.)

ATTENDANT: You can't come in here! You have no right!

YOUTH 1: Try and stop us.

YOUTH 2: What's going on here?

YOUTH 1: Why is it dark in here? Switch on the lights.

ATTENDANT *(trying to gain time in case his client is undressed)*: You have no right. Get out of here.

YOUTH 2: Where are the lights?

(He switches on a light. The Attendant is hugely relieved to see that Vidula is fully clothed. He becomes more aggressive.)

ATTENDANT: Listen, this is a Cyber Café. You have no right.

YOUTH 1: What's this woman doing here? *(To Vidula, who is half-hiding in a corner)* What are you doing here?

ATTENDANT: She is my customer. She has paid to play games here.

YOUTH 1: Games? What games?

ATTENDANT: Video.

YOUTH 2: In this pokey little room! Ha!

YOUTH 1: You have cubicles in the outside foyer for video games.

YOUTH 2: Why does she need a special room for video games?

YOUTH 1: The moment I saw her sneak in alone with him I smelt a rat. I smelt a rotten bandicoot. *(To Vidula)* You are watching porno films, aren't you?

YOUTH 2: You bastard, you show porno films to our Hindu women!

ATTENDANT: I told you she plays video games. We are a licensed Café.

YOUTH 1: Let's take a photograph of her. We need proof she was in this room.

YOUTH 2: Right.

ATTENDANT: No, no. You can't take photographs here.

YOUTH 2: Ha! Ha! No photography allowed. What's this? An airport? Security Zone?

YOUTH 1: Take out your camera, I say. *(To Vidula)* Lady, you are a disgrace to our ancient Indian culture. Come and stand here. By the computer.

(Vidula doesn't move. Youth 1 gropes around the wall and finds the switch board. He switches on all the lights. Youth 2 takes out his camera and aims it at Vidula. He steps back, startled.)

YOUTH 2: You?

YOUTH 1: You know her?

YOUTH 2: I know her brother. She belongs to our caste.

YOUTH 1 *(To Vidula)*: What's your name?

YOUTH 2: Listen, she is one of us.

YOUTH 1: What do you mean 'us'?

YOUTH 2: She belongs to our community.

YOUTH 1: So what?

YOUTH 2: Look. This once we'll let her go.

YOUTH 1: Let her go? Just because she belongs to your caste?

YOUTH 2: If anything appears in the papers tomorrow, I won't be able to show my face to fellow Saraswats.

YOUTH 1: This is ridiculous. After keeping a watch for all these days we have trapped her, red-handed, and you start on this caste nonsense.

YOUTH 2: Sorry. But you know what I mean, Mahadevappa. Please.

YOUTH 1: I don't know what you mean. We should be worried about our total culture. Not our castes. You have sworn to renounce caste, have you forgotten? All right. Listen, lady. You are lucky he is here today. We'll let you go. But don't come back here. We know everything that goes on here.

YOUTH 2: And I won't mention this to your brother. Go now. Don't repeat this mistake. We'll take care of this attendant.

VIDULA *(in a low voice)*: Why don't you fuck off?

(The young men gasp.)

YOUTH 1: Did you hear that? Did you hear what she said? And you say she is one of you?

VIDULA *(her voice rising)*: I have paid for the computer time. I have paid to be left alone in this room. To work here without being disturbed. What gives you the right to come in here? I'll do what I like here. Who the hell are you to question me?

YOUTH 1: We are here as the guardians of our tradition, our ancient …

VIDULA: You have no bloody right. You have no fucking right to harass me.

YOUTH 1: Mind your words, lady. Don't use fuck and bloody to us.

VIDULA: I'll say what the hell I like. Why are you here?

(A new thought strikes her.)

You have come here to rape me, haven't you? You want to attack me.

(Screaming)

Fucking rapists …

ATTENDANT: Easy, madam. Easy now.

VIDULA: You saw it with your own eyes. They pulled away my *dupatta*. You saw it—they tried to molest me. The bastards. I was playing games in the cubicles outside. They dragged me here. They tore my clothes. Help!

YOUTH 1 *(scared)*: Now now, listen.

YOUTH 2: You think I would molest a girl of our own caste?

VIDULA *(to the attendant)*: Please call the police. My uncle, Ramdas Nadkarni, he is the Police Commissioner. Will you call the Police or shall I call him? I'll show these swine. They think they can attack a woman in broad daylight and get away?

(Takes out her mobile.)

ATTENDANT: Madam, madam, not the police, please. I'll handle this. Now are you two getting out or not?

VIDULA *(screaming)*: Get out of here, you bloody bull-shitters. If you don't fuck off this minute …

YOUTH 1: I am not scared of your threats, I say …

(But he lets the other two men drag him away.)

YOUTH 2: I didn't think a woman of our caste could behave like this.

(They exit. Vidula bursts into tears. The attendant comes back.)

ATTENDANT: Don't let them upset you too much, madam. For all their talk of culture, they are only interested in money. I pay them their *hafta*. But when they fall short of funds, they form a splinter group. A new group. Can I get you some tea? Take it easy, madam. Shall I get you the connection again?

(Vidula has already rushed out.)

Scene Seven

Father and Mother in the living room. He is looking through some old files. She is changing cushion covers and arranging the sofa, abstractedly. He looks up.

FATHER: Is the boy coming to visit us today?

MOTHER: Who?

FATHER: The boy from America.

MOTHER: Ashwin? Of course not.

FATHER: Then who is coming?

MOTHER: No one.

FATHER: Then why are you changing cushion covers? It's the third set you have changed since this morning.

MOTHER: No one's coming. I am … I am … I don't know what else to do.

FATHER: That's certainly something new.

MOTHER: I'm all jittery. With Vidu sitting there with him—all alone—a total stranger. She is so unsure of herself. Timid. I don't know why she has to be so …

FATHER: It's Hema. She was always so confident and Vidu has developed this self-image, contrary to hers. Children define themselves against each other. We parents are irrelevant to their growing up.

MOTHER: I wish I knew what was happening there—

FATHER: What can happen? At worst, he can say no. Or she can say no.

MOTHER: They can say yes.

(Father suddenly finds a paper in the file. Looks at it with satisfaction.)

FATHER: There! It had to be somewhere. I knew Ramdas wouldn't let me down.

(Mother reacts to Ramdas's name.)

MOTHER: What's it?

FATHER: The accounts of what we spent on Hema's wedding.

MOTHER: Hema's wedding?

FATHER: I want to settle the argument once and for all. Here …

MOTHER: Are you going to discuss her wedding expenses *now*?

FATHER *(defensive)*: This time she's really overdoing it. I am tired of her nagging us about how we spent nothing on her wedding.

MOTHER: Have we all gone mad? Digging into fifteen-year-old accounts …

FATHER: I didn't mean to. But you know she goes on …

MOTHER: Let her say what she will. She has suffered enough. And so have we. Put it away …

FATHER *(deflated)*: Well, if you don't want me to … will you at least take a look? It won't take a minute. Ramdas was spic and span in his accounts …

MOTHER *(flies into a rage)*: I am sick and tired of your Ramdas. I regret the day I laid my eyes on him.

FATHER *(taken aback)*: Well, well! What's that in aid of? I don't ... I am ...

MOTHER: You go on, Ramdas, Ramdas. About your brotherly love. Helping him out. But have you ever wondered what he thought of you? He hated you for it. ... He was an ungrateful ... jealous ...

FATHER *(calmly)*: I know.

(Mother is taken aback by this calm statement.)

I knew. I knew that. Okay?

MOTHER: You did?

FATHER: Yes. But, poor chap, nothing went right for him. He was smarter than me. Good looking. Good at anything he tried his hand at. I was a plodder—he didn't think much of my abilities. But you know.

(Mother waits for him to go on. He is distinctly embarrassed saying the following lines.)

I knew he deserved success more than me. But what to do? What could I do? I couldn't let him go without a roof on his head. He was my brother, after all. I had to support him.

(Suddenly)

Why are you raking all this up now?

(Mother's face has softened as she listens to him.)

MOTHER: It's my nerves.

(The phone rings. She goes and picks it up.)

Hello ... I am his mother. He is not home. ... You could try his mobile. You have the number? ... He is in some meeting. Try after an hour.

(Puts the receiver down.)

Why is his mobile still switched off? Are they still in the restaurant? I hope not. I told Hema and Rohit. Told them clearly.

Wait till the atmosphere eases a bit. Let them start talking to each other. Then you leave them alone.

(Pause.)

Hema is very tactful. She'll know when to leave.

FATHER: Who was that on the phone?

MOTHER: A call from Bangalore. A job offer. It's the third time today. They want him to join immediately.

FATHER: Oh good! Good!

MOTHER: Good, yes. But the job is in Bangalore.

FATHER: I realize that. What future does a bright boy like him have in Dharwad?

MOTHER *(quietly but firmly)*: And what do we do? Move with him to Bangalore?

(Pause as Father takes that in.)

I am not moving to Bangalore.

(Long pause.)

I am sick of moving.

FATHER: But even if his job were here, in Dharwad, would he want us to live with him?

MOTHER: Actually, even if the daughter-in-law invites us to live with them, I am not going to. I have completed my quota of wet nappies and dirty bottoms and howling babies.

FATHER *(smiles)*: I remember one day—you were feeding her or bathing her or something like that and Vidu was howling away. I was passing by and I said, in a gruff voice, 'Who is that crying?' So Vidu turned to me, gave me a big smile and said, 'It's me, Appa,' and went back to her howling.

(They both laugh. Radhabai comes out with a tray and gives a cup of tea to Mother and another one to Father.)

RADHABAI: Your tea, Ma. And Horlicks, Appa. Ma, you wanted me to remind you to tell Rohit to bring two kg of flour from the grocer. And a packet of light bulbs. And two coconuts.

MOTHER: Yes. I have told Hema.

(Radhabai goes in.)

Whenever we were transferred and we had to move out of a house, Vidu would insist on being taken round on my waist—bidding good-bye to every light bulb in the house. 'Bye, bye, bulb,' to the bulb in the kitchen. Then 'bye-bye, bulb,' to the bulb in the bathroom. Then 'bye-bye, bulb,' in the garage. Every bulb. Every six months. Spent her whole childhood saying bye-bye to light fixtures, my baby.

(Tears well up in her eyes.)

FATHER *(irked)*: What are you making such a fuss about? Every government servant moves to a new place when he is transferred. That's the system. We weren't singled out for harassment.

MOTHER: No. But you didn't have to be in the service. You could have resigned and done even better. Much better. Everyone said you were so good at your job.

FATHER: I know. I know. I was good at it. So?

MOTHER: In Hubli, I pleaded with you. Just resign and start your own private practice. You had built up such a reputation there …

FATHER *(getting upset)*: You mean I should have resigned from the government service when we had three children? Was I insane to take to the pavement with the whole family?

MOTHER: Pavement? That Doctor Shanbhag resigned and begged you to join him as a partner. Now he has a two-storey building for his hospital and a palatial house. But you didn't want risks. You were too timid. We blame Vidu, but she has only taken after you.

FATHER: So it's all my fault …

MOTHER: Forty years of slogging and what do we have to show for it? Not even a house of our own.

FATHER *(angry)*: If you are that worried about a house, I'll tell Hema. She says she is willing to buy this house for us.

MOTHER: Absolutely not—no! We sent her like an orphan from one aunt's house to another. We sent her empty-handed when she got married. ... And now ...

FATHER *(shouts)*: Enough! I said, enough! I don't want to hear any more. I have had enough! After a lifetime of slaving for you, after wearing my fingers to the bone for the family, slogging day and night, this is the gratitude I get from you all. This is what ...

(Hema walks in. Father sees her and suddenly falls silent.)

HEMA: What's this? What's happening?

FATHER: Nothing. Everything is quiet. Peaceful. After forty years of marriage, what is there left to talk about?

MOTHER: What happened, Hema?

(Radhabai has heard Hema come in and rushes out to hear the news.)

HEMA: Everything is just fine, Ma. Rohit and I sat with them for a while. Then we left.

MOTHER: What's he like?

HEMA: You have seen him in the videos. Just like that. Perhaps even better looking. Friendly.

FATHER: Thank god! Now we can relax—and put those cushion covers away.

(Mother, in sheer relief, does a silent namaskar *to the gods.)*

HEMA: It's what happens between them now that matters.

RADHABAI: God's grace. Didn't I tell you everything will turn out right?

HEMA *(taking the packages out)*: Yes. Here. Radhabai, your groceries. Ma, the bulbs.

MOTHER: Good. Radhabai, can you bring me the step-ladder?

(Radhabai goes in. Mother heads for Vidu's room.)

I have to put a new bulb in Vidu's room.

HEMA: Rohit is paying the cab. Why don't you let him handle it?

(Mother shakes her head with a silent smile and goes in, wiping a tear. Hema looks at her, baffled. She takes out her mobile, starts dialling a number.)

FATHER: Three children. All three married and abroad. Have I told you about my friend Phadnis?

HEMA *(not really interested)*: I don't think so. Tell me.

FATHER: He had three sons in the US. His kidneys packed up, he was on the death-bed. So the first son took leave and came. Waited for a month. But Phadnis wouldn't die. So the son went back. Next time Phadnis was critical, the second son came and waited. Used up his holidays. But Phadnis wouldn't oblige. The third son apparently told his mother, 'If Father doesn't die now, I can't come back for two years. I have promised my wife and children a holiday in the Maldives next year.'

HEMA *(almost into the mobile)*: Shut up, Appa! How can you think of such ghoulish things on a happy occasion like this?

Scene Eight

Ashwin and Vidula. Restaurant. He has spent a few years in the US, but speaks without an American accent. Vidula listens expressionless.

ASHWIN: You probably think I should be more affable. Give you more details about life in the States. It probably upsets you that I don't joke more. Or talk more about our future together. Well, I can be quite sociable if I put my mind to it. When I came to the US, I had only two assets. My brains and my charm. As you know, we Saraswat Brahmans are brought up to be nice—to lay on the jam. And that training is just the thing to give you a leg-up in the States, where the major preoccupation is to win friends and influence people. Which I did. I can impress people. I can be charming. Then why do I speak so little with you?

(Pause. He has a habit of being intensely silent for a while and then speaking out suddenly.)

Because this is the real me. I want to be honest with you. I am passing through a crisis. It sounds pompous to use the word, but let me use it, I am passing through a *spiritual* crisis. I am boiling inside like a volcano. I want you to share my agonizing search of myself. It will require an intellectual effort to understand the real me. It may even require an emotional giving-up. If you agree to marry me, you will have to share my inner turmoil. But at the end of the day, I believe you will find it enriching.

(Pause.)

Let me first tell you about myself. I am rich. In the US, I have been a success beyond my own wildest expectations. Beyond anyone's wildest dreams. When I was in college, I was not considered the brightest boy in the class. There were many brighter than me. But where are they now? No one knows, while I have made a fortune. I can buy up the Congress. There's no doubt about it—the US is a land of opportunity. God's own country.

But ... and there are a lot of buts.

The fact is, the white man is played out. The hardworking white immigrant is a thing of the past and today it's we who are keeping the machine ticking. And, of course, making our fortunes. We Indians are right there where the Jews once stood. We shall soon take over the economy. But by peaceful means. My American colleagues keep telling me, 'You Indians. You are honest. Hardworking. Most of all, peace-loving. Not like others. A community that leaves the rest of the world to itself. Great Guys.'

That's what the white man still appreciates about us Indians.

(Pause.)

What am I anguished about then? I have drunk life in the US to the lees. Girl friends, affairs, mistresses, one-night stands. And on the public stage, glamour, success, social connections. I have been through them all. And I have come to the conclusion that *that* whole culture is empty of values now, bereft of any living meaning. It is shallow, you see what I mean, glittering and shallow. The European Industrial Revolution began by rejecting religion in favour of material values. But today that legacy is strangling the West. They have no spiritual moorings left. They are adrift in a godless, amoral world.

I love the US. So realizing where the country was headed was a terrifying experience for me. It threw me into depression. I started delving into myself. What am I? Where am I? I looked to India for guidance.

Unlike the US, India has an ancient civilization. A culture which is full of wisdom and insight. India should have the capacity to lead the world. Yet when I looked back at my country, what did I see?

Again, darkness. All our ancient culture, our spiritualism, our heritage. Everything had been remoulded to fit the market demand. Behind all our spiritual abracadabra, we had hitched our star, and our hope, to global capitalism. Geeta yajnas, Yogic techniques, upanishadic sermons. Systems assembled out of a grab-bag of trendy brandnames. Gift-wrapped in synthetic saffron. The darkness of our souls illuminated with neon lights and stroboscopes. India had become the Walmart of spirituality.

Gradually—and mind you, it has required a lot of painful soul-searching—yes, even painfully, I have realized that Hinduism can indeed save this world from moral chaos, but not through this sort of branded spirituality. No dial-a-solution philosophy is going to help the world. We have to look into our hearts, and discover our ancient values afresh. Begin at the beginning.

(Pause.)

That is why I have come to Dharwad to look for a life partner. I have come here because I believe that it is in places like Dharwad that belief in innocence, the very idea of purity, still survives.

Someone like you carries within you the essence of Hindu spirituality. Woman as Mother, Wife, Daughter. Womanhood as the most Sacred Ideal.

Mind you. There are things we can learn from the West, there is no denying it. Efficiency. Planning. For instance, I cannot understand why your family couldn't at least have had your passport ready. Imagine my surprise and disappointment when I heard that you have still got to apply for it. That means if we both agree to get married, you can follow me only weeks later. I know you have to get married before you get the visa. But the passport? Surely you could have shown me that you are keen to leave? That you are excited by the prospect? It would have made me happy. I don't want to make a mountain out of a molehill. But you see what I mean.

So to come back to the main point. I want you to see this not merely as a marriage but as a mission. I would like you to be my partner in carrying the best of our spiritual tradition to the West and save the West. Yes, I am not ashamed or afraid to say it—*save* it.

I didn't talk about all these things on the video or on email. These thoughts are not for the whole family to sit together and share. This is my innermost communication with you. From the depth of my soul. Meant just for you.

If you find all this unacceptable, please feel free to say so. I don't mind. I expect you to be honest. That is what this meeting is for. We'll get married only if we are agreed on every point implicitly. It is a great responsibility you will be taking on. Think about it. If you disagree, tell me and we shall part friends.

I think I have said all that needs to be said.

(*They sit in silence.*)

Scene Nine

The living room. A huge suitcase lies open on the floor. Hema is unsuccessfully trying to fit some clothes into it.

HEMA: Radhabai … Radhabai …

(A car horn sounds. She goes to the main door and looks out.)

We are coming. Please wait.

(The car horn sounds again. She shouts even louder.)

Please don't make a racket. We'll be coming soon. Just wait.

(Turning to the interior of the house.)

Rohit, Vidu, the cab is here.

(Continues packing the suitcase. Radhabai comes out. In the background, Rohit crosses pulling a big suitcase and some hand baggage and goes out.)

Radhabai, just sit on the lid, please. It won't close.

(They push down the stuff piled inside the suitcase. Then Radhabai, giggling shyly, sits on the lid, pressing it down.)

Where's Ma?

RADHABAI: Resting, poor thing! Sending a daughter away …

HEMA: Radhabai, look. While we are at the station, the boy next door, Vivan—you know who I mean …

RADHABAI: The one that borrows books every day. Him? Does he really finish such fat books in a day? Must be very bright. Or stupid.

HEMA: Yes, him. If he hands you a book, keep it aside for me, please. Don't give it to anyone else.

(By now Hema has managed to press the lid down and snap the lock shut. She nods to Radhabai, who retires into the kitchen, talking, as is her wont.)

RADHABAI: Who else can I give it to? Vidu and Rohit will be gone to Bangalore. Poor Ma. There'll be no one here but you.

(Hema takes out the mobile and starts dialling, when Rohit enters and stands looking at her. She gives him an apologetic smile.)

HEMA: Can't ring them now, I suppose. It's midnight there.

ROHIT *(in a low voice)*: Have you talked to her?

HEMA *(embarrassed)*: No, not yet. I will.

ROHIT: So when is that going to be? On the station platform? Please, don't leave it to me. I won't do it. I can't.

(Hema nods almost in desperation. Suddenly looks at the labels pasted on the suitcases.)

HEMA: Look at this. *(Calls out)* Vidu, what's happened to you? You have put your maiden name on these labels. Vidula Nadkarni. Honestly.

VIDULA *(rushing out)*: Oh, god! I forgot.

HEMA: You forgot? You forget to write your married name?

VIDULA: No, no, it's just that I am uncertain what my legal name is.

(Giggles.)

Does it matter, Hemakka? Ashwin says I should retain my maiden name.

HEMA: Perhaps. You can change it back once you are in the States. At this moment, your ticket has your married name. And so does your passport.

VIDULA: Since this business about Uncle Ramdas, I am never quite sure who I really am. My name keeps slipping, sliding away from me.

(Laughs.)

All right, I'll correct the labels. Do you have a pen? Let me fetch one.

(Starts to go in.)

HEMA: Not now, silly. You can do it in Bangalore. You have a whole day there. *(Suddenly)* Vidu, Rohit and I wanted to talk to you about something.

VIDULA *(surprised)*: Now? Aren't we getting late?

HEMA: Rohit, will you come here for a moment? *(To Vidula)* It's not something one should be discussing in a rush. But you know how it is. The last-minute running around. And it's so difficult to talk of some things. Sit down. Sit.

(Seats her down and sits next to her. Rohit stands behind them.)

VIDULA *(laughs)*: Sounds ominous. All this seriousness. Funereal.

HEMA: Shut up. Don't say such dreadful things. *(Pause.)* It's about Ashwin. How is everything between you and him?

VIDULA: Well, you know how it is. Eight days in a hotel. Was it intimacy? Getting to know each other? ... I don't know.

ROHIT: You said he barely spoke to you.

VIDULA: There was nothing to discuss. Can't blame him. He said we'll get to know each other once I come over there. Fair enough.

HEMA: Now that you are going there, we are sure everything will be all right. We are absolutely certain. But if things don't quite work out ... if you find you cannot live with him ...

VIDULA: Why shouldn't I be able to live with him?

ROHIT: Don't be obtuse. He has not exactly been over-communicative. Barely half a dozen short emails in all these weeks. Hardly any calls.

VIDULA: I told you he is waiting for me.

HEMA: Anyway, we are all sure you are right. But if things don't work out ...

VIDULA: If they don't?

(Hema can't go on.)

ROHIT: What she is trying to tell you is if at any moment you wish to divorce Ashwin and come back, don't hesitate to do so.

HEMA: Leave him and come back if you feel like it. You are timid. We don't want you to suffer in silence for fear of what people here will say. Or what we will feel. We are with you on anything you decide.

(Pause.)

ROHIT: We live in a modern world. A divorce is okay. It's no shame.

(Pause.)

VIDULA *(calmly)*: I'll never divorce Ashwin.

HEMA *(almost rattled by her firmness)*: We aren't asking you to ...

ROHIT: Of course we would be happiest if it didn't come to that.

VIDULA: Ashwin may not speak much. But he was clear about what he expected from marriage. I agreed with him. I gave him my word.

(Pause.)

I have given up eating fish.

HEMA: I noticed.

VIDULA: Look, you are always grumbling about how indecisive I am. This once I am going to be decisive. Aren't you happy?

ROHIT: What about his side?

VIDULA: Of the bargain? I trust him. He is my husband after all.

(Gets up.)

Shouldn't we leave?

(No reply.)

Don't worry. I'll be all right.

HEMA *(pointing to the suitcase on the floor)*: That's done.

ROHIT *(shouts)*: Ma, aren't you finished yet

(Takes the suitcase out.)

VIDULA: Incidentally, Hemakka, thanks for staying on for a week after my departure. Ma needs you. She has always needed you—more than she has ever needed me. Always. More than you have given her credit for.

HEMA *(touched)*: All right, then. Tomorrow when we are alone together the first thing I'll ask her is, 'Ma, can you tell me what caused the change in Radhabai?' Let me see if I get a straight answer.

(They laugh. Outside, Mohan and Mira are heard talking. Vidula runs in. Mohan and Mira enter, accompanied by a surly Rohit.)

MOHAN: Oh, thank heaven. You haven't left for the station yet.

ROHIT: We are about to. Only waiting for Ma.

MIRA: Actually, we went to the station to meet you. The train is forty minutes late. So we thought we would come here.

MOHAN: We were afraid we would cross you on the road.

HEMA: Come in, please. Sit down.

MOHAN: The point is I just spoke to Brother-in-law in Hyderabad. His firm has a beautiful guesthouse in Bangalore. Rohit, you and Vidula could stay there tomorrow.

ROHIT: No, no. We have informed our cousins there we'll stay with them.

MOHAN: Which cousins? The Kabads?

MIRA: Them? We know them. They have a small, two bedroom flat and five of them are packed in it. You won't even have place for your luggage.

MOHAN: Look, we don't want to be difficult. But Brother-in-law says he can arrange to have his office car pick you up at the station tomorrow morning. It'll take you to the guesthouse and be with you all day. Very convenient.

ROHIT: Please ask him not to bother.

MIRA: How are you going to move about in Bangalore then?

ROHIT: No shortage of auto ricks.

MOHAN: Listen, with a car at your disposal, you can visit all your friends and family members in Bangalore. Vidula is going away after all. All your relations will want to see her. The car will go to the airport and then drop you back at the station.

HEMA (before Rohit can remonstrate further): That would be rather nice. But we don't want to be a bother.

MOHAN: No botheration at all. It's not a personal favour. It's an official guesthouse. Official vehicle. That's what official things are for.

MIRA: Squabbling with auto rickshaw drivers in Bangalore. Ugh!

MOHAN: I'll inform Brother-in-law then. Good, incidentally, have you weighed your luggage? It's better to pay excess baggage before you board the train. They can hassle you.

ROHIT: I know. That's why I am trying to rush Ma.

MOHAN: Why rush her? What are we here for? Is all your luggage placed in the taxi outside?

ROHIT: Yes.

MOHAN: Then I'll tell you what, Mira and I will go ahead in the taxi to the station And get the baggage weighed and receipted. You follow at leisure in our car. The train is late anyway.

ROHIT: No, no, we can't let …

MOHAN: Don't worry. Leave it to us.

(Mother comes out with a plate of arati in her hand, followed by Radhabai. Mother sees Mohan and Mira and nods in acknowledgement.)

MOTHER: Please, sit. I'll be with you. *(Calls.)* Vidu—come for the arati.

(Vidula comes out, tearfully clinging to Father. In the mean time, Radhabai has lit the arati.)

MOHAN *(to Mother)*: Don't worry. We'll see you at the station.

RADHABAI: Face the east, Vidu.

(Vidula stands facing the east. Mohan looks at his wife and nods. They move.)

MOHAN *(to Rohit)*: Our driver will wait for you.

(Mohan and Mira leave.)

ROHIT: God, they are unbelievable!

HEMA: What they say makes sense, Rohit, but you can't stay back and send them ahead with the luggage.

ROHIT *(sighs)*: I suppose not. Ma, I'll see you at the station. Okay, Appa. I'll see Vidu off in Bangalore and be back in two days.

(Goes out. Mother finishes her arati and gives the plate to Radhabai who takes it in. Vidula touches Mother's feet and then bows down to Father.)

FATHER: Marriage is a gamble. No escaping the fact—marriage is a gamble.

(Mother pulls Vidula down next to her on the sofa.)

MOTHER: It's time for you to go. And we haven't even sat down together and talked. What can I say? Our lives are over. My father wouldn't even let me finish college. And Hema arrived soon after. And then you all. I never had any time for you children. Just rush, rush. And I achieved nothing in my life. But I was hoping at least you girls would do something. So many opportunities in today's world. We couldn't even dream of such a world. But Hema did nothing with her intelligence and good looks. Has been content to be a housewife. You are capable of anything if you will only make up your mind. But you won't focus. I am told there are lots of openings in America. They say you can take courses in everything—painting, ceramics, pottery, music. Don't throw away your talents in just bearing children. God gave me such lovely children. But I could give them no guidance. We did nothing for you. Don't do the same thing with your life.

(Mother starts to weep. Vidula embraces her. Hema watches from where she is standing, tears in her eyes. The phone rings. Hema picks it up.)

HEMA: Hello—Oh, hello, Isabel. This is Hema. His elder sister. Yes, we met at the wedding.

(Vidula goes to Radhabai, who has entered while Mother is talking and has been watching from the door.)

VIDULA: Goodbye, Radhabai. Here.

(Pushes an envelope into her hand and embraces her.)

RADHABAI: No, no. Now is not the time for me to take anything from you. It's when you come back, for your first delivery. Be back soon and I'll accept an armload from you. Here, some *prasad* from the Maruti temple.

(Radhabai gives her a small bundle tied in a saffron cloth. Vidula then does a quick namaskar to the photograph of the Swamiji on the wall, hugs Father again and quickly moves out taking Mother with her. Radhabai follows them out. Hema continues on the phone.)

HEMA: He has gone to the station. Left a moment ago. ... You know the station road has no network coverage. ... No, they won't be staying with our cousins in Bangalore. Actually, they have been invited to the guesthouse of the Sirurs. ... Yes. You know the Sirurs? ... Ah, yes, the same family. ... No, no, he isn't going to see the girl. The Sirurs have just offered their guesthouse. Nice of them. So much more convenient really. ... You know, Isabel, I couldn't say. I don't think she will be there. But. ... It might be best if you talked to him tomorrow. ... Sorry, I must rush. Bye.

(Puts the phone down.)

We'll be back soon, Appa. Don't get anxious.

(She rushes off. Father suddenly stands up and starts delivering a speech. During his speech, we hear the car drive away.)

FATHER: Before we all part, as inevitably we must, let me say a few words. You have all heard what your mother said just now. Let me tell you she is being unfair ... unfair to herself. If we are all happily gathered together here, if we have been such a loving family, the credit must go to your mother. You don't know what she has been through for the sake of the family. You don't know what she has had to put up with. In my job, I was transferred every six months. From one small town to another. Three children. My salary—there was never anything left for her after the household expenses. But she never asked for anything for herself. Lived on two saris—wearing one while the other one dried on the line. And yet we never acknowledged her sacrifices, her skill at management, her ...

(Radhabai enters and goes up to him.)

RADHABAI: They have left, Appa.

FATHER: Oh, oh, I see. Yes, yes, of course.

RADHABAI *(gently)*: Shall we go in?

(Father nods silently and goes in. In the meantime, Vivan has entered and has stealthily placed a book on the table. She sees him.)

Oh, you! She has gone to the station.

VIVAN: I know. I saw them go. That's why I came in. I mean … I didn't want to disturb them. I only have to return this book.

RADHABAI: They should be back in half an hour.

VIVAN: That's it. I mean. You please tell her. I won't be borrowing any more. My friend Ambuja has come to her grandparents in the Reddy Colony. She is going to be here through the vacation. We are going on a picnic tomorrow. And the day after, we plan to …

RADHABAI: I won't remember all that. You come back tomorrow and tell her yourself.

VIVAN *(as he rushes out)*: That's just it. I can't come tomorrow. Or ever again.

(Radhabai picks up the book, sees the paper peeping out and takes it out.)

RADHABAI: But this is blank. You have forgotten to write your message.

VIVAN: No, no. She wanted it blank. Just give it to her, please.

(Runs out. Radhabai, without more ado, puts the book on the table. Sits down on the sofa and switches the television on. We do not see the screen but only hear the programme music. She watches and then begins to talk to herself.)

RADHABAI: You can't keep a grown up daughter at home, can you?

(The stage slowly begins to darken and finally she is lit only by the reflected glow of the television screen.)

I leaned across the parapet to see what was going on. There she was—this mad woman—stark raving mad. Shouting foul abuses at the kids who were throwing stones at her.

(Pause.)

It took me a few minutes to recognize her. Yamuna! She was shouting and screaming: 'Where's Amma? Which is Amma's house?'

I was paralyzed. Why is she here? What if my mistress sees her? What'll happen to me? I ran and hid in a corner of the terrace. I buried my head in my knees and curled up, so she wouldn't recognize me. I don't know how long I was hiding there. The noise faded. The street became silent again. I crawled back to my kitchen. Safe.

(Pause.)

I had soaked double beans that day. My mistress' family adored the *bendi* I make with double beans. Particularly the children. It's not easy to get the flavour right. Four red chillies and some tamarind paste. Grind them well. Put in a handful of fresh coconut. Two or three triphalas will do. Then add vagar of garlic. The vagar has to be the right shade of brown, mind. That's the trick. I don't eat garlic myself. But the children love it. Then a bit of salt. Again you have to have precise eye judgement—

(The stage darkens as we continue to hear Radhabai speaking and then her voice fades away.)

BOILED BEANS ON TOAST

Note

The title of the play relates to the founding myth of the city of Bengaluru or Bangalore, which is today admired as the 'Silicon Valley of India' and is the subject of this play.

In the eleventh century, King Veera Ballala went out hunting, lost his way in the jungle, and after wandering through the night, arrived exhausted at a lonely hut where an old woman saved his life by giving him a handful of boiled beans (*benda kaalu* in Kannada, the native tongue). In gratitude, the King named the place 'Benda Kaaluru', the place of boiled beans, which in the course of time got corrupted into 'Bengaluru' and was in turn anglicized by the colonial rulers into 'Bangalore'.

The toast is a strictly Western import into Indian cuisine. The Kannada title of the play is *Benda Kaalu on Toast*.

Boiled Beans on Toast was first presented in a Marathi adaptation titled, *Uney Purey Shahar Ek*, at the Yashwantrao Chavan Natyagruha, Pune, by the Aasakta group on 1 March 2013. It was sponsored by the Sahitya Rangabhoomi Pratisthan. The principal cast was as follows, although the names of some characters differed in the Marathi version:

ANITA DATE	Muttu
RADHIKA APTE	Vimala
PRATIBHA DATE	Muttu's mother
UMESH JAGTAP	Shankara/Sundara Rajan
ASHWINI GIRI	Anjana
VIBHAWARI DESHPANDE	Dolly Iyer
SAGAR DESHMUKH	Prabhakar
JYOTI SUBHASH	Anusuya
SIDDHARTH MENON	Kunaal
RAVI SANGVAI	Brigadier Iyer
PRAJAKTA SALBARDE	Sumitra
DEVENDRA GAIKWAD	Inspector/Ravi
PRAJAKTA PATIL	Saroja
RAHUL PARKHE	Head Constable
SHEKH MADAM	Lady Constable
LAXMI BIRAJDAR	Vimala's sister-in-law/ Shankara's wife
VEERA SAXENA	Receptionist
RAHUL PARBHE	'Wipro' guard
SAYALI DEVDHAR	
PRAJAKTA SALBARDE	
VRUSHALI DUBEY	Village women
PRAJAKTA PATIL	
SWAMINI DUBEY	
Directed by	MOHIT TAKALKAR
Set design by	MOHIT TAKALKAR
Lighting design by	PRADEEP VAIDDYA
Translated by	PRADEEP VAIDDYA
Sound design by	DARSHAN PATANKAR
Costumes by	RASHMI RODE

Act One

Scene One

As the lights come on, the entire cast is seen on stage in a phantasmagoric tableau, every character immobile, frozen in the middle of some activity. When the lights are fully on, the actors spring into action, talking, moving about, fighting, shouting, bumping into each other, the background noise of traffic and music adding to the effect of a busy thoroughfare in Bangalore. Then the lights and the music fade out together.

Scene Two

Anjana Padabidri's house. Muttu, the maid, aged about twenty-eight, is ironing clothes in the service room. Vimala, the cook and the chief servant of the house, aged thirty-five, enters accompanied by Muttu's mother and elder brother, Shankara. The mother leans heavily on a triple-hoofed stick as she walks.

VIMALA: Muttu, visitors for you.

MUTTU: Oh god! Why have you come in here? You know Amma—

VIMALA (*to the mother*): You know the rules perfectly well. Amma doesn't like all this crowding in and holding your family conferences here. Muttu's been given a mobile and you know what that's for.

MOTHER: Shankara arrived all of a sudden from our town. He says he has to go back by this evening.

VIMALA: If you'd called Muttu on the mobile, she would've come out for a while. There's no need for you to storm into the house like an army. Please don't do it again.
(*Goes out.*)

SHANKARA: Goodness me! Who's that?

MUTTU: Vimala, the cook. She's been here for ever and she thinks she's the mistress of the house.

SHANKARA (*inspects the house*): A nice big house, I must say.

MUTTU: But she's right. You shouldn't have just come in like this. It annoys Amma. You know that, Mother. We could've met at home in the evening. Or if you'd called me, I would've come out.

SHANKARA: I don't have till the evening. The moment he received his call from Bengaluru, the Boss said let's go and we started immediately. He's been nice enough to let me take the car to meet you while he's at his meeting. I've only got a couple of hours here and then I've to drive him back. And I had to pick up Mother on the way.

MOTHER: I said I won't come. But he wouldn't listen.

SHANKARA: If I knew where this house was, I wouldn't have troubled you, Mother. Do you think I've nothing else to do but hound you? But, I needed you here. There's something very important I've to discuss with you both. I'll do that and leave.

MUTTU (*guardedly*): You could've called me on the mobile.

SHANKARA (*annoyed*): There are things you can't talk about on the phone. Don't you understand? It's a family matter. Don't worry, I won't stay long. Now, I got your letter saying Kalpana's come of age. And you say you want to have all the rituals done here in Bengaluru. Why? Isn't it a matter of happiness for us that your daughter's matured? Who do we have here in this city? All our relations live in Karimangala or Solagiri. They can't come this far for the ceremony.

MUTTU: Husband said Karimangala would mean expense. The remotest relatives'll turn up. In Bengaluru, we can have a smaller affair. More compact.

SHANKARA (*to the mother*): And you agreed?

MOTHER: It's their daughter. Who am I to advise? But what her husband says makes sense. What's the point of spending unnecessarily?

SHANKARA: That's what happens, when people move to the city. The family back home, relatives, connections—they all become dispensable, don't they? They can be put aside. Ignored. Forgotten.

MUTTU: I don't know what to say. You talk to Husband.

SHANKARA: I don't have time now to go searching for Brother-in-law. His factory's beyond the old airport, miles away. Now listen to me. Don't I feel happy if my sister's only daughter comes of age? Should we not celebrate it in our ancestral home in our own town? I refuse to come to Bengaluru with my family for a meal as though I was attending a function in some stranger's house. You and I—we grew up in Karimangala. Our family gods are there. I insist that we celebrate this event in our own house. If you're afraid of the expense, I'll handle it myself.

MUTTU: Husband'll look after all that.

SHANKARA: Leave the money matters to the men. I'll convince him. Let Kalpana finish her exams. There's no hurry. There're only three girls in our family, after all. You have one and I've two. Kalpana is the eldest of the three. Let's invite all the family members— elders, cousins, aunts, uncles—and perform the rites properly.
(*Muttu looks at the mother.*)

MOTHER: As the men decide. What can I say?
(*Vimala enters, looking busy.*)

VIMALA: Have you finished, Muttu?

MUTTU: Yes, yes. Only two pieces left.

VIMALA: When're you going to be done? This is why Amma forbids these family sessions here. Then the grandmother's here from Dharwad. And the old lady needs attention hand and foot. Get on with it.

SHANKARA: All right, all right, we're done. It was just a very important family issue. We won't bother you again, I promise you. Or else next time I shall have the siren on, warning you of our arrival, like in an ambulance.

MUTTU: Brother, please—

Shankara: Or even better, I'll make sure you're not in town when we
     come. All right? Let's go, Mother.
(*Shankara and the mother leave. Vimala's voice is loud enough to ensure
that he hears her comment.*)

VIMALA: Is that your brother? I should ask him to learn a little civility.
     This isn't your backwoods, you know. This is Bengaluru. We can
     do with less rudeness here.
(*Goes out. Muttu continues with her ironing.*)

Scene Three

The living room of the Padabidri house. Anjana and her friend, Dolly. Anjana is in her mid-forties while Dolly is in her late-thirties. Vimala is pouring tea into the cups on the table and laying out biscuits and sandwiches. Intermittently, one can hear Kunaal practising on his guitar in his room.

ANJANA: ... And slowly, you know, you begin to realize that the flip side of life isn't death—it's pain. When they're in pain, the patients can't think of anything else. It fills every crack in their consciousness. It blanks everything out, blinds them, deafens them to the world. But when they're given palliatives and the pain begins to recede—my god! The change! Their interest in life revives. They become human. They begin to discuss their problems with you. Their hopes, plans. It's wonderful!

DOLLY (*to Vimala*): Only one spoon, please.

VIMALA: I know.

DOLLY: But Anjana, they are brought to the Karunashraya and it's only *then* that they know there's no going back? How terrible!

ANJANA: Not always. Sometimes the families tell them what it means. But often they don't. They pretend they're being taken to a new hospital, to another specialist. It can be awful, I agree.

DOLLY: But when they realize they've been brought under false pretences, don't they feel cheated? Throw a fit?

(*The doorbell rings. Anjana calls out.*)

ANJANA: Muttu—

VIMALA: I'll attend to it. Muttu must be cleaning the Master's study.

(*Vimala goes out.*)

DOLLY: That must be awful. To come in the hope of being cured and then find there's no going back. The very thought gives me the shivers—

ANJANA: They do get upset. But the funny thing is, often, when the truth sinks in, the patients feel the family was right not to tell them. 'I would've done the same,' they say. Almost grateful that the lie kept hope alive for that much longer, you know.

DOLLY: But, Anjana, to tell a person that she's going to die—

ANJANA (*smiles*): No, no, no. However terminal the cancer, you never say to a patient, 'You're going to die.' You just say, 'I'm sorry but we won't be able to cure you.' You see, you never know. The patient may not die. There are cases we thought hopeless, still alive.

VIMALA (*enters*): Someone to see the Master. He's given his card.

ANJANA: But Mr Padabidri isn't in Bangalore today. Didn't you tell him? Anyway why's this man here? He should go to the office.

(*Puts the visiting card down on the table without even looking at it.*)

VIMALA: I told him. But he says he was specifically asked to come to the house. Not the office.

ANJANA: How annoying!

VIMALA: There he is.

(*Prabhakar enters. He is about thirty-five, dressed in a cheap suit and a tie. He is sweating profusely. Vimala casts an annoyed look at him for entering so unceremoniously and goes in. He doesn't know which of the two women is Mrs Padabidri.*)

PRABHAKAR: Good morning. My name is Prabhakar Telang. Mr Padabidri had asked me to meet him here this morning.

ANJANA: I'm sorry, but my husband isn't back in town.

PRABHAKAR: Oh but—but he gave me an appointment—for this morning.

ANJANA: I know. I know. He should've been back from Canada two days ago. But he was instructed by his office to go on to Finland. Didn't his secretary inform you?

PRABHAKAR: Actually his secretary doesn't know about this meeting. This was arranged independently. (*Pause. Almost conspiratorially*) By a mutual acquaintance.
(*He is perspiring profusely. Wipes his face.*)

ANJANA: Please sit down. Would you like some tea?

PRABHAKAR: No, no, thanks. (*Pause.*) I don't want to trouble you.

ANJANA: No trouble at all. (*Calls out.*) Vimala, another cup of tea, please.

PRABHAKAR: Thank you. You see, I've come all the way from K.R. Puram in a rickshaw. It took nearly an hour and a half. Actually I'm very late for the appointment. Mr Padabidri would be right to be upset. But the traffic's unbelievable. We were stationary most of the time.

ANJANA: I'm Anjana, Mrs Padabidri. This is Mrs Dolly Iyer, a family friend. I'm afraid my husband may not be back for another four or five days. May be even longer.

PRABHAKAR: Oh, dear! That would be—a huge problem.

ANJANA: I'm sorry. Was it something urgent?

(*Vimala comes in with another cup of tea and a teapot and a bowl of sugar.*)

VIMALA (*to Dolly*): You haven't touched your tea, Madam. It'll have gone cold by now. I'll get you some fresh tea.

DOLLY: No, no, please don't worry.

VIMALA: It's no bother. You like your tea boiling hot, I know that. (*Picks up the tray which she had brought earlier.*)

ANJANA (*to Prabhakar*): Please, have your tea.

PRABHAKAR: Yes, I shall, if you don't mind. Otherwise my tea'll get cold by the time yours comes back and then you'll have to wait while my tea is taken away and heated up again. And so on. (*They all laugh.*)

ANJANA: I'm sorry but I can't understand why my husband should call you home. Most unusual.

PRABHAKAR: It's about a vacancy in his office.

ANJANA: Really? But he moved out of Administration some time ago. He's in Finance Management now.

PRABHAKAR: No, no, let me—let me explain properly. I've a temporary position in my office. I'm on probation. But the prospects are good. The point is—it's a confidential matter.

ANJANA: Then you don't need to talk about it.

PRABHAKAR: No, no. It's not like that. You are, after all, Mrs Padabidri, so I'm sure Mr Padabidri hides nothing from you. And she's your family friend. So—

ANJANA (*smiles*): Relax, Mr Telang. As I said, you don't have to tell us—
(*Anjana and Dolly look at each other and smile, which he notices. It confuses him even more.*)

PRABHAKAR (*anguished*): Please, please, don't misunderstand me. That's not what I meant. The fact is—the boss of the company in which I'm at present employed, is going to quit and join Mr Padabidri's office—and he's taking four of our top-notch managers along with him. His favourites. It's all rather hush hush, as you can imagine. I'm not one of them—yet—but there's a chance I may be taken up along with them.

DOLLY: Oh, congratulations.

PRABHAKAR: But Mr Padabidri's never met me. It's only my boss's recommendation. So he—that is, Mr Padabidri—has asked me to come here and meet him, so we could discuss the situation over a cup of tea. Well, I've got my cup of tea, but I haven't met him.

(*They all laugh. Vimala brings a fresh tray with two cups and places it on the table. She looks around to see if anything more is required.*)

PRABHAKAR (*covering his cup with his palm rather dramatically*): Mine is hot. Piping.

(*They laugh. Vimala is not particularly amused at this familiarity and goes in. A long pause.*)

PRABHAKAR (*almost to himself*): The problem is another four or five days means the news will be out, there'll be pandemonium in our office, I don't know what'll happen then. Anything could. They could target me and terminate my services. That would be the end of my hopes, that's for certain.

ANJANA: I'm sorry to hear that. That's very thoughtless of my husband. (*Pause. They have run out of conversation. But he hasn't finished his tea yet.*)

PRABHAKAR: The road outside your house is like a scene from a war movie.

ANJANA: They're building an underpass there, so they are chopping down the trees.

DOLLY: The problem is our City Corporation is run by people born and brought up in the countryside. They've no time for greenery and environment. They simply love cement concrete, and plastic and glass-fronted buildings. That means modernity to them.

PRABHAKAR: Like me, you mean? But then, you see, you can't blame them. A city is meant for people, so that they can live there. Believe in its solidity. Madam, I grew up in the heart of the Western Ghats—the thickest of forests—near Mundgod—and I grew up yearning for the massive constructions of cement concrete and the towering glass-fronted skyscrapers I saw on television.

ANJANA: You know the main reason for this house being here is that tree outside. Kunaal and I were scouting around Bangalore for a suitable area in which to build our house—that was of course more than fifteen years ago—it was still possible to buy a plot of land you liked on which you might want to build your house—

DOLLY: Ah, for those days, Anjana! Land? You would be lucky to find an apartment today.

ANJANA: We saw this magnificent tree along the wide road—you know with its foliage spreading like an umbrella—and I said to Kunaal, 'Look, Kunaal, that is a rain tree. It has bipinnate leaves—like feathers—they open up in the sun so you've shade under it during the day and they fold in at night, so moonlight filters through.' He was absolutely delighted and we immediately decided to build our house there. We planned the whole layout, standing right there, so that the terrace would be under its spreading branches, and we could have regular dinner parties on it.

PRABHAKAR: You only have to dream of something and you can turn it into a reality. How marvellous!

ANJANA: But of course the City Corporation has other ideas now. They've joined the wide road in front to the Mysore arterial highway and turned it into a ring road. That was the end of our dinner parties. The traffic was deafening. You couldn't hear a word of what the next person said. Now they say the ring road gets choked up, so they've to have an underpass and the trees have to go. There's talk now of widening the road to a hundred and fifty feet! There's simply no end. Kunaal and I—we love that rain tree, and I swear to you the day that tree goes I'm getting out of this house.

DOLLY: My husband was posted here in Bangalore when he was in service and fondly remembered the Cantonment bungalows. The pillars, the porticos, and the monkeytop windows. We come here now and bungalows! Ha! (*Throws up hands dramatically.*) We decided to settle for a comfortable apartment.

PRABHAKAR: Comfortable! Lucky you, Madam! You should see our flat. It's the size of a handkerchief. But then, you see, who asked me to come to Bengaluru? Who asked anyone to come to Bengaluru? With people pouring into the city—
(*Vimala enters.*)

VIMALA: Time for your pills, Amma. I've kept them next to the saucers. I'll find out if Grandma needs anything before she goes out.
(*Goes in.*)

DOLLY: Anjana, I'm willing to put up with the tiniest of apartments, if only I could find someone like your Vimala to run the house. Where did you find her?

ANJANA: We were building this house and she simply turned up and asked if she could work here. I needed a cook desperately and that was it.

PRABHAKAR: And you took her on as a cook without worrying about her caste, customs—

ANJANA: Mr Telang, let me put in a word of caution. If you are going to work for my husband, you would be well advised not to speak of caste and community.

PRABHAKAR (*jumping up*): Oh, Madam, I don't believe in caste at all. I consider myself a secular, leftwing intellectual—
(*Anjana's mobile rings. She checks the caller's name.*)

ANJANA: Excuse me.
(*The guitar music ends on a high note.*)

PRABHAKAR (*embarrassed at his own gaucherie*): That was nice music.

ANJANA (*as she hurries in*): Thanks. My son Kunaal.

PRABHAKAR: I don't understand Western music. But that music's nice. (*Anjana disappears into the house.*)

DOLLY (*lowering her voice*): Listen, Mr Telang, I want to tell you something. Something important. It could help you with your career.

PRABHAKAR (*startled*): My career? What?

DOLLY (*picking up his visiting card from the table*): We can't talk about it here. Let's meet somewhere else. In the next day or two. You know the Café Coffee Day near the Ashoka Pillar? Good. I'll give you a ring on your mobile. (*Looks at her watch.*) Where's my husband? We can't afford to be late for lunch. We are meant to be lunching with Kiran Mazumdar and John Shaw—you know, the Managing Director of the Biocon Empire. They are dear friends.

(*Anusuya, a gracious old lady in her seventies, enters, followed by Vimala carrying her bag which bulges with her needs. Prabhakar stands up.*)

VIMALA: I'll keep this bag in the car, Grandma. (*Goes out.*)

DOLLY: How are you, Auntie? How was the train trip?

ANUSUYA: What can I say? They always allot me an upper berth in the sleeper. And my age is printed, right there on the ticket. (*They laugh.*)

DOLLY: I presume they changed it.

ANUSUYA: The conductor insisted he had no spare sleepers until I threatened to spread my sheet out, right there, in the corridor and go to sleep on the floor. That always works. (*More laughter.*)

DOLLY: And what's the itinerary today? Visiting some temple?

ANUSUYA: No, thanks. My official quota for temples has been long met. Some shopping, probably. Don't know what. All the shops seem to sell the same things. (*Pointing to Anjana*) And she, of course, isn't in the least interested. Busy with her hospice.

DOLLY: But have you seen the hospice building, Auntie? You should. It's so beautifully designed, so tranquil—

ANUSUYA: There was something in the papers today about the race course. It said they're going to close it down and move it out of the city.

DOLLY: It's simple, Auntie. The Chief Minister has his eyes on all that open space in the heart of the city. A gold mine.

ANUSUYA: I've never been to a horse race and if I'm not going to get another chance, I might as well peep in.
(*Anjana enters, obviously upset.*)

ANJANA: Was there anything else, Mr Telang?

PRABHAKAR: No, not at all, Madam. I was just waiting to say thank you and bid goodbye.

ANJANA: I'll tell my husband you were here.

PRABHAKAR: Please. And thank you, Mrs Iyer.
(*Dolly and Prabhakar exchange quick looks and he goes out. Kunaal enters with his guitar in its bag. He is in his late teens.*)

ANUSUYA: Are you keeping me company, Kunu?

KUNAAL: I've arranged an escort for you. A Mr Sundara Rajan. He's the official man-for-all-seasons—looks after our visitors.

ANUSUYA: Thanks. I'll be back soon, Anjana.

ANJANA: Take your time.

KUNAAL: Have fun, Grandma. Mummy, if it gets very late, I may not come home for dinner. I'll sleep over at Nandita's.

ANUSUYA: Who's Nandita?

KUNAAL: The singer in our band. She's absolutely amazing.

(*Startled, Anusuya looks at Anjana, who doesn't show any reaction although she has registered Anusuya's sense of shock.*)

ANJANA: If I'm not going to see you before tomorrow morning, I want to have a word with you. Papa called.
(*Kunaal groans. Anusuya senses the tension in the air.*)

ANUSUYA: I'll be off then.

ANJANA and DOLLY: Bye.
(*Anusuya goes out by the front door.*)

KUNAAL: I've a rehearsal, Mummy. They'll be waiting.

DOLLY (*anticipating trouble*): I'd better go. My husband's probably stuck somewhere. His mobile's busy too.
(*Anjana nods. Muttu comes out running holding a thermos flask.*)

MUTTU: Amma, Grandma's forgotten her thermos flask.

ANJANA: Why're you telling me? Run out and give it to Grandma before she drives off.
(*Muttu runs out.*)

DOLLY: Needs to be told everything, doesn't she?

ANJANA: A good girl. A bit slow though.

DOLLY: Well, you can't expect to find a Vimala every time.
(*Anjana smiles absent-mindedly and nods.*)

I shouldn't have recommended a visit to the hospice to the old lady, should I? She didn't seem to like it.

ANJANA: I don't think she minded.
(*Dolly waves to Kunaal and goes out. Pause.*)

KUNAAL (*defiant*): Yes, Mummy. Papa called. So?

ANJANA: He's seen the credit card statement. You have bought a new, expensive guitar.

KUNAAL: Not expensive. Just a good one. Actually, I need a better one—a resonator—and was tempted by a Dobro. But resisted.

ANJANA: How are you going to make a living playing the guitar? What kind of future—

KUNAAL: Please let's not go over that again. I know every argument. I've to have a guitar. And I need it now, while I'm struggling to make a name for myself. *Not* when I'm bent and old and thirty-five.

ANJANA: I wish you and your father would decide between yourselves.

KUNAAL: But surely that's not what Papa called for. I want to be a musician and I hope Papa will support me till I can afford to be on my own. He knows that.

ANJANA: I think half his worries would be over if you just passed your exams.

KUNAAL (*exasperated*): Mummy, why did he call?

ANJANA: He's received an anonymous letter saying—your drummer is gay.

KUNAAL: I can't believe it! Perhaps he is. Perhaps he is a transsexual. What am I supposed to do about it? He drums like a god.

ANJANA: And that the pad or the club or whatever it is where you play has a reputation for rave parties and drugs.

KUNAAL: I'm going.
(*Starts walking out.*)

ANJANA: I wish you two would leave me out of it. I can't stand it any longer. All I can say is I'm glad his job keeps him away from India. It keeps me sane.

KUNAAL: And I shall also oblige by staying out tonight.
(*He walks out. Her mobile rings. She speaks into it.*)

ANJANA (*on the mobile*): So the ambulance was there on time. Good. I'll start right away.

Scene Four

The gallery of the Bangalore Race Course.
Later that day. Anusuya and Sundara Rajan are watching the end of a race. The soundtrack recreates the excited commotion as a race ends, and the commentator's voice describes the last section of the race and confirms the results. Anusuya is hopping mad.

ANUSUYA: I can't believe it! No Number Eight. No Five. Not even a place. Sundara Rajan, I said let's place a bet on Number Four. But you didn't listen. We lost a fluke win!

SUNDARA RAJAN: Madam, I said nothing. I merely—

ANUSUYA: Don't make excuses now. Didn't I specifically tell you to bet on Number Four? Four. We would have made a killing. But you had to—Did I or did I not ask you to bet on Four?

SUNDARA RAJAN: You did, Madam. But there's no money left. And you don't have a credit card. There was nothing to—

ANUSUYA: Now don't interfere with my instructions any more. Let's look at the next race. I'd actually marked—
(*Refers to her notebook.*)

SUNDARA RAJAN: Madam, we have no money left. We've lost the last rupee we brought.

ANUSUYA: No money? How's that possible? Why didn't we bring enough?

SUNDARA RAJAN: I was only supposed to take you round the city. I didn't know you—we—were going to bet on horses.

ANUSUYA: Nor did I, if that's any help. I didn't realize races were like this. That they gobble up money.

SUNDARA RAJAN: You've placed a bet in every single race since we arrived, Madam.

ANUSUYA: And won. I won the very first race. And won places in two later ones. And then in the fifth race I actually made—

SUNDARA RAJAN: I know, Madam. And staked that amount back again. I told you we should place smaller bets. But you wouldn't listen.

ANUSUYA: Stop advising me. We must look for some more money. Isn't there anyone we could borrow from?

SUNDARA RAJAN: People come here to gamble. Not to lend money.

ANUSUYA: I know, I know. Couldn't you go out and borrow from that Ramayya Chetty shop? They were so nice and polite this morning.

SUNDARA RAJAN: I'll have to go out of the compound for that. And we'll miss the next one.

ANUSUYA: We can't. This's the last one for the day.

SUNDARA RAJAN: I know. Madam, let's just watch the race and go home.

ANUSUYA: But Silver Stallion! We simply—oh god!
(*Inspects the crowds with desperate intensity. Suddenly*)

Sundara Rajan, that man there. Rather stuffy-looking gentleman. In the grey suit. Who's he? Looks familiar.

SUNDARA RAJAN: That's the Brigadier. Husband of Dolly Iyer—you know, Mrs Padabidri's friend.

ANUSUYA: Of course that's him. Will you please call him? Quick. Say I want to talk to him.

(*Sundara Rajan goes to Brigadier Iyer and brings him to Anusuya.*)

SUNDARA RAJAN: Brigadier sir, this is Mrs Padabidri, my boss's mother. She wanted to—

BRIGADIER: Of course I know her. We've met at Anjana's. A couple of times, actually. (*To Anusuya*) As you know, my wife spends so much time in your house you could legitimately charge her rent.

(*Laughs.*) Are you on your own?

ANUSUYA: No, no. Sundara Rajan's there, as you can see. Brigadier, can I bother you for a favour?

BRIGADIER: But of course. What can I do for you?

ANUSUYA: Can I ask for a small loan? Only temporarily.

BRIGADIER (*startled*): A loan? But of course. Except that I don't carry much cash on me.

ANUSUYA: Oh! I don't need much. A few thousand? Ten?

(*The Brigadier, taken aback, fumbles through his pockets, takes out his wallet and starts checking the cash.*)

Even five'll do. You see, I have an excellent hunch for the next race. Not a hunch—a tip—a certain win. I shall return the loan the moment my horse wins.

BRIGADIER: But of course. The point is I hadn't come for the races. I've an appointment with Doctor Gowda, the Chairman of the Turf Club. Let me see how much I have. Hmm! Sorry but I've only four thousand on me.

ANUSUYA: That'll do. Thank you. It's better than nothing. And I shall return it the moment the race's over.

BRIGADIER: I shouldn't worry, Mrs Padabidri. There's absolutely no hurry. I can always get it back from Mr Padabidri or Anjana.

ANUSUYA: That's it, Brigadier. Please, please, please don't say anything to my son or daughter-in-law about it. I shall be most thankful if you mentioned absolutely nothing to them. I shall return the amount the moment the race's over. Now if you'll excuse me. Please, hurry. Sundara Rajan. Three thousand on Silver Stallion for a win. God, I'm excited! And yes, one for a place. Same horse. (*The Brigadier watches bemused.*)

Scene Five

Café Coffee Day. Prabhakar is sitting at a table, immersed in a book. The alarm on his mobile rings. He looks up, sees Dolly arriving from a distance, and quickly shoves the book into his briefcase. And sits, his hands folded, watching the street, seemingly idly. When a bearer approaches him he waves him away as though to say, 'Later'. Dolly arrives.

DOLLY: Good morning. I hope I haven't kept you waiting.

PRABHAKAR: Not at all. Actually you're on time. I chose to be early. Because I love to sit and watch the traffic in the streets of Bangalore. I can sit like this for hours—transfixed.

DOLLY: Really? Most people grumble about our endless traffic.

PRABHAKAR: When I was young I was taken to Gokarn, to the beach. And I had never seen the sea before. I had grown up in the jungles and although the sea was less than fifty miles away, had no idea what it looked like. And I was mesmerized. Waves after waves after waves and then water, right up to the horizon. Our traffic too is like that. Waves after waves of scooters, autorickshaws, buses, cars, every conceivable kind of vehicle, including bullock carts, tractors, and earth movers. It's magical.

DOLLY: I must say you seemed such a scared little yokel when we met at Anjana's. You're a different person now.

PRABHAKAR: When you've grown up in a small town, these city bungalows have a strange effect on you. My entire body begins to shrink, you know. And the tongue refuses to turn the way I want it to. In such situations, I find it's safer to play the innocent fool—it's a safeguard against humiliation.

DOLLY: You're good with words. Do you write poetry?

PRABHAKAR: There was a time I dreamt of it. Plans postponed till I find a roof over my head and a safe job.

DOLLY: Good. We were not properly introduced that day, so let me. I'm Rajalakshmi Iyer but Dolly to everyone. My husband was in the army—retired now. I teach in the girls' public school next to Anjana's house. English elocution. For want of anything better to do. And our house is miles away from the school. So in between classes, I prefer to hang around in Anjana's house. Much nicer than the dreary staff room.

PRABHAKAR: You are obviously very close friends?

DOLLY: Very. She's a darling. Actually she used to spend her whole day idling at home. The idle rich housewife! I introduced her to the director of the Karunashraya, Kishore Rao. Now you have to drag her away from there.

PRABHAKAR: Karunashraya. Yes, that was mentioned that day. What is it?

DOLLY: A hospice. For cancer patients beyond hope. It was started by a dear friend, Kishore.

PRABHAKAR: And Anjana helps out there?

DOLLY: Virtually runs the show now.

PRABHAKAR: And her son? He is a guitar player?

DOLLY (*not interested*): I gather he's very good at the veena. But he plays the guitar. As a rebellion.

PRABHAKAR: Rebellion? Against whom?

DOLLY: His parents.

PRABHAKAR (*astounded*): While he lives with them? While they look after him?

DOLLY: I saw you were immersed in some book. What're you reading?

PRABHAKAR (*blushing as though caught red-handed*): Nothing really.

DOLLY: It's a secret?

PRABHAKAR: No, no, no. But I haven't started reading it. I just bought it the other day.

DOLLY: Tell me about it. I want to know more about you.

PRABHAKAR (*pulls the book out of his briefcase*): 'A Gentleman's Book of Etiquette.' Tells you all about—you know, if someone says 'How do you do' to you, don't say 'I am fine'. The correct reply is, 'How do you do'.
(*They laugh.*)

I learnt that this morning, now, sitting here.

DOLLY: Excellent. That's what I liked about you. Intuitively. That's why I asked you to come here this morning. A simple word from me was enough to get you started.
(*He is unsure of what she means.*)

That's what I like. You're an intelligent, well-read, energetic young man. You should treat the whole brave new world as a challenge, instead of creeping into the Padabidri house for a secret meeting, in search of a job.

PRABHAKAR: I could've been rotting in Mundgod. I'm fortunate to be in Bengalu—Bangalore. That's what I care about. This itself is release. The city air, however polluted, is an oxygen chamber, after the suffocation of a small town.
(*The bearer comes to them.*)

What'll you have?

DOLLY: Nothing, thanks.

PRABHAKAR: Nothing? Cappuccino, latté, espresso?
(*Dolly shakes her head.*)

I'll have a cappuccino.
(*The bearer leaves.*)

I learnt all these names only the other day. Until I came here, I only knew one brand, 'Coffee'.

DOLLY (*smiles*): You've passed all my tests with flying colours. So let me get to the point. Would you go to Singapore if you were offered a job?

PRABHAKAR (*flabbergasted*): You must be joking!

DOLLY: No, I'm not. Wipro has an office in Singapore. Will you accept a posting there?

PRABHAKAR: Please. Please. Don't make such cruel jokes. Wipro!

DOLLY: Azim Premji is a close friend. I was in college with his wife Yasmeen. At Xavier's.

PRABHAKAR: I daren't even dream of that world. Wipro! It scares me even to think of it. It's—it's listed on the Nasdaq!

DOLLY: And when I first met them, they were just plain ordinary people like you.

PRABHAKAR: I'm sorry. I just cannot grasp what you're suggesting.

DOLLY: Let me explain. The other day my husband and I had dinner with Azim and Yasmeen. And he was saying they were looking for a good regional manager for their Singapore office. But they want to fill it without any fanfare. They've their reasons for not advertising the post.
(*The coffee arrives. But he doesn't even look at it.*)

PRABHAKAR: But, Dolly, Mrs Iyer—

DOLLY (*laughs*): Dolly's fine. Go on.

PRABHAKAR: Wipro! It is one of India's largest …. Huge. Enormous. Azim Premji's up there! Will they even look at me? And why should they?

DOLLY: Are you going to listen to me? Or are you going to continue repeating yourself?

PRABHAKAR: Sorry. Sorry. But don't you see—

DOLLY: Look, I didn't ask them. He brought up the subject and asked me to suggest a good person. I've had a word with Azim since I met you. He is agreeable. There's only one proviso—

PRABHAKAR: What?

DOLLY: You've to leave for Singapore almost instantly. Right away. Can you? That's why I had to talk to you first before suggesting your name to them.

PRABHAKAR (*guarded*): How instantly?

DOLLY: Let's say you should've been there yesterday. Look, they've no shortage of people vying to get into the firm. They'll have a rioting mob there if the news leaks out. It's top secret. Don't even mention it to anyone. Or go to the Internet. Do you have to serve notice to your present bosses if you want to leave?

PRABHAKAR: I'm supposed to give them an advance notice of two months. Or pay two months' salary as penalty.

DOLLY: Good. Just pay the penalty and resign. Your monthly salary in Singapore'll be more than what you'll probably get in six months here. You'll be given residential quarters. And a car for your own use. Can you drive?

PRABHAKAR: Yes.

DOLLY: Good. Hand in your resignation tomorrow and get a move on.

PRABHAKAR: Tomorrow!

DOLLY: As soon as possible then. Look, try to understand the situation. You can't tell Wipro that you'll resign your present job only after getting their appointment letter. Things don't work that way. Ask your boss—did he have a formal appointment before he walked into the Padabidri camp? That's not how things are done in the modern business world. You've to prove you're interested in the post!

PRABHAKAR: I understand that. I understand that. But I've just managed to get my job. They've actually given me a probation in spite of the rumpus caused by my boss. They've promised to confirm me. What I always dreamt of. It's not so easy to walk off from it. And my daughter's got into a good English-medium school—

DOLLY: It's up to you, of course. But you must learn to think afresh, see it in its totality. This offer's there today. It certainly won't be there tomorrow. Besides, wake up, Prabhakar! The era in which you were expected to spend your entire lifetime serving a single firm is gone. In this age of globalization you must move quickly, from job to job and upwards. If you get this job, what are you going to do with your wife and child? Are you going to leave them on their own in Bangalore? You have to start thinking about that.

PRABHAKAR: I know. I know.

DOLLY: If you ask me, send them back to Mundgod to your parents— or her parents. It's a question of only a couple of months. Probably less. Then they'll in any case need to move to Singapore. Bangalore isn't a safe place for a woman on her own with a child. (*Long silence.*)

Look, you don't have to agree. If you think it's an unnecessary risk, please don't go ahead. I don't want to arm-twist you.

PRABHAKAR: Do I have a choice?

DOLLY: Splendid. Buy some good new clothes—a well-cut suit or two—and arrange monies for your initial expenses. I shall get the interview fixed at the soonest. You know the Electronic City?

PRABHAKAR: I do.

DOLLY: You'll have to go there for the interview.

PRABHAKAR: Okay.

DOLLY: The first interview is a mere formality. Just for the record. Someone from the Human Resource Development will see you. Azim may ask you to meet him at his house later. You'll be in

Singapore before the end of the month. The real delay will be in getting the passport. You know the Passport Office! But they've someone to look after that. And, of course, they'll handle all the rest. Cheer up!

PRABHAKAR: How can I thank you enough, Dolly?

DOLLY: I've been very lucky in the friends I have. It's a question of spreading the luck around. So good luck!
(*She gets up, waves him a goodbye and leaves.*)

PRABHAKAR (*smiles*): Singapore, here I come!
(*He drinks the coffee in a single gulp.*)

Scene Six

Anjana's house. Anjana on the mobile. Frantic.

ANJANA: I was about to step into the shower when the phone rings and there's a call—from 'the other house where Vimala is employed', if you please—That's it. That's just it. I had no idea until that moment that Vimala had another job—a parallel one—in 'another house', with another family. And the commotion was all about how Vimala had stolen some jewellery. And the mistress of the house was on the phone saying she'd taken Vimala to the Tilaknagar police station. They were both screaming their heads off. Vimala and her, grabbing the telephone from each other's hands, cursing each other, accusing each other of lying. I called Mr Infant instantly—Yes, yes, Mr Infant, the Deputy Inspector General of Police—Please, I *know* one shouldn't call the DIG of Bangalore simply because one's cook's in trouble, but what else was I to do? You couldn't be contacted for more than half an hour and you've strictly forbidden me to call your office for domestic problems. Anyway, I called Mr Infant …. What's the point of having friends in high places if you can't bother them? I didn't know where Kunaal was—So I rushed to the Tilaknagar police station. And I was there for two hours. Oh my goodness!

The sub-inspector and that hysterical woman, Vimala, FIR, complaint—such shouting and screaming and recriminations. It was chaos. Then they said Vimala had to be there till the Inspector turned up. So I've come home. But I've said I'll be back with a lawyer and they can't do this to an innocent woman without evidence and what not. (*Pause.*) But on the way home I've been wondering. I mean I feel sorry for Vimala, but couldn't there be some truth in the accusation? Who knows—recently we've been losing things in the house. Small objects, cash left on the table. Things have been disappearing, from the guest room. I had mentioned it to you—He's not home. Probably—You know he never tells where he's going to be. (*Suddenly exasperated*) Look, here I am, ringing you for advice in the midst of a domestic crisis. And you want to talk of Kunaal's activities—Yes, yes, we have to worry about our son. But at the moment I have more immediate household headaches. Do you mind?

Scene Seven

Prabhakar's apartment. A tiny room now littered with metal trunks, old-fashioned holdalls, and cardboard boxes. His wife Sumitra is sitting on her haunches, weeping openly while packing a box.

PRABHAKAR: Where's the fourth box? Ah! Yes. What's this, Sumitra? Why are you being so silly? It's a question of only a month. Then we'll all be together in Singapore.

SUMITRA: I don't want to go to Singapore. I was so happy when you got a job here. Our own house. Our own life. No parents or parents-in-law to breathe down our necks. No interfering relatives. We were so happy. What more do you want?

PRABHAKAR: No, Sumitra. I'm rotting in this place. I must thank Dolly for making me realize I'm wasted here. I deserve a better job. I can't go on forever with this grind. And you deserve something much better. I'll see to it that you get the best in the world. I shall make you a queen.

SUMITRA: I don't want to go back. Why can't I just stay on here? Vishoo and I could join you in Singapore when you've settled down there. I just hate the thought of going back to that cesspit.

(*Prabhakar has in the meantime dialed a number on the mobile.*)

PRABHAKAR: Oh, you're there? Good. Please, will you please talk to
   her yourself?

(*Hands over the mobile to Sumitra.*)

   Here. It's Dolly.

SUMITRA: I don't want to talk to her.

PRABHAKAR: Please, dear. She's only trying to help us.

SUMITRA (*into the mobile*): Hello—Yes, yes. I know—I know you
   mean well. And my husband says the same thing. But the
   thought of going back to that filthy place—I hate it! We were so
   happy here—I believe you. But Vishoo's got admission in a good
   school here. Back home there are no English-medium schools.
   And she'll miss a whole year—Is that so? They will? I believe
   you. Of course I do. Who else's there to guide us?—I know
   you've been running around for our sake—All right. Thank you
   so much. I'll be brave. Yes.

(*Returns the mobile to Prabhakar.*)

PRABHAKAR (*into the mobile*): Thanks, Dolly. I can't tell you how
   much I appreciate what you're doing for us.

   (*Switching off the phone*) I hope that's convinced you. Such a
   good person. Taking all this trouble. For what? Look, there's
   no question of rethinking the decision now. I have resigned
   from my job. We've taken back the advance on rent. Things
   are happening, darling. What're you shedding tears for? Wipro
   is a dream company. People would kill to get a job there. The
   moment we get their letter, wheels'll go into motion. They've a
   separate department that looks after passports, work permits,
   visas—We don't have to do a thing. Not everyone gets such
   a break!

SUMITRA: I hate her. I don't know in which past birth I harmed her,
   that she should come back again as my tormentor.

Scene Eight

The police station. The Inspector is sitting behind a table. Facing him sit Vimala, Kunaal, and Mrs Saroja Kunigal, a woman of about forty-five, who is fuming.

INSPECTOR: Well, Vimala Thimmegowda, this Mrs Saroja Kunigal has filed a complaint against you. She says that you have unlawfully—

SAROJA: I thought so too, Sir—that *that* was her name. It isn't. Her real name is Vimala Mary Amaldas.

VIMALA: Don't believe her, Sir.

SAROJA: Two days ago, I went to Kamraj Road and met her parents. They're Christians. From Velankanni, who've moved to Bengaluru. Her name is Vimala Mary Amaldas. Her husband's also a Christian. The parents say they spent thirty-five thousand rupees on her wedding and, within six months, she'd dumped her husband.

VIMALA: She's talking nonsense.

SAROJA: I have their address here with me. Here.

INSPECTOR: I'll ask for it if I need it, thanks. Just recount the incidents quickly, please.

SAROJA: She's been working in our house for the past six months.

KUNAAL: Six months! Mummy had no idea at all.

VIMALA: Not six. I'd told Amma but she was of course lost in her own work. She's a busy person.

SAROJA: Don't believe a word of hers. I know she never told your mother she was working for us. She insisted it had to be kept quiet.

INSPECTOR: And you agreed? Didn't you ask for a reference?

SAROJA: We knew she was working in their house. That was reference enough for me. I desperately needed someone to look after my mother. So I accepted. I shouldn't have, of course. I know that now. But she seemed so nice.

INSPECTOR: So you didn't inform her mistress that you were going to employ her.

SAROJA: No. To be honest, I didn't. No.

INSPECTOR: You kept it a secret?

SAROJA: There was nothing to be secretive about. She went to their house to start cooking at eight-thirty in the morning. She agreed to come to our house an hour earlier and finish her duties within the hour. She didn't want to mix up the two jobs. It made sense.

INSPECTOR (*to Kunaal*): Have you ever lost anything in your house?

KUNAAL: No, never. She's been with us for over eight years and we haven't missed a single rupee.

INSPECTOR: No one pinches a rupee. (*Laughs at his own witticism.*) All right.

Go on, Madam.

SAROJA: My mother is eighty-eight. All this woman had to do was to come at seven-thirty, clean up the room, and bathe Mother. Pile up her used clothes for washing. That's all. It took less than an hour and I must admit she was good. She charmed my mother off her feet. Mother adored her.

VIMALA: You see, Kunaal. You do a job well and that's held against you.

INSPECTOR: Please don't interrupt.

SAROJA: My mother had a thick gold chain. A family heirloom. Would easily fetch three-and-a-half lakhs today. She normally took it off and left it on her pillow while she bathed. That was the routine. All these months, things have been going on smoothly. Two days ago Mother comes back from the bath and the chain isn't there! By the time she looks for it, this woman had dressed her up hurriedly and fled, saying she was getting late. I was upstairs doing my daily pooja and it was some time before I heard Mother calling out. I ran down and knew immediately what had happened. I called the driver and chased her in our car. But by that time she was already in front of their house (*points to Kunaal*), chatting with her boyfriend. I forced her back into our car, but of course the boyfriend fled. In his autorickshaw. We should've grabbed him—

VIMALA: Please don't use such foul words. Boyfriend! He isn't a boyfriend—he's my first cousin from the village.

SAROJA: A lover, more likely.

VIMALA (*flares up*): Please mind your words. If it was anywhere else I would have—

INSPECTOR: Please, Madam, please. Let's not have a public fight here.

SAROJA: Well, whatever he is, he's not her husband, that's for certain. She must have called him on the mobile. Or perhaps it was all planned in advance. The moment he saw our car, he scooted off and she tried to disappear into their house. But I got hold of her and dragged her back and we searched her. Of course the chain had vanished. No guesses on where it had gone.

VIMALA: Please don't make these vile accusations. He's from our village. A good boy. Like a brother to me. You ladies you call yourselves educated, you can only think of dirty things the moment you see a single woman.

SAROJA: Single? You? Ha. Who are you trying to fool? I haven't been sitting idle at home since that day you know. I've been investigating every bit of information about her. I've met her parents. She hasn't visited them in years. And now she's settled down with this auto-driver. I can give you his address.

INSPECTOR: We've him under surveillance, please don't worry. We've had his room searched.

SAROJA: They won't keep it at home. More likely they've sold it by now. You should—

INSPECTOR: It's not easy to sell a gold chain worth three-and-a-half lakhs.

VIMALA: Why should I leave my stuff in his room, Sir? I've nothing to do with him.

INSPECTOR: He had two trunks full of saris and women's clothes. When we asked him, he said he'd no idea who they belonged to or how they got there. He claimed he merely used the room to sleep at night.

VIMALA: If he doesn't know, how would I?

SAROJA: Now they have this loot—three-and-a-half lakhs—why should they claim those saris? They can just romp around—

VIMALA: Disgusting lies, Sir. All lies.

SAROJA: Don't think I'll let you get away. If I don't get that chain back I shall wipe the floor with you and your—your—You bitch!

INSPECTOR: Now now, Madam. No foul language. (*To Vimala*) Where do you live?

VIMALA: In Uttarahalli.

INSPECTOR (*looks at his file*): But the address you've given to the Padabidri family is quite different. It says Kadreguppe here.

VIMALA: Oh, that was when I'd just started working in their house. More than eight years ago, wasn't it? That was when my father was alive. I lived with my parents—

SAROJA: Why're you killing off your parents, wretch? They're still alive—hale and hearty. I met them only two days ago. (*To the Inspector*) Can't you see how she's lying!

INSPECTOR: We'll look into that. (*To Vimala*) I'm sending a head constable from our crime staff with you. There'll be a lady constable with him. Show them your house. We have to verify your details.

VIMALA: All right.

KUNAAL: I've got my car. I'll take them.

INSPECTOR (*calls*): Muniraju!
(*A constable appears and gives a half-hearted salute.*)

Check her details. (*To Saroja*) Would you like to go along?

SAROJA: What for? I know her details. She doesn't live in Uttarahalli. She's leading you up the garden path.

INSPECTOR: The head constable'll look into all that. And submit a report. We'll go on from there.
(*Kunaal and Vimala prepare to leave accompanied by the constable and the lady constable. Saroja follows them.*)

SAROJA: Be warned. She's a liar—a confirmed crook. She won't be easy to nail down. But I won't let her go. Let her watch out.
(*They all exit. The lighting changes and a spotlight picks up Kunaal as he speaks on the mobile.*)

KUNAAL: And so the four of us started in my car—me, Vimala, and the two constables. Actually, I was very annoyed with that Saroja woman. She'd continued to insult Vimala even when the Police were promising a proper investigation. I knew Vimala wasn't that kind of a woman—After all, we'd known her for more than eight years.

So we go to some new residential extension in Uttarahalli. I wish you were there, Nandita. It simply wasn't the Bangalore we know. No sign of any modern civic amenities there. An absolute nightmare from which there was no way of waking up. Of course the road had no pavement. In fact, there was no solid ground anywhere to step on—only potholes. Dirt, plastic bags, piles of garbage on which dogs were tearing at blood-sodden bits of menstrual rags. No way could you drive a car through. Stones heaped right in the middle of the road. And in one place, water poured out torrentially, seeming to gush out from the netherworld. And a regular washing ghat had sprung up right there—women washing clothes, pots, and pans by the roadside. And the houses! Oh god! They were like the cardboard containers in my father's warehouse—piled pell-mell almost on top of one another. And in the middle of all this chaos was a pink temple and beside it a livid green mosque. I somehow managed to navigate the car through this mess. There was a peepal tree and around it, a platform. It must have been the meeting place for the panchayat when this area was an independent village. A vestige from its independent past. The tree was intact and I could park next to it.

We got down and followed Vimala through the scrambled streets and reached a house in a remote corner. She took us to its outhouse which was facing away, almost in a sulk.

(*The lights come on the stage and Vimala and the constables join Kunaal.*)

VIMALA: That one in the backyard—that's my house. (*She goes to it and calls out.*) Sister-in-law, sister-in-law—

(*No reply. The constable goes to the house. The lady constable hangs around totally unconcerned.*)

Sister-in-law—

CONSTABLE: It looks empty.

VIMALA: No, no, the kitchen window is open.
(*Goes and knocks on the window shutter. A woman peers out. Looks at everyone without any expression and disappears.*)

Sister-in-law—

CONSTABLE (*loudly*): Listen, lady of the house, will you please come out?
(*The woman comes out of the front door.*)

WOMAN: What do you want?

CONSTABLE (*pointing to Vimala*): Do you know this lady?

WOMAN: The man of the house isn't in.

CONSTABLE: Do you know this lady?

WOMAN: Yes, I do. But we haven't seen her in the last six months.

VIMALA: Why do you say that, Sister-in-law? Don't I live here?
(*The woman gives a blank look.*)

CONSTABLE: Does she live with you in this house?

WOMAN: The man of the house isn't in. You ask him when he comes back.
(*Disappears into the house and shuts the door behind her.*)

VIMALA: That's my sister-in-law. My elder brother's wife. I live with them.
(*Knocks on the door calling out to the woman. When at last the door opens Vimala slips in. After waiting for either of them to re-emerge the constable makes a sign to the lady constable who goes into the house. The door remains open this time. The constable makes some notes. Suddenly the woman comes out.*)

WOMAN: Yes, she's my sister-in-law. She lives here.

CONSTABLE: But you said you hadn't seen her in six months.

WOMAN: Did I? I don't think so.

CONSTABLE: You said clearly you hadn't seen her for six months.

WOMAN: You ask the man of the house when he comes back.

CONSTABLE: I see that, apart from the bathroom, your house has a kitchen and an extra room. Do all three of you live in this space?

WOMAN: I've two children. They've gone to school. They live here too. (*Goes to the back of the house.*)

VIMALA: I sleep in the kitchen—with the children.

CONSTABLE: Can you all fit in?

VIMALA: Don't have a choice.

CONSTABLE: If you live here, you must have your things here—your saris, trunks, bags—something?

VIMALA: I've three saris and blouses. They were washed today. (*The constable looks around for some sign of the saris on the line.*)

Not here. There's no place here. I wash my clothes at Kunaal's place and dry them in their yard.

CONSTABLE: And what about other things? A trunk or a holdall to keep your stuff? Towels.

VIMALA (*laughing out*): My god! I don't have so much property.

CONSTABLE: I want to talk to your sister-in-law. Call her.

VIMALA: Sister-in-law—Sister-in-law— (*No response. Vimala pretends to search for her.*)

Not here. Probably gone shopping.

CONSTABLE: Without telling us?

VIMALA: Ayyo, but you aren't here to question her, are you? The poor thing has enough problems of her own. You can ask me anything. I'll explain.

CONSTABLE (*to Kunaal*): Shall we go?

VIMALA (*helpfully*): She may come back soon. If you're willing to wait—
(*The constable ignores her remarks and moves off accompanied by Kunaal and the lady constable. Vimala goes into the house and shuts the door.*)

KUNAAL: Is that all? Aren't you going to arrest her or do something?

CONSTABLE: Arrest her? What for? What's the point? (*Laughs.*) Our prisons have no spare capacity, Sir. Bengaluru's bursting with women like her. Where they live, how they live, how they move around—it's all a mystery. Impossible to pin them down. Like scorpions, you know. They only have to see a slab of stone and they'll crawl under it and set up house. Drop us near an auto stand, Sir. We'll go back on our own. Thanks.
(*The constables move off. Kunaal speaks into the mobile.*)

KUNAAL: I was flabbergasted, Nandita. Absolutely stunned. She's been with us for nearly eight years—and we've been saying oh such a nice woman, so reliable. And you know, every sentence she uttered to the police and to me was a lie. A bright, white, brazen lie. And she knew that I knew and the police knew that she was fibbing. And what courage! What invention! She was leading us on, she was creating a story from one minute to another. I tell you. She's my heroine. I've never seen such—such—what's the word—creativity! How could we've missed her brilliance!
(*Switches off the phone. And talks to himself.*)

She's simply wonderful. I wish she was my girlfriend. I think—I've fallen in love with her. What a woman! A true heroine!

Act Two

Scene One

The house of Shankara, Muttu's brother, in Karimangala town. As the lights come on, we see women and girls dressed in finery, participating in the coming-of-age rites for Kalpana, Muttu's daughter. She is aged about twelve and is seated on a plank decorated with alpanas. She has turmeric markings on her cheeks, and has oil poured down the parting in her hair. Then the women take their turns at circling a fistful of puffed rice in front of her. A girl sings a Tamil ritual song.

Shankara and Muttu's husband, Ravi, are sitting in a corner of the room. They are both wearing bright-coloured bush shirts and trousers. They are slightly drunk. The other men are in the outer room and cannot be seen.

MUTTU'S MOTHER: Come, Shankara. Now the girl's uncle has to pick her up and place her back on the plank. Come.

(Shankara doesn't move. He continues to ignore her, obviously sulking.)

    Come on. Hurry.

(There is no reply. The mother looks anxiously at Muttu. Muttu comes to Shankara.)

MUTTU: Come, Brother. Come and pick up Kalpana.

SHANKARA: No, I won't come. I won't pick her up. What's she to me? What am I to you? Nothing. No relation. Don't you know that?

MOTHER: Don't say such inauspicious things, Son. Come.

SHANKARA (*snarling*): Why shouldn't I? Look at Kalpana. Decorated. Decked out like a bride. For what you're spending this evening you could've celebrated her whole wedding here. But if it was my daughter sitting there instead of Kalpana—if it was *my* daughter—would you have splurged like this?

WIFE: Please, let's not rake that up now. Not in front of all the relatives.

SHANKARA (*shouts*): You keep your mouth shut, will you? I'm telling them I've nothing to do with them. Don't poke your nose in all this.

(*The guests sense trouble and get restive. The women get up and draw their children closer.*)

MOTHER: Why do you say that, Shankara? Your daughter's my granddaughter too. She's as—

SHANKARA: Oh, is she now? So you've at long last remembered that, have you? And what have you done for these granddaughters, eh? They're rotting in this village. Do you ever think of them in Bengaluru? Do you even remember that they exist? What've you done for my daughters? Tell me.

MOTHER: What could I've done, Shankara? What did I have when I first went there? I was an unlettered widow and I was asked to get out of the house with Muttu, once my husband died. You know that. In the city, I could just about eke out a living by stitching and darning and mending for those Marwadis— mosquito curtains, bed sheets, window curtains—My legs're gone, as you can all see, just pedalling that sewing machine. Eight hours every day. Ten hours. And still there wasn't enough. I lost my legs stitching and sewing. Don't you know that?

SHANKARA: Enough, I tell you. Shut up. We've been through that song and dance routine hundreds of times. I was the older child and yet you didn't take me to Bengaluru. You didn't even bother about me later. It was Muttu, always Muttu—

MOTHER: Shiva, Shiva! How can you blame me? What choice did I have? You were a male child. You think your grandparents would have let me take you with me? They slung me out of the house with Muttu, saying they couldn't look after us. That we were a millstone. We lived like beggars, like roofless orphans, in that monster city. And when I found a job 'twas as a seam-stress, chained to that sewing machine eight hours a day. Often even ten hours. What happiness did I ever see? It was all for you children—

SHANKARA: Don't you dare mention my children. How often did you spare a thought for us once you went there, eh? How often have you visited us?

MOTHER: Would your grandparents have let us into the house? I was the inauspicious woman who'd killed their son. But didn't your daughters come to the city? Didn't they stay with us in their holidays? We all loved having them. Didn't they enjoy the city?

SHANKARA: And came back hating this dump and our life here. You showed off nicely, I grant you that. Displayed how you and Muttu had flourished in the city, without us. How you'd pros-pered. And isn't that what you're here for now? To crow to our friends and relations—

MOTHER: God forbid. It was you who insisted we should have the rites here. You know that. You said we must have it here—

SHANKARA: Yes, so you would remember we're alive here. I had to practically drag you here. Would you've come otherwise? My wife's had two deliveries and you never offered to help.

MOTHER (*bursting into tears*): Why are you accusing me like this, Shankara? What help could I be? I can barely hobble. My legs swell if I so much as run around—

WIFE: Please, Husband, please, stop this now. All our relatives—

SHANKARA: I said shut up! Do you have any brains? Don't you understand if I tell you to shut up? One more word from you

and I'll thrash you in front of them. She treated us like pariahs—
She—she—
(*He virtually foams at his mouth.*)

Are you my mother? No, you're not. You are the mother of
Bengaluru Muttu. You've been no grandmother to my children.
Have you ever fondled them? Caressed them? You're a demon.
If we'd let you, you would even drink their blood. Aren't you
ashamed to call yourself my mother? You, you, I'll show you—
(*He attacks her. Starts beating her. Ravi, Muttu's husband, who has
so far been watching warily from a distance now jumps up and grabs
his hand.*)

RAVI: Are you in your senses, you drunken fool? If you're so sloshed,
go and sleep it off in a corner. Don't create a rumpus here.

SHANKARA: Ah! The great son-in-law himself. His royal self! Don't
you think I know who pays the fees of the English-medium
school? My daughters are condemned to Tamil schools, while
you stand pulling your locks in front of your mother-in—

RAVI: Hey! If you utter one more word I'll settle your hash right here.
Are you saying I can't pay for my own daughter?

SHANKARA: Go away! Your daughter—

RAVI: I warned you—
(*Attacks Shankara. They struggle. But Shankara is too drunk to fight
and Ravi beats him up. Pushes him into a corner from where his wife
helps him up and takes him away. There is pandemonium in the room.
The women gather their children and bundles and leave hurriedly.*)

WOMAN (*to the mother*): Ayyo, we've cooked food for thirty people.
They're all leaving. It'll all go waste. Please at least you have
some food.

MUTTU: Let's go, Mother. We've had enough of this home. Let's go
back to Bengaluru. I'm never going to step into this cursed town
again. I'm done with it. For ever. Come, Ma. Husband. Kalpana.
Let's go.

Scene Two

A new extension of the city, a virtually random arrangement of shapeless blocks of flats. Kunaal is sitting waiting patiently in a corner. Vimala arrives riding a scooter. She is surprised to see Kunaal.

VIMALA: Oh, Kunaal. What're you doing here?

KUNAAL: What else? Waiting for you.

VIMALA: How long have you been here? How did you get this address?

KUNAAL: I asked your sister-in-law.

VIMALA: She knew?

KUNAAL: Actually she didn't. I got it from Saroja Kunigal—you know, the lady who's accused you of stealing.

VIMALA (*suddenly rattled*): You mean—she had my address?

KUNAAL: Yes, and gave it to me without any fuss. She also added, 'Tell Vimala she can't escape me. I'll get her.'

VIMALA: Oh god! Such an evil woman.

KUNAAL: Is that your scooter?

VIMALA (*distracted*): What? Oh, this scooter? Where can I afford a scooter? It belongs to a cousin. He had to go away for a couple of days and has lent it to me.

KUNAAL: Why have you disappeared into thin air, Vimala? Mummy was waiting for you all day next day. The kitchen doesn't feel like one without you.

VIMALA: Who's been cooking?

KUNAAL: Mummy's got some temporary help. A Malayali woman.

VIMALA: Once the police have your address they start hounding you. They start visiting you. Every day. It's so embarrassing—attracts comments from the whole neighbourhood.

KUNAAL: My parents can help you there. You know they have friends in the police.

VIMALA: I don't want to bring you a bad name.

KUNAAL: No, you won't. Start coming to our house again from tomorrow.
(*An autorickshaw comes and stops nearby. A young man in the khaki uniform of a driver gets out, stands giving Kunaal a hostile stare, and then disappears round the corner.*)

KUNAAL: Will you come?

VIMALA: I don't know.

KUNAAL: Why not? We've no complaints against you. (*Laughs.*) Let me tell Mummy you're coming.

VIMALA (*horrified*): You aren't going to tell Amma you came and saw me here, are you? Please, don't. That'll only make matters worse.

KUNAAL: Why? I'm meeting you in broad daylight—in the open. Surely there's nothing wrong there.

VIMALA: There, that only means you don't understand. Please don't tell Amma you came to see me. She won't let me step into the house again.

KUNAAL: If she sends for you—
(*The young man comes out of the house and stands, glaring at them.*)

VIMALA: I'll give her a ring. I'll call this evening. No, tomorrow morning. But please, Kunaal, don't tell anyone about this house. I'm
tired of running.

KUNAAL: All right. (*To the young man*) Hello, I am Kunaal. I'm sure
Vimala has talked about me.
(*There is no reply.*)

VIMALA: He is my first cousin.

KUNAAL (*laughs*): Goodbye.
(*Goes off.*)

VIMALA: Don't let him worry you. Come in.

Scene Three

The Reception Room of a Wipro office. Prabhakar is wearing a new suit, a bright new tie, and shoes.

PRABHAKAR: Good morning. My name is Prabhakar Telang. I've an appointment here for an interview.

RECEPTIONIST: And with whom would that interview be, Sir?

PRABHAKAR: Mr A.K. Gopalan.
(The receptionist looks into her computer.)

RECEPTIONIST: Are you sure, Sir? He's not in today. I doubt if he's in India since even his Personal Secretary's on leave.

PRABHAKAR *(taking out a letter from his pocket)*: Here, I've a letter from Mrs Dolly—Mrs Rajalakshmi Iyer—confirming the interview.

RECEPTIONIST *(scans the computer)*: But I'm sorry, there's no one of that name on our staff. I can't see that name anywhere. What department—

PRABHAKAR: No, no, Mrs Iyer is not a staff member of Wipro. I know that. She's a friend of Mr Azim Premji's. Mr Premji has confirmed to Mrs Iyer that Mr Gopalan will interview me today here. It's all there in the letter.

RECEPTIONIST: I'm sorry but this isn't Mr Premji's office.

PRABHAKAR: I know that. I know it's not his office. You see, there's a post for the Regional Manager in the Singapore office of Wipro.

RECEPTIONIST: I'm sorry, Sir. I know nothing about all those things. I'm only a receptionist here.

PRABHAKAR: I know. That's why I'm explaining it all to you. I've already been selected for the post of a Regional Manager in Singapore. What's on today is not an interview really. The selection's already been made. This is just a show to—

RECEPTIONIST: Sorry, Sir. If you were to meet Mr Gopalan, it should've been there on my schedule for today. And it isn't. And he isn't here. I can't help you.

PRABHAKAR (*slowly panicking*): Please don't say that. This is an important matter. A matter of life and death, you could say. I have resigned from my permanent job, paid the penalty of two months' salary, vacated my house, sent my family back to the village. Please, please, help me.

RECEPTIONIST: I'm doing my best to help you, Sir. That's what I'm here for. But Mr Gopalan isn't in office today and I've no idea when he'll be back. You don't even have a proper letter of appointment from this office. So what am I supposed to do?

PRABHAKAR: Look, it's not just a matter of my job. It's my whole life. I've taken a loan of seventy thousand. My entire future—everything hinges on this—this one meeting. Call it an interview, a meeting, anything. You understand what I'm saying, don't you? I've resigned a very nice job—

(*The receptionist presses a button and a security guard comes in silently. Prabhakar notices him and laughs.*)

No, no, I won't become hysterical and attack you, I promise you. But try to understand my plight. If Mr Gopalan isn't there, is there anyone else? There must be someone who looks after his work in his absence—perhaps Mr Premji himself? He knows Mrs Iyer. And I've borrowed—pawned our village land—for the preliminary expenditure. Wait. Wait. I know. I'll call Mrs Iyer. Will you talk to her?

(*The receptionist nods. Prabhakar presses a button on his mobile. Listens. Then with great relief speaks.*)

Oh Dolly! Thank goodness, you're there. What a relief! I was beginning to panic. I'm in the Electronic City. In the Wipro office—as planned—That's it. That's it—The interview hasn't taken place. The receptionist says she has no information. I'm baffled too. Can you speak to her? Please. (*To the receptionist*) Here. That's Mrs Iyer. Can you talk to her? Please.

RECEPTIONIST (*speaking on the mobile*): Yes, Ma'am. Tell me—Yes, yes. He's explained all that but I've no intimation from my office about it. None at all—He's not in the office—Please, Ma'am. Don't shout. I'm only doing my duty. I don't have to talk to you. (*Hands back the mobile in exasperation to Prabhakar and waves him away. Goes back to her computer.*)

PRABHAKAR (*on the phone*): So, Dolly. What am I to do? All right. All right. I'll wait. (*To the receptionist*) She says she'll talk to Mr Premji and call me back.

RECEPTIONIST: You can wait here. No problem. (*When Prabhakar moves to a chair in the corner*) I hope you don't mind my saying so, Sir. But since I joined Wipro I've never heard of Mr Premji or his colleagues recommending anyone like this personally. It's entirely against the spirit of Wipro. People are selected on merit—

PRABHAKAR: But they've checked my merit and passed me.

RECEPTIONIST: Fine. Fine. Excuse me. I must get on with my work. (*Prabhakar dials Dolly's number on the phone. But it's quite clear it's busy.*)

PRABHAKAR (*half to himself*): It's a nightmare! Seventy thousand—the village land—and then—

Scene Four

The garden outside Anjana's house. Anjana is trimming the hedge but it is clear her mind is not on the job. She is visibly upset. A mobile starts ringing inside the house and keeps on ringing. Muttu picks it up and comes rushing out.

MUTTU: Amma, Amma—Amma, your phone.
(*Anjana hurriedly wipes her tears.*)

ANJANA (*takes the phone*): Who's it? Oh, Vimala—Where are you? And when are you coming?—What?—Oh please don't tell me that. You can't do that to us! When are you coming back?—Ohho! All right. Come back as soon as possible.
(*She has been sniffing while talking on the phone. So ...*)

Nothing, nothing. Just a bad cold.
(*Switches off the phone and calls.*)

Muttu—
(*Muttu is right behind her near the door, having come to a sudden halt as soon as Vimala's name was mentioned.*)

MUTTU: Amma—

ANJANA: That was Vimala. She says she can't come back for another week. Some problem—has to go to her village. What're we going to do if she goes off like that? And Karunashraya is chock-a-block this week. They need every hand desperately. I can't let the nurses down at the last minute. We'll have to ask the hired cook—what's her name—if she can come for another week. Has she arrived?

MUTTU: Shalini rang earlier. When you were near the gate. Her child is sick. She won't be coming for the next two or three days, she says.

ANJANA: Oh dear! What then? Restaurant food for a week? I hate the thought.

MUTTU (*softly*): Amma—

ANJANA: Yes—

MUTTU: I can cook.

ANJANA: You can? And you didn't mention it all these days?

MUTTU: Vimala told me not to mention it. 'Just stick to your job,' she said.

ANJANA: Can you then handle the kitchen till she comes back? Bless you. You know Mr Padabidri's rarely home. And Kunaal loves eating out—UB City, Mainland China. It's just me. And of course there's Kunaal's grandma, for the next couple of weeks. But she handles her own food. You know that. Just basic food will do for me.

MUTTU: Yes, I do, Amma. And, Amma, I'm a Mudaliar by caste so—

ANJANA: Oh, for goodness sake, I'm not interested in your caste. Can you cook a decent meal? Rice and lentils?

MUTTU: Yes, I can, Amma.

ANJANA: Good. That's all that matters. Just whip up something for me then. Anything. With whatever's there in the kitchen.

(*Muttu doesn't move.*)

Go on. If you need any help, call me.

MUTTU (*in a low voice*): Amma, we've run out of cooking gas.

ANJANA: No gas? Nonsense. We have four cylinders.

MUTTU: There are only two in the house. And they're both empty.

ANJANA: I can't believe it. There should be four. Come. Let me see.
(*Starts to go in.*)

MUTTU: Vimala has lent the other two to Professor Menon's family.

ANJANA: Who? Who's this Professor Menon?

MUTTU: Our neighbours. Recent arrivals. Their gas connection hasn't
been sanctioned yet. So they've borrowed two of our cylinders.
They've promised her they'll return them the moment—

ANJANA (*incredulous*): Vimala's given them two of our cylinders
without telling me? I can't believe it.
(*No reply.*)

Does she take money from them for the cylinders?

MUTTU: I don't know, Amma.

ANJANA: Since when's this been going on?

MUTTU: I don't know, Amma. That family moved into our neighbourhood some four months ago. We've only had two cylinders
since then.

ANJANA: How terrible! Muttu, go to their house instantly and say we
want the cylinders back. Right now.
(*Muttu doesn't move.*)

Hurry. And don't accept any excuses. The shameless—

MUTTU: Amma, shall I also bring the microwave back?

ANJANA: The microwave? But our microwave—

MUTTU: The old one. Actually it wasn't working too well when they took it. But they've got it repaired and ours is giving a bit of trouble. And also the mixer—

ANJANA: Have they looted our entire kitchen? What else has she gifted to these Menons?

MUTTU: That's all. But they can keep the mixer. Our new one's very good.

ANJANA: And what about the fridge? Has she hired that out too?

MUTTU (*smiles*): No, Amma. It's too heavy.

ANJANA: Heavens! And all this under my very nose! I'd never have— Now go and tell them we want everything back. Even forks and spoons, if they've taken them. And this has been going on for four months!
(*Muttu is about to leave but stops.*)

MUTTU: Pardon me, Amma. Is there any bad news?

ANJANA: Bad news? Why?

MUTTU: Your eyes—
(*She indicates tears rolling down her cheeks with her two index fingers.*)

ANJANA (*wiping her cheeks*): Our rain tree. It's lying there looking so helpless. Like a baby. Just the trunk and the roots. I can't bear it.
(*Tears well up again and she wipes them. Muttu looks amused and goes in.*)

Scene Five

The race course. Anusuya and Sundara Rajan, poring over the racing notes.

ANUSUYA: Good. Let's go through it again so we're sure. Read that list again please.

SUNDARA RAJAN: Win and place for Number Three. Then Numbers Five, Eight, and Eleven for the second place?

ANUSUYA: Do you think Number Three is okay for a Win? Or should it be Eight, do you think? You know Eight won twice in Hyderabad. But somehow Three seems—why aren't you saying anything?

SUNDARA RAJAN: I won't say anything, Madam. You ask my opinion now and if the horse loses, you hold me responsible. I don't want anything to do with it.

ANUSUYA (*laughs*): Why would I grumble if your advice was anywhere near right? But look, look, look. I missed that completely. Flash Past. His father was Kubla Khan. And mother—what do you know? Queen Serenghetti. I would have missed him completely. They print these details in such small print. Queen

Serenghetti. Do you know Serenghetti? My daughter Leena lives in Nairobi and she wrote to say that she went with her friends to the Serenghetti Park. I received her letter only yesterday and here it is! What a coincidence! Not a coincidence but a sign, surely! How much time do we have before the next race, Sundara Rajan?

SUNDARA RAJAN: Barely five minutes. Some two horses are to get into the boxes.

ANUSUYA: Then hurry up please! Bet on Flash Past. Twenty thousand for a Win.

SUNDARA RAJAN: Twenty thousand?

ANUSUYA: Yes, yes. Hurry, Number Four! Flash Past. Son of Queen Serenghetti. How could I miss him!

SUNDARA RAJAN: But look at the odds. That horse can't possibly win. Perhaps we can place a smaller—

ANUSUYA: Don't argue with me for god's sake. This is the last race of the season. Our last chance. Go. Run. Number Four. Flash Past. Twenty thousand.

SUNDARA RAJAN: Madam—

ANUSUYA (*fiercely*): I said go!
(*Sundara Rajan rushes to the booking window. She moves to the front of the gallery and leans on the balustrade. Sundara Rajan comes running and stands next to her.*)

ANUSUYA: Done? Good. Now!
(*The race begins and its progress is covered by the commentary on the soundtrack. They both watch eagerly and she gets wildly excited as the noise of the crowd swells.*)

ANUSUYA: Ayyayyo! Seven—Two's leading. Where the hell're our horses? They can't all be dead! Ah, there. There it is. Number Eight. Hurray. Keep it up. Eight!

SUNDARA RAJAN: Please, Madam. Be careful. Don't get too excited. Madam—

ANUSUYA (*screaming*): Ayyo! Look, it's Number Four coming up. *Our* Number Four. It's our Flash Past. Son of Queen Se—e— That's it. He's overtaken the rest. He's leading. That's it! Four! Four! Sundara Rajan—My fluke. He's won—He's won—Four! Hurrah—

(*Falls down in a faint.*)

SUNDARA RAJAN: Madam, Madam—

Scene Six

Anjana's living room. Dolly, sitting alone. A cement mixer which is roaring on the road outside goes suddenly silent. Dolly starts speaking on the mobile. At that exact moment the doorbell rings. Dolly ignores it, but while she is speaking, Muttu runs in from the kitchen and goes to attend to the door.

DOLLY: God, the racket outside! Can't hear a word. They're building the underpass. Thanks for the message. But, actually, tomorrow evening we've been invited to the Governor's Residence. A special concert. And do you know my husband forgot to tell me? What can you do with him?—It's Ayaan and Amaan, sons of Ustad Amjad Ali Khan.

(Muttu comes and stands signalling. Dolly, covering the mobile, gestures to ask her what she wants.)

MUTTU: Someone to see you, Madam.

DOLLY: Me? Here?

MUTTU: Says his name is Prabhakar Telang.

DOLLY: Oh? Ask him in.

(Muttu goes to the front door.)

I'll call you back. Someone to see me.

(*Switches off the mobile and prepares to meet Prabhakar. Muttu comes in followed by Prabhakar and goes in.*)

DOLLY: Oh, you! What're you doing here?

PRABHAKAR: I've come to see you. What else?

DOLLY: This isn't my house, you realize?

PRABHAKAR: I know. But I knew Anjana and Kunaal wouldn't be here now and you would. I'm without a job, you see. I spend all my time studying the movements of people.

DOLLY: Following someone around is called stalking. It's a legal offence.

PRABHAKAR: Why did you do it? Was it really necessary?

DOLLY: Was what necessary?

PRABHAKAR: That's great. You ask me. My wife's refusing to come back to Bangalore. She says what humiliation she's suffered will last her a lifetime. I'm penniless. Why did you do it?

DOLLY: You're right. Why do I do it? I keep asking that question to myself. Why do I want to run around and then get blamed in the end? I know some influential people; they could be of help; they're willing to help. But in the end I get the blame. My husband keeps asking me that question. I run around for months arranging everything and you don't show me the courtesy of waiting there for half an hour more.

PRABHAKAR: Where?

DOLLY: In the Wipro office. I rang after half an hour and you were gone. You threw a tantrum, the receptionist told me.

PRABHAKAR: And what was I to do sitting there? And for how long? Do you know how desperately I tried ringing you? And you were busy. Busy. I couldn't get through to you—

DOLLY (*flares up*): What else did you expect me to be if not busy? Talk of ingratitude. Of course, my mobile was busy. Because I was trying to get in touch with Azim Premji, to find out what'd gone wrong. You think he's so easy to contact? Fortunately he was in Malaysia. At least I could talk to him. In the States it would have been midnight. And he got in touch with his office. He didn't know Gopalan was away. But he told Phillips. And insisted the arrangements had to go through.

PRABHAKAR (*incredulous*): He called the office? That day?

DOLLY: Yes, immediately, for my sake. And instructed Phillips to proceed as planned. That day. But where were *you*? You'd simply vanished.

PRABHAKAR: I was seriously contemplating suicide.

DOLLY: And didn't go ahead, I can see. Instead you've created the most embarrassing situation for me. Dreadful. I've never been in such a predicament before. I can't face my friends. I haven't seen Azim and Yasmeen since that day—and we used to meet every other day. And then you've the gall to ask me if that was necessary! You've the bloody cheek!

(*A long pause. Then*)

PRABHAKAR: Before I came in now, I was standing outside, for nearly ten minutes, wondering if I should enter. The concrete mixer was bellowing away, so I knew we wouldn't hear each other anyway. And I was fascinated by that mixer with its huge grotesque striped belly. And those bright yellow long-necked earth diggers and extractors with sharp claws and fangs. What are they here for? For me. So I could use these streets. Go over flyovers. Flow with the crowds. To give meaning to all this—this mess, this chaos. I keep asking myself: what keeps things working at all in this city? What drives these crowds? Hope. Ambition. Whatever. It's our version of the American Dream, which would've horrified my parents, but has brought me to Bangalore. It seemed poised to lead me on to Singapore. But no matter. Despite the lesson you've taught me, Dolly, I promise you, I shall pursue that dream. I shall be relentless in a—

(*Suddenly the concrete mixer erupts into action again outside, with a deafening roar. They can't hear each other. He shrugs his shoulders, laughs loudly, waves goodbye, and moves to the door. There he runs into Brigadier Iyer coming in, bows to him elaborately as though they were old friends, and walks out. Baffled, the brigadier turns to his wife to ask who that was. Dolly gestures that she hasn't a clue. They go out. The noise outside continues.*)

Scene Seven

Muttu's house in another part of Bangalore. Vimala arrives on a scooter. Calls out.

VIMALA: Muttu—Muttu—
(*Honks loudly. Muttu enters.*)

MUTTU: Oh, Vimala! How nice. Come in. Come in.

VIMALA: No time to come in. Let's talk here. How're you?

MUTTU: Okay. As usual.

VIMALA (*smiling*): Oh, better than usual, surely. You've got a promotion.

MUTTU (*confused*): What was I to do? Amma said you hadn't come or you weren't coming or something like that. Asked me to take charge till you came back. That's all.

VIMALA: And you got stuck for good. Very nice. I worked there for eight years. You've set yourself up for the next eight now.

MUTTU (*her eyes fill up*): No, I swear to you I didn't mean to steal your place. If you decide to come back today, say so and I'll happily go back to the cleaning and washing. I promise.

VIMALA: Is your mother in?

MUTTU: Yes. Busy with her stitching and sewing. As usual.

VIMALA: Can I say hello to her?

MUTTU: Of course. Mother, Vimala's here!

MOTHER (*from inside*): Why don't you ask her to come in? Sit down for a while?

VIMALA: Do you mind coming out? Please. I don't want to leave the scooter in the street. You can never be sure.
(*Muttu's mother hobbles out on her stick.*)

How are you, Gangamma?

MOTHER: What can I say? You know my legs. They're gone. All that—

MUTTU: I asked her to step in and sit for a while. But she won't.

VIMALA: Let's skip the formalities now. What I've come to tell you is, when I was in trouble your daughter grabbed my job. It was nicely done.

MUTTU: That's not true. I promise you—

VIMALA: Shut up! Who snitched to Amma about the gas cylinders? Those two cylinders were lying idle, and my only thought was to help the Menons, poor them. That's all. I didn't steal them for myself, did I? And yet you tattled to Amma—

MUTTU: No, no, listen, please. There was no gas in the house—

VIMALA (*almost fiercely*): Stop whining and listen to me. You swiped my job and saw to it that I would never get it back. (*To the mother*) Now let me give you a piece of news. Your son Shankara. He's in Bengaluru.

MUTTU: Really? Where?

MOTHER: How do you know my Shankara?

VIMALA: Don't you remember? You brought him to Amma's house to see Muttu. About her daughter's growing-up ceremony. I never forget a face. How else do you think I've survived in this city?

MOTHER (*already getting panic-stricken*): Shankara's here? Where's he?

VIMALA: Listen to me. A few days after that row he had with you and Muttu's husband in your village, he moved to this city. He's left his wife and daughters back home and bought himself an auto-rickshaw. He lives here.

MOTHER: Oh god! Why didn't he tell us?

VIMALA: Why would he? He hates you like poison. Get in touch with you? He hasn't let on to anyone here anything about himself. Where he's from. His name. Address. Nothing. I went to see my cousin at the auto stand and who should I see there but ...? When I said, 'Aren't you Muttu's brother, Shankara?' he almost jumped out of his skin.

MUTTU: Where's he?

VIMALA: He shares a garage with some half-a-dozen young men—all auto drivers.

MOTHER: Ayyo, why does my son do things like that?

MUTTU: How's he?

VIMALA: That's what I came to tell you. He's in the hospital.

MUTTU and MOTHER: Hospital? What happened? Oh mother of mine—

VIMALA: Half a dozen boys in a room together. Can't you imagine the shenanigans? Drinks. Drugs. Street women. Apparently there was a fight the other day. They brought out their bicycle chains and knives. Now he is in the general ward of a hospital wrapped up in bandages. And the hospital won't keep him for long if he doesn't produce some cash. (*Pause.*) And in this entire city, only I know who he is.

MOTHER: Please, please, I must go and see him immediately. Right now.

MUTTU: Hold on, Mother. Let's at least find out the name of the hospital.

VIMALA: There you are, practical as usual. You've a permanent job now. You've eight years in which to find out where he is. If he lives that long. Bye—

(*Turns to go. The mother tries to stop her, but cannot catch up with her and collapses on the road. Muttu grabs hold of Vimala.*)

MUTTU: Please, Vimala. Please. Tell us where he is. You can't do this to us. Mother'll die of anxiety.

VIMALA: I don't give a damn. Enjoy your job. Let go of me!

Muttu: Vimala—please—

(*Vimala pushes Muttu aside, gets on the scooter, and drives off. Muttu runs to her mother and helps her up.*)

MUTTU: Don't believe her. I won't swallow a word she's saying. She's a liar. Always was.

MOTHER: No, no, she's telling the truth. I can feel it in my bones. My Shankara's in trouble, Muttu. We must find him. He's lying in some hospital! I know she's telling the truth—

MUTTU: All right, all right. I'll tell Husband. We'll look for him. Don't worry, Mother. Husband's bound to find him. Come in now.

(*Helps her up.*)

Scene Eight

Night. Bedroom in Anjana's house. Anusuya is resting and Kunaal is sitting by the bedside.

ANUSUYA: What's this band of yours, Kunu? And why are your parents so unhappy about it? You used to play the veena and so well too. We all thought you would grow up to be a great veena player.

KUNAAL: Will you come and listen to my band?

ANUSUYA: No, I won't, if you don't mind. I just can't come to all those places. But send me a cassette and I'll listen to it.

KUNAAL: No one makes cassettes any more, Grandma. And I haven't managed to get an album out yet.

ANUSUYA: Why not?

KUNAAL: The music companies want me to add something 'Indian' to my music. 'Add a flute,' they say, 'or some tabla. You know. Sitar, Indian culture. A few strains of veena. Then it'll have a market.'

ANUSUYA: But what's wrong with that? It is our music.

KUNAAL: It's not my music, Grandma.

ANUSUYA: But you were so good at the veena.

KUNAAL: I know. Papa and Mummy would've been happier—or let me say, less unhappy—if I'd continued with that. Veena is so prestigious!

ANUSUYA: But all those years of training—are they going to be wasted?

KUNAAL: No, no, they've proved most useful. My fingertips had got calloused thanks to the veena. They were in condition for the guitar.

ANUSUYA: I suppose I should leave it all to you. You know what it's about. But do you know where you get your talent from? Your mother. She was so gifted—a divine voice she had. Every time she sang, the women of my age in Dharwad would sigh and say, 'I wish I could have her as my daughter-in-law.'

KUNAAL: She did become your daughter-in-law.

ANUSUYA: To tell you the truth—I suppose I can tell you now—when she agreed to marry your father, it broke my heart. He has no art in him whatsoever. You get it all from her. I often wonder why she said yes to him. (*Kunaal is amused and laughs.*) Somehow, after marriage, she lost her gift. And I don't suppose he's even noticed.

KUNAAL: She hums—rarely. A nice voice. The problem with her is that she feels she must support Papa. I've a suspicion that deep down she doesn't at all mind my heavy metal band. But she stood behind Papa when they struggled in their youth. Now she must be at his side in their old age. The devoted Hindu wife.

ANUSUYA: You should've heard her sing—specially the compositions of Saint Purandara Dasa. The entire audience would be moved to tears.

KUNAAL (*excited*): That's it, Grandma. I consider myself an avatar of Purandara Dasa too. Truly. He composed his own songs. So do I. He broke away from traditional music. So have I. And he never played in the royal courts. He took to the streets. You told me that. And I don't play in the pompous concert halls either. For me it's the clubs, garages, and pubs. I don't believe in God. But in a way, I suppose, music is my god.

ANUSUYA: That's all right then. If that's what you believe. You know Purandara Dasa searched for God all over the world. And then he didn't even know it when God came and stood, right in front of him. I thought all that was possible in earlier ages. Treta. Dwaapara. But I tell you, Kunu, when that Number Four, Flash Past, suddenly shot out and overtook the other horses, I—I—I suddenly had that vision. How can I describe it? At that moment I saw God. Vividly. For a moment He was there—for me. Real. I saw Him. Then I don't know if it was the Truth or just an illusion. I'm not that erudite. And perhaps that's why Flash Past lost at the last moment. If he'd won and I had collected all that cash, it wouldn't be a divine experience, would it? It would've been just a fluke, not a vision. God's not there to keep us company permanently. He shows Himself and is gone. And for me that was enough. God showed himself to me. (*Her eyes fill up with tears.*) What more could I ask for in this life?

(*She wipes her tears. He too is deeply moved by her words. They continue to sit in silence.*)

Scene Nine

The Padabidri living room. Dolly, alone, talking to someone on the mobile.

DOLLY: … And what your boyfriend told me simply amazed me. (*Muttu enters.*)

Excuse me, just hold on.
(*Dolly lowers her mobile to listen to Muttu.*)

MUTTU: Madam, Amma called. The train left on time. But the traffic's so bad they're stuck on South End Circle. They may not be home for another fifteen minutes.

DOLLY (*eager to continue her phone conversation*): Thanks.

MUTTU: It was just like that here outside our house too, Madam. Noise, honking, petrol fumes. Thank god for the underpass. It's so peaceful now. Shall I make you some tea in the meanwhile?

DOLLY (*waving her away*): Not to worry. My husband will be here any moment.

MUTTU: It won't take a minute. Boiling hot and just one spoonful of sugar. I know.
(*She goes in. As she continues on the mobile, Dolly peers out of the window to make sure her husband hasn't arrived and continues.*)

DOLLY: No, no, it's no favour. I just happen to know some influential people. Two years in ballet and then Bharatanatyam—that's some training, Asha. You can't just throw all that away! I know the director of the Trinity Laban Dance School in London and he was asking me why they didn't get enough students from India. Despite all the facilities—No, money's no problem. That's the thing. There are scholarships. And bright girls like you must make use of them.

(*Brigadier Iyer enters and stands silently listening. She is so carried away by her own words she doesn't notice his arrival.*)

It's laughable that a dancer like you should be a dance teacher in a school. That's no better than being a drill teacher, is it? My advice is resign the job and get out. Launch out. Don't wait. You must leave immediately and go for an—

(*Notices her husband and switches off her mobile, halfway through the sentence, and waits tensely for his next move. He glares, then goes up to her, and starts slapping her. She puts up with it as though she is used to it. In a low voice*)

Not here. Not here. Please.

(*Muttu steps in with her tray carrying a pot of tea. She pretends not to have noticed what's been happening.*)

BRIGADIER (*in a flat voice to Dolly*): We had a flat tire. I've asked the car to be taken home directly once the puncture's repaired. Took a cab here. Let's go.

(*He goes out. Dolly turns to Muttu.*)

DOLLY: Tell Anjana I had to go back urgently. And here, if you're ever in need, just call me.

(*As she puts the mobile back into her handbag, she takes out a five hundred rupee note and gives it to Muttu who takes it without a thank you and tucks it in the sari-knot on her waist. Dolly leaves. Muttu's mobile rings. She speaks.*)

MUTTU: Oh god, Mother, I've told you a hundred times not to ring me here. Amma doesn't like it. Yes, yes, Husband's in touch with the police and they're looking for him. Bye. I must rush.

(*Switches it off. To herself in exasperation*)

As though we've nothing else to do. The brute. He'll get in touch if he needs to. I don't give a shit.

(*Anjana and Kunaal come in.*)

Dolly madam and her husband were here and said they had to go.

ANJANA: Yes, I saw them.

MUTTU: Some Mr Raykar called three times. Wanted your mobile number but I refused to give it to him. He's left his number.

(*Gives a piece of paper to Anjana. At the mention of Raykar, Kunaal becomes attentive.*)

And I've brought a woman to do the cleaning and ironing. She's a neighbour—

ANJANA (*transferring the number to her mobile*): Ask her to wait, please.

(*Muttu leaves. Anjana, almost to herself*)

Raykar? Some new admission?

KUNAAL: He's a pawnbroker. A moneylender.

ANJANA (*startled*): How do you know?

KUNAAL: There is only one person in our house who is aware of everything that's going on here. Not you, not me. Our driver, Francis. I asked him and he told me. Grandma often dropped in at Raykar's on the way to the races. So I went and met Raykar. Grandma's been borrowing money from him. Regularly.

ANJANA: You knew all along! And didn't let me know?

KUNAAL: I didn't see why I should if she didn't want to. I assured him the deal was safe and told him to carry on. I said not to disturb the arrangement until she was gone. (*Pause.*) Now she's gone and he's on the phone. She's borrowed close to two-and-a-half lakhs from him.

ANJANA (*horrified*): She has what? (*He shrugs.*) But two-and-a-half lakhs, Kunu!

KUNAAL: Did you never wonder where she got all the money to bet on the horses? Week after week?

ANJANA: But—but—this Raykar—he trusted her with that amount?

KUNAAL: She pawned her jewellery.

ANJANA : Oh my god! Kunu!

KUNAAL: What?

ANJANA: Her gold bangles and diamond earrings and pearl pendants— Two-and-a-half lakhs splurged on horses!

KUNAAL: Why not? Her son can afford it. Why shouldn't she indulge? If she'd asked for money, she would have been treated to long sermons by both of you. And I know how *that* feels. Actually I feel decimated that this method of conning Papa never occurred to me. I feel such a dunderhead. She's a true genius.

ANJANA: Don't you feel ashamed to say these things against your father? He would be heartbroken if he heard about his mother—

KUNAAL: Not for the first time, I'm sure.

ANJANA: Yes, he's made money. So what's wrong with that? Do you know how he's slogged for it—travelled all over the world— worked through the nights? And what gives you the right to run him down? I haven't seen you have qualms about spending his money.

KUNAAL: I know and I don't care. What amazes me is how you stick by him. Does it really matter to him what you or I do? Even Grandma says you've let your singing go to pot for his sake and he hasn't even noticed.

ANJANA (*astounded*): Did Grandma really say that?

KUNAAL: Something like that. She should know.

ANJANA: No, she doesn't. She is wrong. (*Pause.*) Very wrong.

KUNAAL (*turning away*): There you go. I knew—

ANJANA: No, no, that's one thing I won't let you blame your father for. She's wrong. All right. Since you've asked me, let me tell you—

KUNAAL: What?

(*Pause, as Anjana gathers courage to continue. Kunaal, impatiently*)

What?

ANJANA: You should probably know about it anyway. You're old enough now. You were not even two then. We'd just moved to Bangalore and were living in a chawl—two tiny rooms in a corner. And Papa worked. He travelled around day and night as an Operations Manager. He was making plenty of money. But he was never there when I wanted him. I don't blame him. I could feel myself slowly going crazy. And to keep myself sane, I used to sing out—loudly.

(*Pause.*)

One day there was a knock on the door. It was a young man who lived next door to us. A Bengali. He too was alone. No friends, no relations. I can't remember what he did. Some kind of a software job that kept him mostly at home. When he realized how welcome he was, he started coming regularly to our house. He would come. Laugh. Crack jokes. Play with you.

(*Pause.*)

He had a nice voice and we often sang together—mostly Hindi film songs. But also Rabindra Sangeet, which he taught me. Even the correct Bong pronunciation. With him around, time just flew.

(*Pause.*)

I woke up one day and he was gone. He had vacated his room and left. He had tacked a note for me on my door. It said, 'I don't

wish to be trapped into a relationship with a married woman.'
Trapped!
(*Pause.*)

I used to suffer from insomnia those days. Had a large caché of
sleeping pills. I ground some pills in milk and fed them to you. I
swallowed the rest. I then prayed to the gods, clasped you to me,
and went to sleep—never to wake up again.
(*Pause.*)

I don't know how long we were sleeping like that. No one
would've known for days if we'd died. But I suddenly opened
my eyes and sat up. Bright and wide-eyed. I was alive and so
were you. Death had cheated us both.
(*A very long pause. At last*)

I could never sing again after that. I'd lost my voice.
(*Pause.*)

KUNAAL: Why do you say that? I've heard you sing—or at least hum
in your bathroom—

ANJANA: I found it again, years later, in Karunashraya. One evening,
I was sitting with a patient—she'd only a couple hours to live—
and she said to me, 'Can you sing? Will you sing something
for me?' And I suddenly found myself singing. A composition of Purandara Dasa's. 'When you've been given human life,
and have a tongue, shouldn't you sing of Krishna?' The song
just poured out, on its own. (*Pause.*) And so did the tears. At
long last.
(*Pause.*)

But somehow singing never meant the same again.

KUNAAL: Have you ever told this to Papa?

ANJANA: No, but perhaps I should tell Grandma.
(*They laugh. A long pause.*)

KUNAAL (*with great difficulty*): I'm only asking because you mentioned him—but did you—were you in—Did you love that
young man?

ANJANA (*as though trying to sort out her memories*): I don't think so. If
I had, do you think I would've reacted as I did?
(*Kunaal's face brightens.*)

KUNAAL: That's all right then. Nothing really happened!

ANJANA: I could have lost you!
(*Suddenly she hugs him. They stand still for a couple of minutes, holding
on to each other, in a rare, tight embrace. Then Anjana moves back
wiping her tears.*)

KUNAAL: You know what, I'm going to set those words of Purandara
Dasa's to music. To *my* music. And then we'll have a proper
show. We'll present you on stage: 'The Kunaal Padabidri Band
presents Anjana Padabidri, the Singing Sensation …'

ANJANA: Spare me, please. Do what you like, but leave me alone. In
any case, no one'll hear my voice in all the racket you make.
(*They both laugh. Anjana moves calling out to Muttu.*)

Muttu, this new cleaning woman—
(*She goes in. Kunaal sits, brooding. Then slowly he pulls out his mobile
and speaks into it.*)

KUNAAL: Nandita, I've just realized something I'd never thought of
before. I might not have been here at all now. I may never have
existed, and yet the world would've continued to be, exactly as
it is now. I mean. This world, this city, Bangalore, my friends,
family, you—everything would have existed, but not me. I
could be inside some black hole! I wouldn't be existing. What
an utterly horrible thought! But if I didn't exist, whether the rest
of the universe existed or not, *that* wouldn't have mattered in
the least, would it?—
(*As he speaks, behind him, the stage fills with the characters of the play.
They are not stiff now or frozen, and stand at ease listening to him. A*

girl, presumably Nandita, comes and sits close to him, smiling at what
he is saying. He puts aside his mobile, takes out his guitar from its case
and starts strumming it as he continues to speak to her.)

That's going to be my new composition—yes—my paean to
Bangalore that might never have existed. You know what's the
first line? 'Big Bang Bangalore is a Big Black Hole!'
(*Gentle laughter from the crowd. He starts humming a tune and trying*
it out on his guitar.)

(*Fade out.*)

Plays by Girish Karnad

Translation

Evam Indrajit by Badal Sircar   1974

Dates refer to the year of publication. All the plays have been published by Oxford University Press, except *Talé-Daṇḍa*, which was initially published by Ravi Dayal, Publisher, but is now an Oxford University Press title.

Appendix
Note on Translating My Own Plays

During my teens I wanted to write poetry in English and become an internationally renowned poet. But unexpectedly, before leaving for Oxford at the age of twenty-two, I found myself writing in Kannada— that too a play, inspired by a myth. That traumatic experience literally dictated my future. I decided to continue to write plays and only in Kannada. I didn't think I would ever look beyond.

However, the decision of the National School of Drama in the 1960s to become truly 'national' and look for plays from regional languages created a demand for dramatic texts translated from vernacular drama into Hindi. The success of the NSD production of Adya Rangacharya's *Kelu Janamejaya* (*Suno Janmejaya*), translated by B.V. Karanth and Nemi Chandra Jain, led to a sudden interest in whatever was available in Kannada and my *Tughlaq* was discovered. I personally had nothing to do with the process of translating it. Karanth translated it sitting by a lantern during the blackout that enveloped Delhi during the Indo-Pak war of 1965. I was only pulled into the swirl of self-translating when Alyque Padamsee asked me for an English version for presentation by the Theatre Group in 1968.

That's when I took a decision which was to affect my entire career as a playwright: I decided to do the English translation myself, a decision prompted by the following reason. Unlike in a novel, in theatre words need to be *spoken* and that too in front of an audience, which means the dialogue needs to have the kind of structuring of sentences, and allow for the kind of articulation, in which the actors can *breathe* through it. Most Indian translators have no awareness whatever of the problems involved in writing words which have to be pronounced aloud on stage, because normally they only deal with prose as it is read silently on the page.

I had been dealing with this problem since going to Oxford. There, I was active in the Oxford Union, a debating society, and was familiar with the demands speaking on stage makes on the words and rhythms one chooses to use. On my return to India, I became active in an amateur acting group called the Madras Players, with whom for over seven years, I dealt with the works of writers as varied as Arthur Miller, Tennessee Williams, Peter Shaffer, and Harold Pinter. We were none of us professionals, our use of language was crude and second-hand, but for me it nevertheless meant a hands-on experience of language on stage.

I need scarcely add that the use of language in the Oxford Union, with its pretence to authority, confidence, and charm is very different from its use in theatre with its attempts to catch the nuances of human frailty. Not just the words and voice but the use of breath is different in the two enterprises.

During my later years with the Madras Players, thanks to the notion of an 'Indian theatre' encouraged by the NSD, new plays by writers of the calibre of Mohan Rakesh and Vijay Tendulkar began to emerge from regional languages, and tired of the foreign fare, which was technically accomplished but culturally remote, I plunged into translating Badal Sircar's *Ebong Indrajit*. I was excited by the Bangla production I saw in Calcutta, there was an excellent Hindi translation available by Pratibha Agrawal which I used as a basis, and Sircar vetted the translation himself for accuracy. The experience of producing this translation on stage for the Madras Players gave me a new confidence, so when Alyque asked for an English version of *Tughlaq*, I took on the task myself.

I should add that my guru, Professor A.K. Ramanujan, had expressed interest in translating *Tughlaq*, but I declined most reluctantly. Turning down a request from such a towering figure in the field of translation was not easy, but Ramanujan's entire approach, as he has so brilliantly explained, was conditioned by how the text could be re-mapped on the printed page rather than breathed out by actors moving about on stage. The problems to which I sought solutions were different.

One great advantage of this decision was that I was able to improve the text while translating it. I didn't have to treat the original as sacrosanct and often took liberties with it, which often exasperated Karanth, who after struggling with a difficult passage translating it into Hindi, found that in my English translation I had simply chosen to skirt around the difficulty by taking an entirely different route. It has even happened that after watching my play enacted on stage or hitting upon more felicitous phrasing in English, I have altered the original in the Kannada reprint of the text.

A whole new dimension was brought to the situation when Ravi Dayal, who was with Oxford University Press then, decided to publish the English translation of *Tughlaq*. I, as a friend of Ravi's and colleague from the OUP days, opposed the move as I thought no one would be interested in buying an English version of a Kannada play. But I was proved wrong. In the 1960s many new universities were burgeoning in India, they all had departments of English and needed to teach drama as a subject. We are all children of Shakespeare and Wordsworth, but Terence Ratigan and Noel Coward—even George Bernard Shaw—meant nothing to this generation, and texts like *Silence! The Court Is in Session* and *Tughlaq* were exactly the texts to which the students responded directly. *Tughlaq* as a published text in English proved a success, was prescribed as an academic text in several universities, and sold in large numbers. This was an entirely new audience for my work.

Thereafter I translated all my plays into English myself for publication by OUP, which helped the plays to reach out to a much larger audience than would have been accessed by the Hindi version alone. My plays have been translated into almost all Indian regional languages, and when someone, who has no access to Kannada, wishes to translate my plays into his or her language, I advise the translator to refer to both the English and Hindi versions as the basis: the English, being the playwright's translation, contains as precisely as possible what he means to say, while the Hindi has the ability to use Sanskrit and Hindi words lost in the English, overcoming the disadvantage of a foreign language.

And I have been fortunate in finding translators like B.V. Karanth, Ram Gopal Bajaj, and Padmavathi Rao, who, apart from being at home in Hindi, were also friends and happy to work with me.

The only exception is the Hindi translation of *Yayati* which is poor since the late B.V. Narayana's Hindi is turgid and it was published without being shown to me. In point of fact, I am now unhappy with the original Kannada text itself as it was my first play and many moments in it sound immature to me. I have completely rewritten the play in Kannada and English (which is included in this volume) and can only hope to get a new translation in Hindi to replace the current one.

To sum up, I translate my own plays in English because I don't know a more reliable translator for my plays in English. Three years at Oxford, seven with OUP and the Madras Players, and then the last thirty-odd years conversing in English with my wife and children at home—these are qualifications that few other Indian translators can match!

The other reason is that even if someone wishes to use the Hindi version as the basis for taking my play into Kashmiri, Malayalam, or whatever language, the English will be there as a 'conduit' of my intent.

Let me point out that not all these texts are translations.

Nāga-Mandala was jotted down in a rough draft in Kannada which I then shaped into an English text for the students of the University of Chicago.

The Dreams of Tipu Sultan was commissioned by BBC Radio, and since the resource material was available only in English, there seemed to be no point in contorting one's way through Kannada first.

The Fire and the Rain was commissioned for a theatre workshop organized by the Guthrie Theatre, Minneapolis, with American actors and, therefore, although I started with a very rough draft in Kannada, the work evolved as I worked along with them and my excellent Dramaturge Barbara Field in English, almost from scratch.

Bali: The Sacrifice was commissioned by the Leicester Haymarket Theatre for a British cast and audience. I discarded an earlier Kannada draft and wrote the play afresh in English.

Flowers was written in English, for an actor who knew no Kannada.

So having started as a translator of my plays, I have slowly morphed myself into a playwright in English.

Finally, do I have a non-Indian audience in mind when I write plays in English or translate my plays into English? There was a time, I must confess, when I thought the ultimate destination of my play in English would be the British or the American stage, but not anymore. Apart from whatever I have said so far, Time has created a new demand for English versions. There is much more English spoken and understood today in India itself than half a century ago, there is much more theatre in English.

More importantly, I have realized that a play is a product of a specific cultural milieu and often makes no sense to someone outside it: a play carries with it an audience with a definite cultural and emotional background that it cannot shake off.

For example, I am gratified by the response *The Fire and the Rain* normally evokes from Indian readers or audiences. After reading it, the musician Bhaskar Chandavarkar faxed to me, 'Not only is this your best play, I am sorry you will never write a better one.' It won the Bharatiya Jnanpith, India's most prestigious literary award.

But most readers unfamiliar with Indian society fail to make sense of the play. And who would blame them?

About the Playwright

GIRISH KARNAD is a playwright, film-maker, and actor. He writes in Kannada, the language of the state of Karnataka, and has translated his plays into English. Some of his more recent plays however were written originally in English. His plays have been performed in most of the Indian languages as well as abroad.

He graduated from Karnatak University, Dharwad, in mathematics (1958) and was a Rhodes scholar at Oxford where he received an MA in philosophy, politics, and economics (1963).

After working with Oxford University Press, India, as editor, he resigned to freelance, and was awarded the Homi Bhabha Fellowship for creative writing. He used this opportunity to explore techniques of traditional theatre forms and write *Hayavadana*, which initiated a new movement in Indian theatre.

Subsequently, he went on to serve in cultural institutions of national importance, as the Director of the Film and Television Institute of India, Pune; the Chairman of the Sangeet Natak Akademi (the National Academy of the Performing Arts), New Delhi; and the Director of the Nehru Centre, Indian High Commission, London.

While he was at the University of Chicago as Visiting Professor and Fulbright-Playwright-in-Residence, he wrote *Nāga-Mandala*. The play was premiered in the USA by the Guthrie Theatre, Minneapolis, which then commissioned him to write *The Fire and the Rain*.

The Haymarket Theatre, Leicester, UK, commissioned and premiered *Bali: The Sacrifice.*

His radio play, *The Dreams of Tipu Sultan*, was commissioned by BBC, London, and broadcast on the fiftieth anniversary of Indian Independence. He further celebrated the occasion by directing *Swarajnama*, a television programme in thirteen episodes on India's struggle for independence, for Doordarshan.

He wrote and presented the telefilm *The Bhagavad Gita* as part of the programme *Art That Shook the World* for BBC Two (2002).

His plays have been produced by most of the major directors in India, like Ebrahim Alkazi, B.V. Karanth, Vijaya Mehta, Satyadev Dubey, and Mohit Takalkar.

Vanraj Bhatia has composed a full-scale opera based on *The Fire and the Rain*, the first of its kind in India.

The International Theatre Institute of UNESCO, Paris, has declared Karnad the 'World Theatre Ambassador'.

He has also been active as actor, director, and scriptwriter in Hindi, Marathi, and Kannada films and teleserials, and acted for film-makers like Shyam Benegal, Satyajit Ray, Mrinal Sen, Nagesh Kukunoor, and Kabir Khan.

He has been awarded the DLitt by Karnatak University, Dharwad, Vidyasagar University, Midnapore, and Ravenshaw University, Cuttack, as well as the degree of Doctor of Humane Letters, *honoris causa*, by the University of Southern California, Los Angeles.

He has been conferred the Padma Bhushan by the President of India and has received the Bharatiya Jnanpith, the country's highest literary award.